"The most important, useful and powerful book I have read on couple therapy since Virginia Satir's *Conjoint Family Therapy* . . . one of the rare books that is both useful to the lay audience and indispensable for the clinician."

Dennis Jaffe, Ph.D., President
Association for Humanistic Psychology
author of *Healing from Within*

". . .fascinating material for readers to test in their own lives."

Ruth C. Ikerman,
Los Angeles Times.

"A book which makes all other texts about relationships finally understandable."

Eddie Schwartz,
Skyway News, Minncapolis

"Jordan and Margaret Paul have written something very wonderful that speaks to everyone. I enjoyed it immenscly and learned a great deal."

Ali MacGraw

"I have read and enjoyed your very valuable book. It is a real gift to those in relationship. . ."

Rev. Terry Cole-Whittaker,
author of *What You Think of Me Is None of My Business*

"Excellent! Fresh, useful insights, great diagrams, terrific dialogue — upbeat — it's got it all!"

Harold H. Bloomfield, M.D.
author of *Making Peace with Your Parents* and *How to Survive the Loss of a Love*

Do I Have To Give Up Me To Be Loved By You?

JORDAN PAUL, Ph.D. AND MARGARET PAUL, Ph.D.

HAZELDEN

Hazelden Educational Materials
Center City, Minnesota 55012-0176

ISBN: 1-56838-068-2

Editor's note
Hazelden Educational Materials offers a variety of information on
chemical dependency and related areas. Our publications do not
necessarily represent Hazelden's programs, nor do they officially
speak for any Twelve Step organization.

To our children — Eric, Joshua, and Sheryl

For your love
your laughter
your sensitivity
your wisdom
your patience

Acknowledgments

The end of our seven-year struggle to complete this book gives us this joyful opportunity to acknowledge those people whose contributions were so important. We wish to express our warm and loving thanks to:

Jane Jordan Browne, who, through many frustrations and disappointments, never lost faith in us and went far beyond her duties as an agent to shepherd us through every phase of this book.

Joyce Fleming, Elva Kremenliev, Nancy Bryan, and Bonnie Hesse, the wonderfully talented writers and editors we worked with at different times, who helped us organize, clarify, simplify, and add life to our writing.

Diane DuCharme, who saw the value in our work and had the faith to commit to publish.

Al Ross, friend and advisor, who gave us invaluable help and guidance.

Our son Eric, who patiently helped us open our traditional minds to the thinking needed to use a computer/word processor.

Our dear friends Jeanne Segal, Will McWhinney, Dennis Jaffe, and Michael Leibman, who read our material, asked questions, and suggested ideas that helped our theory and our book to evolve, and who supported us through the difficult times.

Our family, friends, and clients, too numerous to name, who sympathetically asked, year after year, "What's happening with your book?" and patiently put up with hearing, year after year, "It's almost finished." Now it is.

Contents

Section Two
Explorations on the Path of Evolution

Introduction

We are psychologists and marriage counselors, married to each other. Our earlier book, *Free to Love* (1975), told the story of the first eleven years of our marriage. We wrote *Free to Love* to help other couples understand how turmoil in a marriage can gradually give way to a spirit of mutual understanding and acceptance. At that time, however, we were just emerging from a very difficult period, and things were often touch-and-go even as we wrote. Many of our insights were truly new and fresh — from an argument we had just finished!

As we continued to study our relationship and those of our clients, we put together an important new theory about why couples behave as they do, how relationships get into trouble, and how conflict can be handled so that two people may always return to loving feelings. As we formulated our theory, we came to question traditional therapy, including our own.

At the beginning of our careers we saw ourselves as problem solvers, applying everything we had learned in our training: Gestalt Therapy, Transactional Analysis, psychodrama, systems theory, behavior modification. We specialized in sexual therapy and seemed successful at it. Nonorgasmic women became orgasmic, impotent men became potent, and rapid ejaculators were taught how to solve that problem.

But again and again we kept running into the same puzzling result: these changes rarely affected the *quality* of the relationship. Couples were still not emotionally intimate: people who had made love infrequently before coming into therapy eventually went back to their old patterns, even after their problems had seemingly been solved. Or the problems would be solved briefly only to crop up again a few months later. And, of course, some problems didn't change at all. So, we began to re-examine our ideas about how change occurs.

People enter therapy unhappy and usually blaming others, especially their partners, for their difficulties. A wife blames her husband for staying too late at the office too often. A husband blames his wife because she doesn't want sex often enough. Both partners generally believe that if only the other's "bad behavior" could be changed, everything would be all right. When we, as therapists, tried to help our clients change their behavior (rather than understand and respect it), we were tacitly agreeing that they were wrong and needed to be "cured." We were also expecting them to be able to make any "necessary adjustment" in their bad behavior.

We were victims of the false notion that change comes about merely by decision and willpower. Most professional advice-givers (pop psychology books, religious leaders, newspaper columnists, etc.) reinforce this notion. Ideas for "better" ways of living include the unspoken expectation that change is easy. For example, if you want to be thinner, then choose a diet, and force yourself to stay on it. Just do it — get thinner, or be sexier, communicate better, express your feelings more openly, listen to each other's feelings, stop feeling guilty, be stronger, be more loving, take time to meditate. But what do you do when your attempts to change fail, which they often do? Give up? Try harder, only to fail again? Either way your self-esteem is eroded.

The truth is that whenever we are unable to accomplish what we want, something very important is hindering us — something so compelling and so powerful that even great efforts of willpower cannot prevail. *The only effective way to accomplish the change we seek is to understand and overcome the powerful hidden motives that keep us fixed in our present behavior.* The term we use for these deep motives is "intent." Intent is the purpose or the unspoken motivation behind what we do. It is always expressed by our behavior and reacted to by our partner, though usually invisible to both.

While it may be easy to understand the idea of intent, most people find it difficult to see in their daily lives. For example —

> Behavior: "Well, you're finally home! It's the third time you've been late this week!"
>
> Visible reason: I am angry *because you were wrong to come home late.*
>
> Intent: I am angry *to protect myself from facing my fears and feeling bad — what if you don't want to come home?*

Our Intention Therapy concentrates on understanding and respecting the one intent that dominates our lives and creates almost all the difficulties in our relationships — the intent to protect ourselves against any pain, especially disapproval and rejection. Also, we focus not on "solving the problem," i.e., teaching one partner to come home on time and the other to forgive tardiness, but on helping people understand and take responsibility for their fears and the resulting need to protect themselves.

Most of our behavior, in relationships especially, is self-protective, e.g., anger, withdrawal, overeating, drinking, frigidity, or impotence. We act protectively simply because we feel too insecure to do anything else. Once we recognize and respect this most basic aspect of our lives, many positive changes can happen:

- We can stop judging ourselves negatively; these judgments only lower our self-esteem.
- As we feel better about ourselves, we don't need to protect ourselves so rigidly and are willing to take more risks.
- As we understand our part in a problem, we no longer have a need to blame and be angry.

Attempts to change without understanding one's intent will usually fail. For example, most couples leave the popular Marriage Encounter weekend with renewed optimism and loving feelings. It is usually a positive experience and many good communication techniques are taught. But since protections are not dealt with during the weekend, when couples get into conflicts that bring up their protections, they retreat back into old patterns. They find themselves feeling distant with each other again and have no idea why or what to do.

This book does not merely tell "how-to" but concentrates on "why-not," exploring the blocks to change. When the "why-nots" are taken care of, anyone can put into practice the many wonderful ideas available for achieving intimacy and greater self-esteem. This book is process-oriented rather than solution-oriented. Our aim is to help you become more aware of your own self-created obstacles to joy *and aware of the process by which you can help each other remove these obstacles.*

Those partners who enter this process move through it haltingly and at times with difficulty. *But they do move!* Solutions come, problems are resolved — by a process that may seem indirect but actually encourages the changes the partners are seeking for themselves and each other. We are in this process ourselves, and we have personally counseled hundreds of couples who are creating freer and more joyful, yet profoundly intimate relationships. You can join us.

Jordan and Margaret Paul
Los Angeles, California
February, 1983

Section One

From Conflict to Intimacy

·1·

Do I Have to Give Up Me to Be Loved by You?

How to preserve warmth and closeness while at the same time holding on to the new freedom to choose? This is the preeminent question the culture confronts on the domestic scene . . .

DANIEL YANKELOVICH
New Rules

We all know that falling in love is ecstasy, but we're also just as convinced that most love relationships will wither or even die with time. In fact, being in love and being married seem mutually exclusive. When we think of love, we think of excitement, joy, and sexiness. Marriage is compromise, giving in, routines, security, obligations. It seems that in-love feelings go away as a natural result of familiarity, responsibilities, and the passage of time. The cynical question "Why spoil a good relationship by getting married?" asks why one should give up delicious excitement for dutiful loyalty.

All of us hunger for a love that will stay intimate and secure, yet also encourage our individual fulfillment.

Freedom and intimacy are to a person what sun and water are to a plant: both must be present at the same time for a person to flourish. In 1956 Erich Fromm wrote in *The Art of Loving,* "The question is how to overcome separateness, how to achieve union, how to transcend one's own individual life and find at-onement." The question today is how to overcome separateness, achieve union, and so forth, *without losing oneself in the process.*

All of us need to be ourselves *and* to be loved. In childhood we see-sawed between the fear of losing our parents' love and the determination to have our own way. As adults we try to keep our love relationship without losing our individuality. So, all of us, whether we know it or not, are constantly asking ourselves how much we can let ourselves think, feel, and act freely without being rejected by those we love.

The people we want most to love us are those who pressure us most to do what *they* think is right. Deeply in love, most new mates make what seem like minor adjustments in their behavior in order to please each other. Whether you agree to squeeze or roll the toothpaste tube doesn't make much difference at first, but as time passes, such small concessions can become large issues. To paraphrase Judith Viorst in *Yes, Married! A Saga of Love and Complaint:* "Before we were married we knew each other's positions on all the fundamental issues . . . Then we found we were taking positions on things we didn't know *had* positions."

Primary relationships — those between committed mates, siblings, or parents and children — often operate from an implicit threat: "If I don't like what you do, I won't love you any more." Each partner says covertly: "Do things my way; think the way I think; believe what I believe. Don't be you. Be what I want you to be or I won't love you." The message always comes down to:

"Give yourself up." But people can't feel deeply loved unless they are approved of and respected for being who they really are.

So, whether you conform or rebel, the result is the same: you lose touch with what you want, or you stop believing you have the right to feel what you feel and want what you want.

Do you say "I love you" when you don't mean it? Make love when you don't feel turned on? Give presents grudgingly? Grin and bear the housework you hate? Come home early when you'd rather be somewhere else? Stay home when you'd rather be out with friends? When you do what you do because you care — even when that means doing what the other person wants you to do — you do not give yourself up. *You give yourself up when whatever you do comes from fear, obligation, or guilt.*

The answer to "Do I have to give up me to be loved by you?" leads to one of two different directions. The path marked "Yes" — giving yourself up — moves you closer, slowly but surely, to severe problems. The other path marked "No" is not often taken, but it leads to a relationship that can remain loving, joyful, and challenging.

Answering "No" creates a most unusual relationship — what we call an Evolving Relationship. In an Evolving Relationship partners engage in a process that leads to individual freedom and integrity while increasing intimacy. Each partner encourages the other to express and understand himself or herself on ever-deepening levels. Loving feelings flourish, and with them come support, mutual acceptance, fun, sensuality, and passionate sex. Each partner *and* the relationship evolve.

Such a relationship is as rare as it is hard to build. To get there, partners have to become vulnerable and take emotional risks. Carl Roger's credo in *Becoming Partners* evokes the spirit of the Evolving Relationship:

> Perhaps I can discover and come closer to more of what
> I really am deep inside — feeling, sometimes angry or
> terrified, sometimes loving and caring, occasionally beau-
> tiful and strong and wild and awful — without hiding
> these feelings from myself. Perhaps I can come to prize
> myself as the richly varied person I am. Perhaps I can
> openly be more of this person . . . Then I can let myself
> be all this complexity of feelings and meanings and values
> with my partner — be free enough to give of love and
> anger and tenderness as they exist in me. Possibly then I
> can be a real member of the partnership, because I am on
> the road to being a real person. And I am hopeful that I
> can encourage my partner to follow his or her own road
> to a unique personhood, which I would love to share.

In an Evolving Relationship couples slowly dismantle
the barriers that get in the way of freedom and intimacy.
Almost all of these barriers are built by the typical ways
people respond to conflict.

Conflict and Intent: The Key

Conflict! Mere mention of the word is enough to raise
anyone's anxiety level. Conflict is thought of as fighting,
losing, compromising, rejection, humiliation. We think of
George and Martha tearing at each other in Albee's *Who's
Afraid of Virginia Woolf?* Romantic love, on the other
hand, is idyllic days and nights unmarred by bickering or
snide remarks. If only these could last forever. You may
sometimes think to yourself, "Wouldn't it be wonderful if
we could go back to those days before we started to
fight?"

But conflict occurs in all close relationships. Since
people are by definition different from each other, it is
inevitable that any two people will sometimes come into
conflict — which can be defined simply as a difference in
what two people want, need, or think. You want to talk
and your partner wants to make love. You want to relax

and your partner wants to play tennis. You think it's okay to spank your child and your partner is shocked at the very idea. Conflicts occur over any difference of opinion or desire. However, *it is not the conflict itself, but how we handle the conflict that creates difficulties.* A conflict is merely a catalyst that precipitates a predictable chain reaction of responses and consequences.

For example, David wants to make love. He reaches out to Barbara when they get into bed and begins to caress her. Barbara sighs and turns her back to David, indicating that she's not interested. Inside, David feels disappointed, hurt, and anxious, but rather than experience and express these feelings he gets mad at Barbara. David's anger hurts and frightens her, but rather than allowing herself to feel hurt, she either gives in to him or shuts down completely, effectively shutting out David so she won't be affected by his anger.

Our theory is based on the unique idea that *all of the many varieties of responses to a conflict stem from only two intents — to protect or to learn. Intent,* as we use the word, is the purpose, the goal, the motivation behind our responses. Even though our intent is usually subconscious, our behavior always follows directly either from an intent to protect or an intent to learn.

Curiosity, the openness to learning, is our natural intent, the state in which we were born. Protections, on the other hand, are learned strategies for dealing with fearful situations. For example, had we feared failing or being hurt, we would never have attempted to walk or would have quit trying after the first fall. Being open to learning, we got up and tried again each time we fell until we learned to walk. Each fall taught us something that moved us close to our goal. A subconscious intent to learn determined our behavior. As we became more fearful of disapproval and rejection, we became more and more protected, and our openness to learning, especially about ourselves, diminished.

In *The Search for Authenticity,* James Bugental says that there are only two possible paths in life, which he calls "the path of dread" and "the path of courage." In our Intention Therapy we call these "the Path of Protection" and "the Path of Evolution." Our intent on the Path of Protection is to defend against everything we fear. On the Path of Evolution our intent is to learn, particularly about ourselves and our partner, and to understand how things really are with us.

Every interaction with people in our lives is governed by these two intentions. *All behavior and all feelings come from them.* We choose our intent freely, but the choice is made so automatically we usually don't know we've made one. We can choose protection one moment and learning the next, but the two are mutually exclusive. We cannot be protected (closed, hard, defensive) and open to learning (open, soft, and curious) at the same time. Whichever intent is stronger at the moment will prevail. Picture the simple example of the ground squirrel: When he feels the need to protect himself, he stays in his hole; when he feels safe, he ventures out cautiously, exploring the environment outside. But he cannot do both at once — be inside his hole (protected) and outside exploring (learning). The squirrel may want the tempting acorn outside very much, but has no way of getting it until he's willing to leave his hole. The same thing is true for all of us. That's why when we make a conscious decision to change, the decision itself will not bring about change. We can want something very badly — to stop smoking, be thinner, be less critical, express more feeling — but we will be unsuccessful when our primary intent is protective.

We are usually unaware of our true intent since it is subconscious. Also, we probably won't be aware of the strength of this unacknowledged intent — all we will know is that there are mysterious hidden obstacles preventing things from getting better.

An unacknowledged intent is like a shape you stumble over as you're walking through your own living room in the dark. It's your living room; you know it well. Walking through it ought to be easy. But when it's pitch dark all you can know is that there's something there hindering you — and you won't find out what it is or be able to avoid it in the future until you're willing to turn on the light and look.

The first step to meaningful change is *to become aware of our intent and then to connect it to the behavior and inescapable consequences that follow it.*

The Intent to Protect

The intent to protect is a basic motivation to defend oneself against any threats, real or imagined, of emotional pain. To do this people use a variety of means to keep themselves from feeling the real emotions generated by any particular conflict. For instance, a person may protect himself or herself from fear by feeling angry, anger being a much easier emotion to tolerate than fear.

People protecting themselves run the gamut from the most timid to the most aggressive. A man who threatens his opponent with towering rages, a woman who dissolves in self-pitying tears, or the debater who uses calm rational logic to carry a point are all being equally self-protective. None of them wants to learn. *Any response to a conflict other than openness to learning is protective.*

All protective behavior in a conflict falls into one of three categories: 1) Compliance — giving ourselves up to avoid a conflict by denying our own feelings or needs and going along with what the other wants because we fear rejection. 2) Control — trying to change the other's mind

7

or behavior by making him or her feel guilty or afraid. Disapproval (in the form of anger, criticism, tears, threats, lectures) tells the other: "You are wrong" and "I won't love you until you do things my way." 3) Indifference — ignoring the conflict, withdrawing into separate preoccupations (TV, work, drugs, sports). This implies "I'm not affected by you, and you can't hurt or control me."

When one partner becomes resistant or indifferent, the other feels shut out and unimportant. On the other hand, attempts to get one's partner to change are invariably met with indifference, resistance, or rebellion. After all, to give in to another's control is to give up oneself.

When both partners protect, they create what we call a protective circle. When both run from conflict, there is a distant peace. Attempts to get the other to change brings on power struggles, each person bent on winning — or at least not losing. Giving oneself up may eliminate power struggles, but the submission itself becomes part of the problem. Protective circles set in motion all of the gnawing difficulties in most ongoing relationships: boring or infrequent sex; poor communication; emotional distance; a lack of fun; bitter struggles over money, in-laws, or child-raising; or any other large or small issue.

If your partner's behavior is upsetting you, should you give up wanting change? Definitely not! In fact, we can't give up wanting our partner to change unless we stop caring, which is as destructive as trying to force change. *The desire for change does not create the problem, but rather how we go about getting it.* Problems arise when our primary intent is self-protective — to *make* the other change. An intent to learn, on the other hand, opens the way to significant changes.

The Intent to Learn

Only one response to a conflict breaks the protective circle and opens the door to intimacy: *an intent to learn.*

What do we mean by an intent to learn? It is the willingness to be vulnerable and open, to feel our feelings directly rather than through the filter of our protections, and to discover why each of us is feeling and behaving as we do. We engage in a process of exploration to discover the answer to such questions as:

- What important reasons does my partner have for behaving that way?
- What part do I play in this problem?
- How is my partner's behavior affecting me? (threatening? irritating?)
- Why does it affect me that way? What personal issues does it stir up?
- Why is it so important to get my way, or to be right?
- What fears, values, expectations, and beliefs lie behind my feeling threatened or irritated?
- How does my anger, irritation, or indifference affect my partner?
- How does my partner respond?
- What are the consequences?

Searching questions such as these may succeed in breaking through deeply entrenched battle lines. Barry and Marilyn, clients of ours, had been fighting for years over child-raising. After a few sessions with us, they began to accept the novel proposition that each had good reasons for his or her present behavior. When they finally opened to knowing themselves and each other, they approached each other with genuinely interested curiosity instead of their usual steely anger. Barry explored what he wanted from his children and where those ideas came from. Did his parents have similar expectations? Why did he get so angry when anyone in the family did something he didn't like? Marilyn explored her beliefs about the kind of father Barry should be. Why wasn't Barry interested in understanding her point of view? Why wouldn't he read any books about bringing up children? Why did it exasperate her when he wouldn't? Was she trying to make Barry over into her ideal image? Were they in a power struggle with child-raising as their arena? Gradually, as they addressed these questions together, they shed light on the blind and deaf spots in their communication. As they learned more about themselves and each other, many changes began to creep into their lives; eventually this conflict reached a satisfying resolution.

Seeing conflict as an opportunity rather than as a calamity puts it in a new light. You may think it sounds ridiculous (if not impossible) to face emotional pain willingly. But it does make sense. Protection against physical pain is a physiological response (the fight or flight syndrome), but protecting against emotional pain is a pattern *learned* in childhood, once necessary for a child's survival, but no longer productive for adults. Most of us still react to conflict in our childhood patterns. Being open in a conflict is the only way we can learn what the conflict has to teach us and unlearn our self-limiting protections.

When we stop blaming our partner, we assume responsibility for our own lives. We are willing to be vulnerable and to risk feeling and expressing pain. When we are softer, our partner will be less likely to respond protectively. When our partner joins us in the task of learning, we begin to understand ourselves and our partner more and more deeply. Understanding each other better naturally gives us deeper feelings for each other. Together we create Intimate Love and an Evolving Relationship.

Since some people respond to visual presentation better than to the written word, we have prepared the chart on the following page to illustrate the Path of Protection and the Path of Evolution as they unfold from a conflict. Further explanation will follow in Chapter 2.

The Blocks to Moving from Protection to Learning

When we see that behavior comes from only two intentions, understanding our own and others' behavior becomes simple and clear. However, because protections are subtle and deeply ingrained, moving from an intent to protect to an intent to learn will be very challenging. The crucial first step is to recognize your protectiveness. This in itself is enough to set you on the Path of Evolution. You may even believe you have been open to learning all along — until you take a close look at what you do when your partner upsets you. Do you explore until you understand why you got so upset in the first place, why your partner is behaving as he or she is, and what might be going on between you? Or are your conclusions based on *assumptions* about why things are as they are? Have you explored your protections with your partner? Use these questions as check points to find out your intent. When we believe it's wrong to be protective (calling it weak, hostile, cold, unfeeling) we make it harder to see our own protectiveness. And yet we all protect in a conflict to some degree — mostly for the following three important reasons:

1. We have never seen people act any other way.
Most models of family conflict seem to come from the world of boxing or from the battlefield: strike hard to put fear into your opponent, and protect your own flank. We live in a competitive culture and are conditioned to want to win. Most people are not aware that they have any other option than to protect. Unless you were raised in a

THE PATHS THROUGH CONFLICT

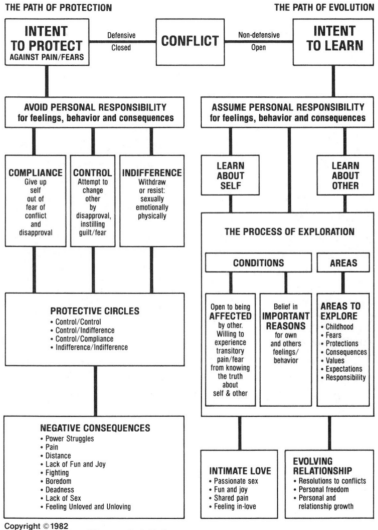

THE PATH OF PROTECTION

THE PATH OF EVOLUTION

| INTENT TO PROTECT AGAINST PAIN/FEARS | Defensive Closed | CONFLICT | Non-defensive Open | INTENT TO LEARN |

AVOID PERSONAL RESPONSIBILITY for feelings, behavior and consequences

ASSUME PERSONAL RESPONSIBILITY for feelings, behavior and consequences

COMPLIANCE
Give up self out of fear of conflict and disapproval

CONTROL
Attempt to change other by disapproval, instilling guilt/fear

INDIFFERENCE
Withdraw or resist: sexually emotionally physically

LEARN ABOUT SELF

LEARN ABOUT OTHER

THE PROCESS OF EXPLORATION

CONDITIONS

AREAS

PROTECTIVE CIRCLES
• Control/Control
• Control/Indifference
• Control/Compliance
• Indifference/Indifference

Open to being **AFFECTED** by other. Willing to experience transitory pain/fear from knowing the truth about self & other

Belief in **IMPORTANT REASONS** for own and others feelings/behavior

AREAS TO EXPLORE
• Childhood
• Fears
• Protections
• Consequences
• Values
• Expectations
• Responsibility

NEGATIVE CONSEQUENCES
• Power Struggles
• Pain
• Distance
• Lack of Fun and Joy
• Fighting
• Boredom
• Deadness
• Lack of Sex
• Feeling Unloved and Unloving

INTIMATE LOVE
• Passionate sex
• Fun and joy
• Shared pain
• Feeling in-love

EVOLVING RELATIONSHIP
• Resolutions to conflicts
• Personal freedom
• Personal and relationship growth

most unusual home, you may not be able to recall your parents' responding to something they disapproved of by trying to understand why you acted as you did or — even more rare — why your behavior upset them so much. Most of us were punished, not understood, when we broke the rules. Parents protect themselves by telling children they're wrong and trying to get them to conform. After all, parents were also raised this way.

2. We all have fears of learning.
Fear is the major short circuit to an intent to learn. When it comes to learning about our partner and ourselves, we fear knowing the truth about many things. The universal fear of being rejected and losing our partner's love underlies all the fears activated in conflict. To open to learning leaves us vulnerable. The truth may be threatening; it may seem easier to avoid the inner search than to pursue it. Usually, even those who *seem* intent on learning have only developed less obvious protective strategies than the rest of us.

3. We are a solution-oriented rather than a process-oriented culture.
The Western mind has been programmed very narrowly: define problems, seek solutions, set goals, make decisions, fix things. Fix your spouse, fix your children, fix yourself. When we see something we don't like, we judge it and want to change it rather than understand it; we look for the immediate solution rather than seek to understand why the problem arose. Do you take aspirin for headaches, sleeping pills for insomnia, and tranquilizers for anxiety rather than deal with the underlying conditions? Do you look to others to tell you how to behave rather than search inward for the source of your problems?

Most conflict-resolution theories usually skip over the process of understanding the sources of the problem.

When problems are objective, as in business, immediate solutions may be perfectly appropriate. But conflict occurs in personal relationships over highly sensitive feelings. Before a mutually satisfying solution can be arrived at, people must understand more about themselves and their partners.

Working diligently at solving a problem may, paradoxically, make it impossible to understand why it occurred. Without understanding, the solution probably won't work satisfactorily for both people, or the symptom may disappear only to emerge as another set of problems.

A Process Approach

When couples think their estrangement is caused by their running conflicts, they often try to solve their problems with legalistic techniques: contracts, compromises, trade-offs, or promises. But these encourage "peace at any price" — even if the cost is giving up oneself. Couples may get peace, but no real resolution that leaves both people feeling good.

The alternative is entering into a process of exploring the problems. Shifting focus from solutions to understanding can turn a battle into an adventure. You may think this sounds too time-consuming or impractical, but we have found that in the long-run, exploration is more efficient and more effective than any packaged formulas. Why? Because since each conflict (out of an infinite number of possible conflicts) has many complex components, the search for answers never ends. What works once may not work again. What works for one couple may not work for you, especially if your solutions mistake the symptoms for the disease, treating the headache without looking for the cause.

Think of a relationship as a delicate toy horse, powered by a hidden set of elegant cogs, wheels, and springs. Suppose that the horse is not working the way it should. Destructive reactions to the breakdown would be to smash the toy to pieces or toss it in a corner — reactions exactly equivalent to the protective responses we discussed earlier. A more curious observer might notice that the toy horse's legs were not moving properly and do something to prop them up a bit. But the only approach that would solve the problem would be to take apart the hidden mechanism of the little horse, noticing how the springs and wheels, designed to oppose each other in a synchronized balance of tensions, were a little out of whack, and now worked against each other instead of together. With the inner mechanism understood, the toy horse could be made to gallop again, as his intricate inner mechanism intended him to.

Here is a sample of the variety of typical issues most couples fight over. (You can add your own to the list.)

TIME — how to spend it, being late, missing appointments, compulsive promptness

MONEY — extravagance, stinginess, greed, generosity, over emphasis, lack of, distribution

SEX — with each other, importance, frequency, quality, outside the partnership, prudishness, education of children

CHILDREN — having them, raising them, goals for, discipline, medical care, schooling, recreation, transportation, daily care, religion

SOCIAL BEHAVIOR — appearance, manners, sense of humor, discretion, attention-getting mannerisms at social gatherings, public/private, roles (male-female), at work, toward the other's friends and family

RESPONSIBILITIES — around the house, for children, in decision-making, sharing of

WORK — getting, keeping, losing jobs, over-time, choices, moving, changing fields, remuneration

In addition to the issues they habitually fight over, partners also criticize each other for their temperamental differences. Most partners will find themselves on opposite sides of many of the following polarities:

Spontaneous — Controlled
Intense — Low-key
Silly — Reserved
Rebellious — Conventional
Open emotionally — Closed emotionally
In-depth relating — Superficial relating
Practical — Impractical
Experimental — Stable
Emotionally up and down — Emotionally even
Sociable — Antisocial
Emotional — Logical
Open-minded — Opinionated
Easy-going and relaxed —Tense and anxious
Leader — Follower
Reliable — Unreliable
Organized — Disorganized
Self-centered — Self-sacrificing

The resolutions of these issues and differences vary greatly, but the process for reaching resolution is the same for any issue. When we let go of the anxious search for solutions in favor of fascination with the process of discovery, then we can explore — not how to change or what to change to — but why things are the way they are and what is getting in the way of each of us having what we want.

How Resolutions Occur

If partners are willing to keep on exploring, all conflicts can eventually be resolved. A conflict is resolved when the issue is no longer an issue — when a solution has been found which truly satisfies both partners. The time it takes to resolve a conflict varies greatly. You can resolve some conflicts easily once you unlock the issue from the power struggle. But some issues may require days, months, or even years of exploring before being resolved.

When you resolve a conflict that has tapped into fundamental beliefs and fears, *the resolution will be a synthesis,* meaning that both partners will have changed as a result of their new awareness. The emerging resolution is often one that was not even imagined before the exploration began. Each of us sees reality through an automatic perspective very much like a pair of glasses we don't know we're wearing. As we share ourselves with each other, each of us can become aware of our lenses; then our vision clears.

What Do We Do Until We Find a Resolution?

When partners stop accusing each other, they can start being concerned for one another. If one partner's feelings about a given issue are particularly strong, the other can meet those needs without feeling misused. For example, Mike and Carol were always at odds over being on time. Mike was very punctual, Carol was late. In exploring why he was so upset whenever Carol was late, Mike realized that he was afraid of others' disapproval if he kept them waiting. Once he accepted that his feelings were his issue and stopped thinking Carol was wrong, the power struggle ceased. Released from the power struggle, Carol found herself caring more about Mike's anxiety and therefore better able to be on time. (If Carol had also been highly motivated to be late — perhaps to exert power over others by keeping them waiting — they would have needed to explore more deeply before the issue could be resolved.)

The process of exploring can leave you feeling intimate and satisfied even before a resolution is found. In fact, the resolution itself is actually less important than the process you go through; *it is not the resolution that creates intimacy, but the process of getting there.* When you do not feel in-love feelings after an exploration, you know something more needs exploring.

People often ask, "Are we going to have to go into this exploration process for every issue that comes up?" Of course not. When you differ on a trivial issue such as what movie you want to see, that conflict can be resolved easily and immediately. But if an apparently trivial issue continues to cause bad feelings, time is needed to explore the issue more deeply until you discover what the real issue is.

Subsequent conflicts become easier and easier to deal with as they arise. If Carol and Mike had kept on thinking narrowly that punctuality rather than the underlying power struggle was the problem, they would have failed not only to solve the punctuality problem but also to gain the essential insights into themselves that helped with similar problems.

We all want freedom and we all want intimacy — at the same time. But we'll never get that by giving ourselves up or attempting to get our partner to give up themselves. The path to intimacy and freedom demands that we approach conflict with an openness to learning rather than with protections. Openness, however, means being vulnerable and as Andrew Greely wrote, "Everyone wants intimacy, but few of us are very good at vulnerability."

But when we finally understand how and when our protective intent governs our actions and interferes with our relationship, we have a real chance to be "good at vulnerability." Then — and only then — personal freedom *plus* intimacy between partners becomes a possible dream.

·2·

The Paths through Conflict

Two paths diverged in a wood, and I —
I took the one less traveled by,
And that has made all the difference.
                    ROBERT FROST
                    "The Road Not Taken"

Chapter 1 has shown that there are two possible chain reactions — one positive and one negative — which will occur whenever a couple gets into conflict. The chart on page 12 showed the inevitable progression toward negative consequences on the Path of Protection and the unfolding of intimacy and loving feelings on the Path of Evolution, where an intent to learn predominates. The pages that follow show the step-by-step progression with comments on each stage. This will help you see exactly what it is you're doing that keeps you from the closeness you seek, then show you what you could do instead, so that the conflict in your relationship will lead you closer together, not farther apart.

The Path of Protection and the Path of Evolution — A Step-by-Step Illustration

CONFLICT

Relationship problems begin with a conflict such as:

Differing desires or needs
(One partner wants to make love and the other is not in the mood . . . again.)

A difference of opinion, a values conflict
(One partner doesn't think, feel, or behave the way the other thinks he or she "should.")

Unmet expectations
("If you loved me, you'd . . . .")

A conflict is any situation that creates *upsetting feelings:*
disappointment
sadness
hurt
fear
irritation
insecurity
pain

Conflict will occur in *all* relationships.

THE PATH OF PROTECTION   **THE PATH OF EVOLUTION**

| INTENT TO PROTECT AGAINST PAIN/FEARS | Defensive / Closed | CONFLICT | Non-defensive / Open | INTENT TO LEARN |

All of the many varieties of responses to a conflict stem from *only two intents:*

> *to protect*
> or
> *to learn.*

The intent underlying the responses predicts and determines the couple's future interaction.

It's *not the conflict,* but *what we do* in the face of the conflict that leads either to difficulties and distance or to freedom and intimacy.

We protect when we are upset.

We are protecting ourselves against having to experience some pain we fear.

These protective responses, learned in childhood, become *automatic, instantaneous,* and for the most part, *subconscious.*

We become *defensive:*
> closed
> hard
> unavailable
> cold

(The fears associated with conflict are discussed in Chapter 7.)

THE PATH OF PROTECTION   THE PATH OF EVOLUTION

| INTENT TO PROTECT AGAINST PAIN/FEARS | Defensive Closed | CONFLICT | Non-defensive Open | INTENT TO LEARN |

AVOID PERSONAL RESPONSIBILITY for feelings, behavior and consequences

Protections let us avoid personal responsibility for our own feelings, behavior, and any resulting consequences.

We have stopped being open to learning about ourselves.

The primary intent of a protective response is *not against another,* but *for oneself.*

All of us have very good reasons for wanting to protect ourselves. But when one of the partners thinks protectiveness is "wrong" or "bad," the defensiveness that first led to the protection is intensified.

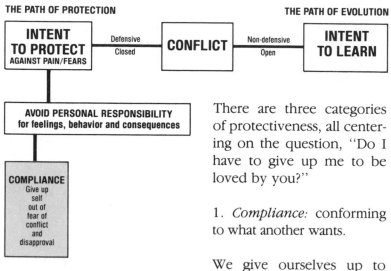

There are three categories of protectiveness, all centering on the question, "Do I have to give up me to be loved by you?"

1. *Compliance:* conforming to what another wants.

We give ourselves up to avoid the conflict that we fear will lead to *disapproval/rejection.*

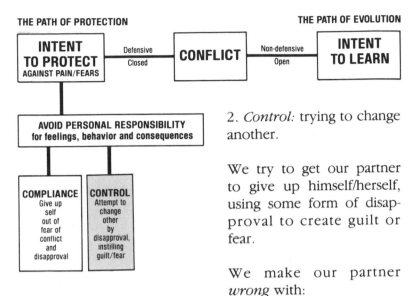

2. *Control:* trying to change another.

We try to get our partner to give up himself/herself, using some form of disapproval to create guilt or fear.

We make our partner *wrong* with:
    anger (overt or silent)
    threats
    criticism
    accusations
    complaints
    sarcasm
    tears
    lies
    lectures or explanations

(A detailed description of these protections is found in Chapter 8.)

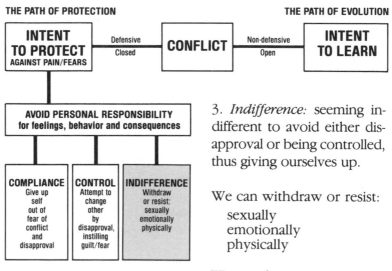

THE PATH OF PROTECTION

THE PATH OF EVOLUTION

3. *Indifference:* seeming indifferent to avoid either disapproval or being controlled, thus giving ourselves up.

We can withdraw or resist:
    sexually
    emotionally
    physically

We can shut out our partner by means of:
    work
    TV
    newspapers or books
    drugs or alcohol
    overeating
    sports or hobbies
    sleep, fantasy or
        meditation
    illness
    depression

(These protections are detailed in Chapter 8.)

THE PATH OF PROTECTION

THE PATH OF EVOLUTION

| INTENT TO PROTECT AGAINST PAIN/FEARS | Defensive Closed | CONFLICT | Non-defensive Open | INTENT TO LEARN |

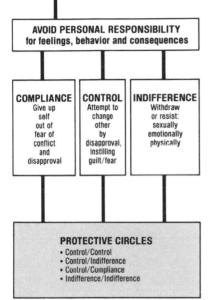

AVOID PERSONAL RESPONSIBILITY for feelings, behavior and consequences

COMPLIANCE	CONTROL	INDIFFERENCE
Give up self out of fear of conflict and disapproval	Attempt to change other by disapproval, instilling guilt/fear	Withdraw or resist: sexually emotionally physically

PROTECTIVE CIRCLES
- Control/Control
- Control/Indifference
- Control/Compliance
- Indifference/Indifference

When Partner A protects and Partner B responds protectively, a protective circle is created.

Since protective responses vary, a couple will find themselves in different circles under different circumstances.

Control-Control
Each attempts to change the other.

Control-Indifference
One partner attempts to change the other and the other resists or withdraws.

Control-Compliance
One partner attempts to change the other; the other gives in, going along with the control demands.

Indifference-Indifference
Each becomes indifferent, withdrawing and living essentially separate lives.

(Protective circles are discussed in Chapter 9.)

THE PATH OF PROTECTION   **THE PATH OF EVOLUTION**

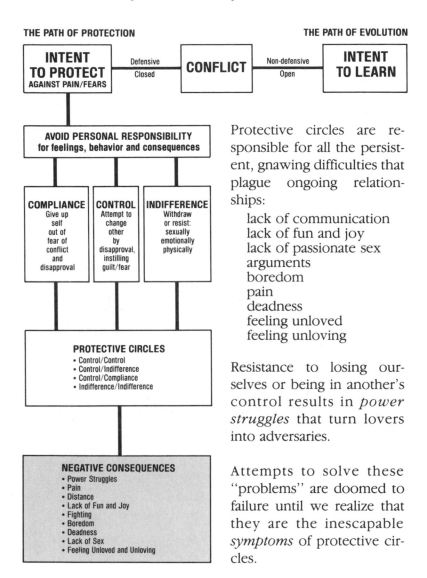

Protective circles are responsible for all the persistent, gnawing difficulties that plague ongoing relationships:

> lack of communication
> lack of fun and joy
> lack of passionate sex
> arguments
> boredom
> pain
> deadness
> feeling unloved
> feeling unloving

Resistance to losing ourselves or being in another's control results in *power struggles* that turn lovers into adversaries.

Attempts to solve these "problems" are doomed to failure until we realize that they are the inescapable *symptoms* of protective circles.

(Negative consequences are discussed in more detail in Chapter 9.)

THE PATH OF PROTECTION   THE PATH OF EVOLUTION

| **INTENT** **TO PROTECT** AGAINST PAIN/FEARS | Defensive Closed | **CONFLICT** | Non-defensive Open | **INTENT** **TO LEARN** |

The only responses to a conflict that are not protective come from an intent to learn from the conflict.

When we want to learn, we are *non-defensive:*
open
soft
curious
warm
available

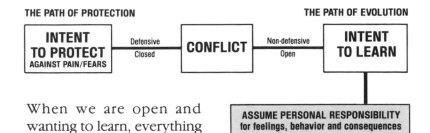

When we are open and wanting to learn, everything changes.

We give up *blaming others* and assume personal responsibility for our own feelings, our behavior and any resulting consequences.

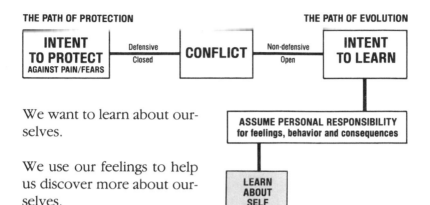

THE PATH OF PROTECTION — THE PATH OF EVOLUTION

INTENT TO PROTECT AGAINST PAIN/FEARS — Defensive / Closed — **CONFLICT** — Non-defensive / Open — **INTENT TO LEARN**

ASSUME PERSONAL RESPONSIBILITY for feelings, behavior and consequences

LEARN ABOUT SELF

We want to learn about ourselves.

We use our feelings to help us discover more about ourselves.

We ask questions like:

Why am I so upset?
What are my fears?
Why am I so afraid?
What do I hope to gain from feeling or acting this way?
Why do I see things as I do?
What are my unmet expectations?
Why do I get angry when I'm hurt or disappointed?
What is the purpose of my anger?
Why is it so important for me to get my way, to be right and not to be wrong?
What are my fears of not being in control?
What part am I playing in creating this present problem?
How is my partner's behavior affecting me? (Threatening? Irritating?)
Why does it affect me the way it does? What personal issues does it stir up in me?
How do I respond when I feel threatened or irritated? Why?
What are the consequences of the way I respond?
How does it affect my partner? What happens between us?

THE PATH OF PROTECTION   **THE PATH OF EVOLUTION**

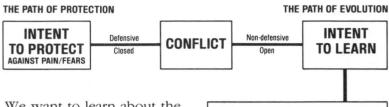

We want to learn about the other.

We can ask and listen to the answers to the same questions we asked ourselves:

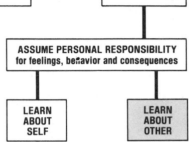

What are your fears?
Why are you so afraid?
Why do you see things the way you do?
What are your unmet expectations?
Why do you get angry when you're hurt or disappointed?
What are your fears of not being in control?

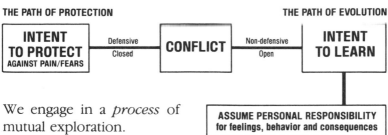

THE PATH OF PROTECTION   THE PATH OF EVOLUTION

| INTENT TO PROTECT AGAINST PAIN/FEARS | Defensive / Closed | CONFLICT | Non-defensive / Open | INTENT TO LEARN |

We engage in a *process* of mutual exploration.

We want to understand ourselves and our partner on a deeper level *and* to help our partner understand himself/herself more deeply.

We help each other feel and express our feelings so that we can learn from our feelings.

The focus of the exploration is *not* a search for *solutions* to our problems or a commitment to change behavior. We search for the new *understandings* which give respect and dignity to behavior. Resolutions and meaningful changes will automatically follow. Explorations are complete when each person feels understood and each feels loving toward the partner.

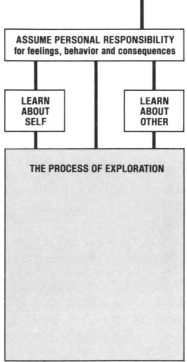

ASSUME PERSONAL RESPONSIBILITY for feelings, behavior and consequences

LEARN ABOUT SELF

LEARN ABOUT OTHER

THE PROCESS OF EXPLORATION

We explore both
  the *issue* of the conflict
  (sex, tardiness, etc.)
        and
  how we are talking about
  the issue (our intent).

(The exploration process itself is discussed in Chapters 3 and 4.)

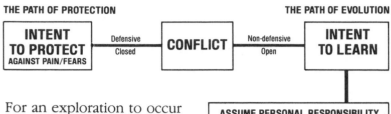

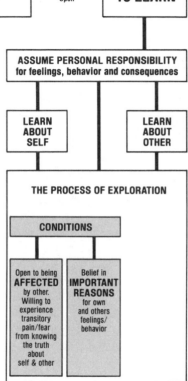

THE PROCESS OF EXPLORATION

For an exploration to occur the following conditions must be met:

A willingness to experience the *transitory* pain and/or fear that may accompany *knowing the truth* about ourselves and another.

The belief that feelings, thoughts, and behavior are *always* motivated by very important reasons — our *needs, hopes,* and *fears.*

When we believe there are very important reasons for behavior we stop accusing our partner of being wrong and the door is opened to *understanding* and *respect.*

Our partner will accurately sense whether our intent is an openness to learning or protective.

(The conditions for exploration are further discussed in Chapter 3.)

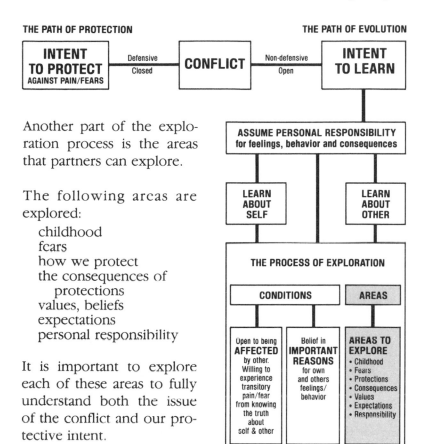

Another part of the exploration process is the areas that partners can explore.

The following areas are explored:
childhood
fears
how we protect
the consequences of
protections
values, beliefs
expectations
personal responsibility

It is important to explore each of these areas to fully understand both the issue of the conflict and our protective intent.

(These areas are discussed in Chapters 6 through 11.)

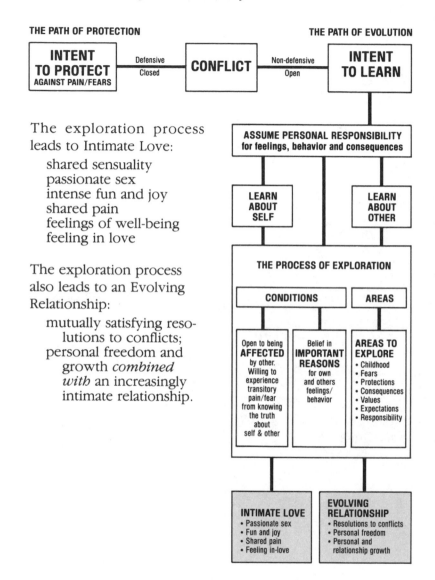

The exploration process leads to Intimate Love:

> shared sensuality
> passionate sex
> intense fun and joy
> shared pain
> feelings of well-being
> feeling in love

The exploration process also leads to an Evolving Relationship:

> mutually satisfying resolutions to conflicts;
> personal freedom and growth *combined with* an increasingly intimate relationship.

(Intimate Love is discussed in Chapter 5.)

(The Evolving Relationship is discussed in Chapters 1 and 12.)

On the previous pages we have seen the natural progression as one step leads to another on the paths through conflict. However, it is important to look at the overall picture, for some crucial understandings then become clear.

Most of us would like to play it safe and act protectively, yet we want the results of having been open. As you can see from the following chart, we cannot begin with an intent to protect and go directly to the benefits of an intent to learn.

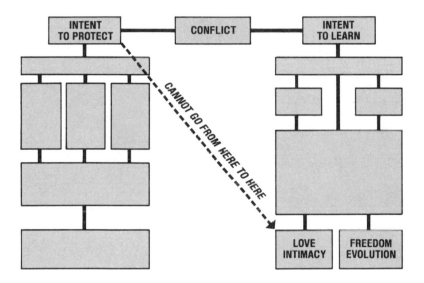

☐ There are always some predictable negative consequences attached to the choice to protect ourselves.

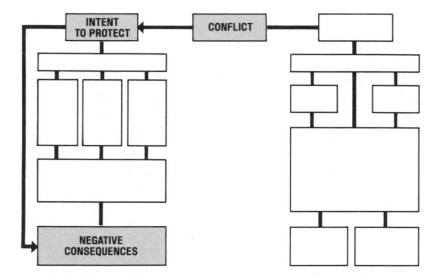

☐Consequences will change only when intent changes. Likewise, behavior will change only when intent changes, since behavior results from intent.

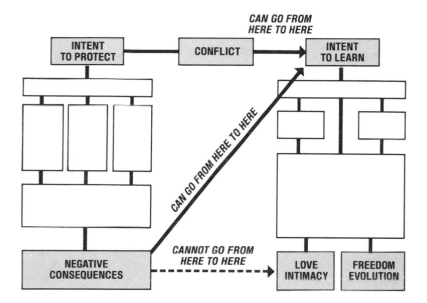

Can You Go Directly from a Conflict into an Exploration?

Just becoming aware of the option to learn will not necessarily help you move easily into an exploration. Protective responses run deep, and the protective circle is activated in an instant. Usually people proceed through the Path of Protection to the negative consequences. At that point, if they feel enough pain or dissatisfaction, they set out with a new intent on the Path of Learning. It is possible to go directly from a conflict to an intent to learn, but this is quite difficult since protections arise so quickly and automatically.

As your protections lessen, you will move more easily into explorations. However, it is not reasonable to expect to leave your protections behind completely or permanently. You move onto the Path of Evolution when you're feeling strong, then leap back to the Path of Protection when frightened. All you can do is to become aware of which path you're on and the important reasons for choosing it. Once you're open to knowing about yourself, *you have already changed,* and will continue to change as long as you continue to become aware.

From Conflict to Exploration — Our Own Experience

We personally still often act protectively with each other. In fact, we may not even be aware that we are feeling anxious, hurt or frightened. Like everyone else, we are at times unwilling to open up — and like everyone else, then we suffer the consequences. But the more we understand and work through our protections, the less defensive and more open to learning we become. It is our increasing awareness of the futility and unhappiness of our protective choices that eventually leads one (and then both) of us to want to learn.

Even when we get locked in the protective circle, we are able to get out of it much more quickly. Knowing how great it feels to go through an exploration, we are unwilling to spend the weeks (and sometimes months) we used to spend huddled in our protective shells. We go directly from a conflict into learning more often now, but our usual pattern is still the progression from conflict into our respective protections and their negative consequences. When our protections make us feel worse rather than better, we become willing to learn. Then we explore, and through the exploration, reach intimacy again.

In our work with individuals and couples, we've discovered that openly sharing the dynamics of our personal struggles has helped our clients understand the ideas we've presented. So, throughout this book from time to time, we'll relate in the first person our own struggles, beginning here with an example of how we avoided getting caught in a protective circle — at least on this occasion!

MARGIE:
One evening when I was not feeling well I told Jordan I was exhausted and needed to go to sleep early. Our daughter Sheryl, who was also sick, came into our bedroom three times during the night with various needs and complaints. I would have been so relieved if Jordan had taken care of Sheryl that night, but each time she came in, he just groaned and rolled over. I felt neglected as I did the necessary mothering, and the next morning I was feeling very distant from Jordan.

Although I don't like feeling distant, I felt trapped by my emotions. I knew that since I was upset with him, if I told him my feelings he would feel attacked, would probably react defensively, and we'd be in a battle. But I also knew that unless

I dealt with my feelings in some way I would not feel close to him.

Finally, late in the afternoon the thought crossed my mind that there must be some good reasons for Jordan's behavior. I saw that I did indeed have the option of wanting to learn. When I wanted to understand him instead of judge him, I could approach him without accusations. I said to him, "I felt really awful last night when you didn't help with Sheryl and I've been angry all day, but it just occurred to me that there is something to understand about the situation. I'd really like to know why that happened."

His answer wound down into many issues, as explorations sometimes do. We talked about the role his mother played in caring for the children, as opposed to what his father did. We explored the fear he feels when I'm not feeling well and his desire to pretend it's not so. We discussed his "selfishness" at wanting to sleep and being worried that he wouldn't fall back to sleep and would be too tired to work the next day. We talked about his fear that he wouldn't do it "right" and I would be upset with him. We dealt with his fear that if he took some responsibility for things like that, I would ask more and more of him, so he was trying to hold the line by not doing it and by not learning how to handle the children's illnesses. After talking about all these things, he was then open to feeling sad that his behavior had caused me pain. All of his concerns were not magically overcome just by becoming aware of them, but the process of overcoming them had begun. He was now open to hear my feelings and needs. I talked to him about wanting a more equal sharing of responsibility, not just dumping more responsibilities on him. I shared with him my pain at not feeling cared about when he didn't see that, at times, I need him to take over and give me some rest. I told him I often didn't ask for help because I believed that I should be able to do it all. When he really understood more about my needs and how I felt in those situations, we both felt better and we ended with loving feelings.

In the heat of battle, calm discussion like the above doesn't seem possible. At that point it probably is not! But if we can learn from any conflict — even if it's after protections and negative consequences have occurred, we will have taken a step in the right direction. As a friend of ours once wrote, "Life provides us with two possible kinds of experiences — positive and negative. For those who learn from their experiences, there are only positive experiences."

·3·

Exploration: The How of Learning

You always ask me, "What is your problem?" On the day you ask me, "What is your mystery?" our relationship will begin.

CLINT WEYAND
Thank You for Being

When both partners really want to learn about themselves and each other, the process we call exploration can begin. An exploration is simply spending time talking to each other about things that matter. Lovers do this a lot without even being aware they are "exploring" — they do it simply because they are very curious about each other. Explorations in the beginning of a relationship usually consist of revealing things already known about oneself. In an ongoing relationship, explorations probe *what is not yet consciously known about each person* — the mystery in Weyand's epigram above. These explorations help us understand why we do what we do. With a partner who accepts and cares about us, buried feelings can surface. Not knowing what exactly will surface is always scary, but, as Marilyn Ferguson observes in *The Aquarian*

Conspiracy: "Uncertainty is the necessary companion of all explorers."

As we define it, exploration involves both a method and a spirit — the "intent to learn." When both partners are willing to "come out," i.e., not hide behind their protections, issues can be explored fairly easily. But we, in our relationships, aren't really as simple to picture as the ground squirrel described in Chapter 1, because our protections aren't as easily recognized or identified. We can't see our partner run into his or her hideaway; instead, we see and feel coldness, anger, and other signals. The partner who is retreating often has as much trouble recognizing when he or she has run for cover.

The difficulty in identifying or recognizing the intent arises because it is expressed on a level of communication that is usually ignored. Communication always occurs on two levels:

Level 1 is *what* you are saying about the issue (money, sex, etc.)

Level 2 is *how* you are saying it.

It is Level 2 which reveals the person's intent and which always determines the course and outcome of any interaction. We *always* react, (although usually subconsciously), to the way we are being talked to. It's not the words we react to but the intent behind those words. For example, when we talk to each other accusingly and coldly, we get into a fight, not an exploration. When we want to prove ourselves right and fear being wrong we are definitely not open to exploring and learning.

When protected, we are defensive and battle to win, or at least not lose. Explorations are cooperative efforts to make sense out of things. When protected, all we can do is go round and round without real understanding or resolution; we cannot begin to explore the issues and resolve them until we can be more open with our partner.

Working on a relationship often means working on projections rather than just on issues. Resolving conflicts without new awareness is not exploration. For example, while an apology can be a genuine expression of regret that opens the door to better understanding, it is often no more than a ritual to keep the partner's anger at bay and avoid exploring the underlying cause of behavior.

There Are Always Good Reasons

Sincere exploration depends on certain background assumptions. First we must accept the fact that all of us always have very good, respectable, important, and appropriate reasons for feeling and behaving as we do. Understanding these important reasons will help us to better understand each other and to have more self-respect. Reasons are *not* justifications: they do help us understand the purpose our behavior serves. We do what we do not out of habit or because our past experiences make us do it, but because our behavior continues to benefit us, usually by protecting us from something we fear. Labeling behavior "sick," "neurotic," or "masochistic" demeans the individual by disregarding the very important reasons behind his or her behavior. The underlying intent of so-called "self-destructive" behavior is not masochistic but self-protective.

For most of us, *the pain we feel is preferable to the pain we fear.* People stay in unhappy, often miserable marriages to avoid loneliness or to keep from having to make new decisions. Some stay in unsatisfying jobs or continue to drink or abuse drugs rather than face what they would have to face if they didn't have these behaviors to protect them. Indifference, resistance, and rebellion, even when it leads to unhappiness, makes perfect sense when they are seen as attempts to protect against the greater pain of losing oneself. Protective behavior is neither right nor wrong, but it does make sense and is respectable.

Questions That Work

Some psychologists and counselors claim that asking "why" calls forth explanations and excuses from each partner. As John O. Stevens puts it in *Awareness: Exploring, Experimenting, Experiencing:*

> "Why do you feel bad?" is at best a request for explanation and justification, and at worst a demand that you deny the fact that you feel bad if you can't justify it. "How do you feel bad?" or "What do you experience?" and your answer "I feel tense in my stomach and my head aches," brings you into closer contact with your own experience. Your answer is a real communication that tells me more about yourself. When you ask "how" and "what" you request information about facts and processes. When you ask "why" you only ask for endless explanations — the cause of the cause of the cause of the cause of the cause.

In our view, "how," "what," or "why" is not what's important. It's the spirit in which questions are asked and answered that matters. Questions and answers can blame others and excuse oneself, or lead to more self-knowledge and responsibility, *depending on the intent.* If you ask "Why are you shutting me out?" then the question can be a blame, and the answer can be an excuse or a justification, according to the intent. If the answer is, "I'm angry because you're shutting me out," then the answer is a blame. If you explore and discover that "I'm angry because when you shut me out it scares me. I'm afraid to cry and let you see my fear because I think that's weak, so I get angry to try to change you," you are understanding your protections.

Questioning can, of course, turn into a kind of courtroom procedure when the purpose is to trap the other into making admissions that will be used later as evidence. Questions of this type say: "Go ahead, see if you can prove your case," rather than "I really want to understand your point of view and why you see things the way you do." Sue and Ray have a running battle over what time he gets home in the evening. Every morning Sue says, "What time will you be home tonight?" and Ray answers, "Oh, I don't know. Around 6:30, I guess. I'll call you if I'm going to be late." Often he is at least a half hour, and sometimes two hours, late and hasn't called. Invariably Sue's reactions range from irritation to rage. "What was it this time?" she yells, not really wanting to know the answer. Ray gives some excuse, hoping to pacify her.

After taking a class in how to communicate better, Sue learns that she has a better chance of getting through to Ray (i.e., getting him to do things her way) if she tells him her feelings rather than getting angry at him. So when Ray walks in forty-five minutes late, rather than yelling, Sue says in a calm voice, "I really get upset when you're late. I have terrible fantasies of you being in an accident." But nothing changes. Ray continues to make excuses and come in late. What Sue doesn't realize is that her basic *intent* has not changed; she still thinks Ray is wrong and hopes to change his behavior by making him feel guilty. As long as her intent is to change him rather than know him, he will probably react defensively.

An angry or withdrawn person will not soften and open to self-exploration when feeling judged or manipulated. You may have found that when you share your feelings with your partner you get defensiveness rather than concern for you. When this happens you need to ask yourself *why you want your partner to know your feelings.* If the answer is to get him or her to change so that you won't feel what you're feeling (hurt, frightened, or embarrassed), then your remarks really said, "I'm feeling bad and *you are wrong.*" When you realize that your partner was reacting to an accusation, it's not surprising that he or she didn't care about your feelings.

Comments about your partner's behavior like "You're holding back from me," or "You seem upset a lot of the time," will also usually be met with defensiveness. Unless accompanied by an overt attempt to learn, such as "I wonder why?" or "You must have good reasons," observations are merely attempts to change your partner. When you comment on something about your partner because you really do want to understand him or her, your caring will come through and your partner will be much more likely to respond warmly and openly.

Individual Responsibility

You, as an individual, can be responsible only for your own intent; it does no good to believe that your partner's intent must change before the two of you can resolve your difficulties. Many people can admit how they are feeling, but still try to evade personal responsibility by saying, "Well, if he wouldn't be so withdrawn, I wouldn't be so angry." The converse is, of course, equally valid: "Well, if she wouldn't be so angry, I wouldn't be so withdrawn." In this standoff each person recognizes only the consequences of the other's actions, not his or her own.

Marriage theorists claim that couples need to fight and to express anger. But merely venting anger is usually a dead end. Expressing anger is helpful *only* if it eventually leads to a change of intent and opens into exploration.

Moving from Anger or Indifference to an Exploration

If you are fighting or feeling withdrawn from your partner, starting an exploration is one of the hardest things in the world. Each partner wants only to keep from feeling hurt, and each is waiting for the other to soften, apologize, or reach out. You feel so vulnerable when you are the first one to reach out, it feels almost humiliating, as if you're admitting you're wrong. Keeping your pride intact may seem more important than bridging the distance. If you make the first move, you don't know whether or not your partner will use your vulnerability against you. Will he or she remain protected and defensive, or soften and want to learn? It's much safer to wait for your partner to reach out to you. But most people wait too long, finally settling for a distant relationship or a divorce rather than risk being vulnerable. As Pierre Mornell observes in *The Lovebook,* "To start talking, one person must accept responsibility for ending the power struggle. He must not really care who saves face and who loses it."

First Steps

Anger can actually be the first step toward learning. Anger is generally self-protective, covering up more vulnerable feelings. Dorothy Briggs explains this in *Celebrate Your Self,* "When anger is spent, almost invariably a helpless, powerless feeling eventually surfaces. Why? Because *anger is a second feeling* — a cover-up for a more primary emotion. That first feeling may be hurt, frustration, fatigue, deprivation, shock, disappointment, worry, fear, rejection, embarrassment, failure or any other." A person who finds it impossible to get through anger usually believes in the illusion that this anger has been caused by the other's unacceptable behavior.

MARGIE:

Sometimes, even though I feel as if I want to learn, I'm so angry at Jordan that I can't seem to open. When this happens I often ask his permission to be angry and blame him. I say something like "I know I'm blaming you, but I'm very angry and I want you to just listen and not say anything." (I generally say this with anger, too.) What I am really asking him to do is attempt to understand me even though I am protected. If he agrees, then I let him have it. Yelling at him usually releases me to my pain. I used to dislike myself for getting angry, but now I realize that often I can only get to my softer feelings by getting angry first; my anger is sometimes the doorway into myself. Once I've gotten it out, I'm generally much softer and more available to looking inward. But if I just stop with the anger and never get into exploring the softer feelings underneath, all I'm doing is being a victim and blaming. I do not learn new things about myself and we remain distant.

What Do I Want Most Right Now?

Before you can move out of protections into exploration you must acknowledge your present intent. Ask yourself:

- "Is my primary intent to be safe?"
- "Is my primary intent to be right, to avoid the pain of being wrong and disapproved of?"
- "Do I want to know myself and my partner? Do I want to get closer?"
- "Is it worthwhile right now to open myself to unpleasant feelings for the sake of intimacy, or would I rather remain distant and safe?"

Until you know your intent, you can't change it.

JORDAN:

Often when I ask myself the question, "What do I want most right now?" I realize that I want to be safe (remain protected). When I see that, I stop blaming Margie for our fight. There's no point in trying to get her to change her intent when I'm not willing to change mine. Sometimes I want to get her to soften first to make it safe for me, but even that doesn't usually work. *If I want to be safe, then she can never make it safe enough for me even if she does soften first, since I can't guarantee her reaction if I open up.* When my "safety" becomes painful enough (and it always does) my intent changes; then I'm willing to risk the pain of opening, because *the pain of the distance has become too great.* When my intent changes my whole demeanor alters immediately: I become soft, open, and willing to learn. But I can't choose to be open until I admit, first to myself, that I have been defensive.

Many therapists or writers of how-to books claim that you "should" be open with your feelings or that you "should not" try to manipulate your partner — in other words, that being defensive and protected is wrong. When you believe it is *wrong* to be protective, you may get caught in an exchange like this: "What's the matter?" "Nothing," or "Why are you angry?" "I'm *not* angry." The denial itself is a protection against being wrong — for protecting! Until you can say — at least to yourself — "Yes, I'm blaming you," or "Yes, I am shutting you out," you are simply stuck.

Everything changes when you acknowledge that you are protective. When you stop blaming your partner, the atmosphere between you changes instantly. Now you can explore the very good reasons each of you has for protecting — which is the first achievement of your exploration.

Becoming Aware of Intention

You can become aware of your true intent by paying attention to your feelings. Protected, you will feel one of two ways: angry, irritated, hostile, resentful; or empty, removed, or indifferent. If you feel hurt, you will feel the victim. You may feel angry, believing that your partner is "making" you feel bad and is therefore at fault. Your partner will see you as defensive — cold, hard, blaming, critical, closed, tense, unavailable, unyielding.

Unprotected, you will feel curiosity, compassion, sadness, or excitement. If you are sad or disappointed, you still remain soft, nonblaming. Your emotions seem to you something to be learned from rather than avoided.

You can also pay attention to your behavior. As we said earlier, *behavior always reflects intent* — sometimes contradicting what is being said. Explorations that get nowhere (or degenerate into another fight) do so because the partners become defensive. Although people are often able to hide their primary intent from themselves *their partner can see it clearly.* Regardless of the words that are used, tone of voice, body language, and facial expression reveal intent. The subtleties of the human voice are hard to capture on the printed page, but anyone can hear the difference between "Why did you do that?" said with irritation and disapproval and "Why did you do that?" said with genuine interest and curiosity.

The vibrations of disapproval are so powerful that they can not be camouflaged. If you say to your partner, "Why are you so distant?" having already decided that this is wrong, no matter how sweetly or softly you ask the question, you will always betray your intent. Each of us is phenomenally sensitive to and perceptive about nuance: *when one person senses another to be hard and judgmental, they are almost always right.*

MARGIE:
Jordan and I have found that when we deny each other's perceptions we cut off learning. If we talk like this, we are trapped:

M: I feel shut out. I'd really like to know why.

J: But I'm not shutting you out.

M: But I still feel shut out.

J: Well, that's your problem. I'm not shutting you out.

M: Yes, you are.

J: No, I'm not.

We are caught in a no-win battle. If we talk like this instead, we will probably discover something:

M: I feel shut out. I'd really like to know why.

J: Well, I'm not aware of shutting you out. What am I doing that's making you feel that way?

M: Well, I guess it's your tone of voice. It's got that flat sound, as if you're holding back from me. Are you angry at me?

J: No, I'm not angry, but I guess I *am* a little irritated.

M: About what?

Now we can explore whatever it is I did that upset him.

Exploring Together

Learning about oneself and another is a many-faceted process: intellectual, emotional, and intuitive. The questions that occur rarely evoke simple or immediate answers. The first answer is often "I don't know," or a superficial reply — only the tip of the iceberg. Deeper answers may come only after a long time, though each answer lets us pursue the remaining questions further. Having a dialogue with someone who really wants to know us makes learning new things about ourselves far easier. Many people, in fact, go into therapy to find this kind of support, but having it from our mate means a great deal more. Examples of this process are found in Chapter 4.

The emotional phase of the exploration is extremely important, though you may not reach it with each exploration, since most of the time is spent intellectually trying to focus and understand the issue. When you make an emotional connection — either to past painful memories or to a buried present pain — the exploration undergoes a crucial shift from an intellectual discussion to an emotional experience. When we deeply experience present pain (for example, the pain of rejection), the past is illuminated; intense recollected emotions may flash before our eyes. An exploration reaches a peak when an intellectual awareness of the causes of the moment's pain connects with an emotional response arising out of the past. Most of us have been taught to try to "get over" upsetting feelings, *but you do not get over them until you get into them.* When we go deeper into our feelings we get new information that takes us a step closer to getting rid of our personal demons.

As you explore your partner, pay close attention to signals that say "I'm sad, scared, hurting. What I'm talking about is painful to me." Notice if your partner's eyes fill with tears, if the corners of the mouth pull down, if the chin quivers. Pay attention to whether you are being emotionally moved by your partner's pain. When you see or sense your partner's pain, you can encourage it with a touch, a hug and a comment such as "I can see this is very painful for you." Helping your partner release his or her emotional pain is one of the most important parts of an exploration.

Often, when one person has explored himself or herself with the help of his or her partner, the explorer feels very loving but the partner does not. Expressing painful feelings and getting understanding in return has released loving feelings: now the other partner may need to do the same before he or she is released. When we are open and vulnerable together, we have made an intimate connection.

Exploring Yourself

When exploring, all you can know is what is going on within you at the moment. You start with that and talk about it, or just feel it. To begin you can tune into your protectiveness — your disapproval of your partner or your lack of feelings — and sense whatever pain (fear, hurt, anxiety, disappointment) is being covered up. When in a conflict, you must first understand what you reacted to, then explore why you reacted as you did. Getting to the bottom of your feelings and understanding them takes time, so please be patient both with yourself and your partner.

The first feeling you are likely to confront is the feeling of being at fault. Everyone reacts differently to the feeling of being in the wrong: some get angry, some start to cry, some become very distant and feel nothing, some become embarrassed, some become rigid and defensive. When you see how you feel and behave when you suspect you've done something wrong, you know that you are both judging yourself and keeping yourself protected from your partner's judgments. Seeing this, you can explore what the judgment is and where it comes from. *The more*

*you explore and discard your self-judgments, the deeper
your knowledge about yourself will become.*

As you become more aware of what is inside you,
you begin to question why you feel the way you do. At
first your talking may sound confused: you are not yet
sure where you are headed, exactly what you are feeling,
or why you are feeling it. The path to discovery is not
straight. But if you keep paying attention to whatever is
going on inside you and trust these feelings to lead you,
you will eventually reach the awareness you seek. However, if you have already decided that your true feelings
are so deeply buried in your unconscious that you cannot
know them, you will not learn much. Our experience
with ourselves and our clients has taught us that the
unconscious is available to conscious awareness when we
really want to know and do not prejudge what may be
there.

In his book *The Search For Existential Identity,*
James F. T. Bugental describes the process he goes through
when exploring himself:

> First, I kind of "soak in" the issues for quite a while. I let
> all angles of it hit me, and I experience the anxiety, anger,
> tension, or whatever emotions go with it. But I don't, if I
> can help it, try to solve it right away. Then, when the
> process is working best, I talk to someone . . . And all I
> do when I talk is say whatever comes to me about the
> matter I'm concerned with — what it feels like and how
> blocked I feel and whatever else comes to mind about it.
> And the person I'm talking with just helps me say it all
> out and avoids advising, criticizing, or getting in my way.
> At this point, an interesting thing begins to happen. As I
> open myself inside so that I say whatever comes to mind,
> all sorts of new perspectives open up also. What seemed
> a hopeless situation gradually comes to have other possi-
> bilities.

When you are willing to ask yourself why you feel
and act as you do, you can explore any area of conflict.

Why do you get so upset when your mate is late? Why
are you always late? Why are you so stingy? Why do you
spend money so recklessly? Why do you watch so much
television? Why do you rarely desire sex or feel excited
sexually? Why do you always drink a lot at parties? Why
do you spend every weekend on the boat with your
buddies instead of with your mate and/or children? Why
are you always so tired that you fall asleep on the couch
at 9:00? Why are you sick so often? Why do you work
such long hours? Why do you rarely want to be alone
with your partner? Why do you lie to your mate? Why do
you promise things and don't follow through? Why do
you take so many drugs? Why do you feel the need for
extramarital affairs? Any conflict, no matter how trivial it
seems, can teach you something new about yourself. By
asking "Why?" with an intent to learn and then pursuing
the reasons behind the reasons, we begin to understand
ourselves and our partner more deeply.

Exploring Your Partner

Many people cannot comprehend what we mean when
we talk about "wanting to know" one's partner. "I do not
need to know any more about him," a woman may snap.
"I know him so well I can tell you exactly what he's going
to do at any moment of the day." When people claim to
know their mates, what they really mean is that they can
reliably predict the others' behavior. But you can predict
someone's behavior without having any idea of how that
behavior came about.

When you don't know what questions to ask your
partner, it may be because you are afraid to know the
answers. Conversely, when your partner repeatedly
answers you with "I don't know," he or she is probably
afraid to know. As William Ofman observes in *Affirmation
and Reality,* "When you say 'I don't know,' it means to

me that you don't wish to look or to attend; it is not so deeply hidden that you can't discover the reason for it quite soon."

When you really want to pursue knowing your partner, you are open to understanding his or her *perceptions and feelings*. But it's extremely difficult to listen to your partner when his or her words hurt or frighten you. When your partner is upset, angry, or withdrawn, those actions are covering fear, anxiety, or other pain, but it is hard to want to get through your partner's blame or indifference and understand what is really there when this very behavior is causing *you* pain. To do this requires your willingness to acknowledge that much of what your partner says about you is probably true. This does not mean that you are wrong for doing it, but you are doing it. If you don't judge yourself for having done whatever is upsetting your partner, then you won't become defensive in return.

Suppose your partner says to you in an accusing tone, "You don't love me" (obviously wanting to change you rather than know you). Your automatic reaction would probably be defensive: "I do so. How can you say that? Only yesterday I bought you a present. I tell you I love you all the time. What's the matter with you? What do you expect, anyway?" You don't really want to know what your partner expects — you just want to talk him or her out of feeling that way (and make him or her feel ashamed of it, too).

But when you really want to understand, you will ask questions with softness and curiosity. First you might try to find out whether your reading of the other's feeling is correct:

"You seem angry to me. Do you feel angry?"

"You seem a long way away from me. Are you feeling distant?"

"You must have some good reasons for feeling as you do. Can you tell me what they are?"

"Have I done something that upsets you?"

"Why does that upset you? There must be some good reasons and I'd like to understand what they are."

"What do you want that you're not getting right now?"

These questions are not a formula, merely examples. When you really want to learn, questions will automatically occur to you. The exploration itself is different for every couple; there are no prescribed questions and no right answers. When you are genuinely curious the questions will flow, just as they do from an inquisitive child.

What ultimately happens will depend on both partners' true intent. Consider the difference between the following two greatly condensed exchanges. Mary is silently angry with Jim:

Both Protected

JIM: (distant, voice slightly hard)
   What's wrong? (His tone of voice shows he doesn't really want to know; he just wants her to stop acting that way.)
MARY:
   Nothing.

Jim plunks himself down in front of the TV and nothing more is said. The distance continues, even widens.

Jim Wanting to Know; Mary Protected

JIM: (genuinely soft and curious)
   You seem upset. What's wrong?

MARY: (closed and hard)
Nothing.

JIM:
Look, hon, I hate this distance. It makes me feel awful. Have I done anything that hurt you?

MARY: (angry and accusing)
Yeah. How come you told Sam and Anne that we'd go out with them Saturday and you never asked me or even told me about it? It's so embarrassing when other people know my plans before I do. Why do you always do that to me? (Mary is still protected, not wanting an answer, just wanting to put Jim in the wrong and get him to stop the behavior that has made her so angry.)

JIM: (still soft and open)
Mary, I'd like to talk about this, but it's hard to understand what the problem is when you're yelling at me. Do you think we could just talk about it for a while?

MARY: (finally softening)
Yes, I guess we do need to talk about it . . .

Now that they are both open, they can start exploring.

At times, you are open and vulnerable but your partner is not. You may then withdraw to lick your wounds. When you are withdrawn, your partner may open and want you to open up again, but you may not be ready yet. Such pulling back says, "Because you would not open when I wanted you to, now it's too late." More than wanting to learn or wanting intimacy, one or both of you wants control over the other's availability. Under these circumstances, the intent to protect oneself and control the other predominates over the desire to explore and share.

You may find it very difficult for both to open up at the same time, either emotionally or sexually. In troubled relationships, it is common for one partner to be open while the other is closed. When one gives up trying to make the other open, the other often feels new freedom to risk and express openness.

When Your Partner Is Closed to Learning

Sometimes one partner is simply unwilling to look inward, though this does not have to shut off exploration for the partner who *does* want to know. If your partner refuses to talk or continues to blame you even when you remain open for a long time, all you can do is accept this decision, after making it clear that you would like to continue exploring when he or she is ready. With the pressure off, he or she may become willing to explore sometime later.

We hear many people, especially women, say, "I want to know myself and my partner. I really love getting into things and understanding them. But my partner is not interested. I don't think he even understands what I'm talking about. He says he doesn't see the point. What can I do?"

One person will rarely remain closed when the other is *truly* open and nonblaming. Before you decide it's your partner's fault, you could thoroughly check out how open you really are. This is hard to do, since casual friends and even a therapist may not see you the way you actually are with your mate. Only your mate, children, an especially close friend, or a therapist who personally engages with you in the therapeutic process, can help you see your long-standing protections.

If you want to look inward but your mate remains protected, you can expect turmoil. Should your mate remain closed, the relationship will eventually end. But people usually choose that alternative far too soon. Before ending the relationship, you can use the present situation to learn some important things about yourself. Most people leave relationships convinced that the other person is at fault, never understanding their part in creating the difficulties. If they can't see that, however, divorce is merely the prelude to another marriage in which two protected people make life difficult for each other. *Divorce without awareness of our protections is an exercise in futility.*

Matt is a client of ours who remained in a troubled relationship long enough to grow considerably. Matt first entered therapy reluctantly, at the insistence of his wife, Sandra, who was fed up with his constant criticism. When he entered therapy, Matt was a hard, controlling male chauvinist who was perpetually angry at Sandra, complaining that her clothes were too revealing, her behavior in public embarrassing. He told her she wasn't sexy enough at home, was a messy housekeeper, and had dreadful friends. He was angry when she wanted to go back to school and furious when she didn't want to make love. They remained in therapy a number of months but got nowhere, since neither was willing to look inward; both wanted only to blame and were unwilling to acknowledge it.

A few years later they returned to therapy, this time at Matt's suggestion. Sandra had decided never to have sex with him again, though she was willing to keep on living with him for the sake of their child. This time Matt was willing to look inward, even though Sandra wasn't. He became fascinated with discovering why he felt the way he did and what had created his feelings. Eventually Sandra began to have a series of affairs, was rarely home, and quit therapy. This was a bitter pill to swallow for a man with rigid values: all Matt's worst fears were coming true. But he never gave up: he stayed with both the marriage and the therapy, continuing to explore his values and fears and his need to control. Slowly, very slowly, Matt opened to his softer nature. Today he is a completely different person: warm and likable, with a sense of deep inner security. Sandra never did open to learning, and Matt finally left that relationship, but he learned a great deal about himself and is now equipped to establish a fuller, more satisfying relationship.

Learning Possibilities When Your Partner Is Protected

1. You can pursue understanding your partner's reluctance, if he or she is willing. Later on he or she may be willing to risk exploring further in return, although *expecting* such reciprocity is really an attempt at control.

2. You can feel the pain of wanting someone to be there for you and not having it. (When this turns into blaming the other for that pain, the spirit of learning is gone.) When you are really open, coming up against another's unavailability is very painful, but a valuable learning experience. For example: How do you deal with rejection? How have you contributed to your mate's protected state? What fears have been activated? What do you do for yourself when the other is unavailable? Does this remind you of experiences in your past?

3. You can play both parts, your partner's and your own, either aloud or silently, asking yourself the questions you would like your partner to ask and then answering them:

> "Are you upset with me?"
> "Yes."
> "How come?"
> "Because I hate it when you yell at me."
> "Why do you hate it?"
> "Because it scares me."

"What scares you about it?"
"It reminds me of when my father used to
yell at me."
"Tell me about that."

Doing this aloud can help your partner understand that
your real intent is to explore yourself rather than blame
him or her.

4. You can go off by yourself and write out your
feelings. In *At a Journal Workshop*, Ira Progoff offers very
helpful patterns for writing to increase self-awareness. You
write as you would talk, starting from whatever you are
aware of and winding down into deeper awareness. You
ask yourself questions that will lead you inside: "Why do
I feel this way? What am I afraid of right now? Am I hurt?
What hurt me? Do I think my partner is wrong? Do I think
I am wrong? What do I really want right now?"

Sharing your writing with your partner may open the
locked door between the two of you. Often a person will
be open to the written word while being closed and
defensive when you say the same thing, probably because
your critical stance and tone of voice are absent from the
written page. If the entire writing, however, is focused on
blaming your partner rather than exploring your own
feelings, your partner will probably remain distant.

Some People Open to Learning Only in a Crisis

Sometimes the person who complains that his or her mate
is not willing to look inside lets the partner go on thinking
that everything is all right, protecting against the other's
anger or hurt. It is the *fear of finding out the truth* that
creates much of the dishonesty in primary relationships.
Telling the truth about what you are doing or feeling may
either bring about the end or create a whole new
relationship. Until you are willing to risk the possibility of

being in pain, it is hard to be honest, but until you are honest, your mate may not see any reason to explore with you.

Earlier in this chapter we described our own tendency to remain protected until the pain of the distance between us was so great that we chose to soften and open to learning. Everyone does this to some degree. People with especially crippling fears and therefore especially rigid protection mechanisms may find it nearly impossible to shed protective behavior until the pain of the bad marriage has become intolerable.

Joe and Helen are clients who opened to learning only in the midst of crisis. Joe had spent most of their fifteen-year marriage ignoring Helen, working long hours, coming home tired, and falling asleep in front of the TV. Sex between them was perfunctory. Helen, who had felt unhappy and unloved for years, finally persuaded Joe to come with her for counseling. But while Helen was feeling unloved, Joe was not in any pain; he saw no reason to be any different from what he was.

Finally, after she found out that Joe had been having affairs for years, Helen began to have a series of affairs, and after a short time fell in love. For the first time in her life, she felt loved and realized that she was a highly sexual person. Her lover called several times a day, shared his deepest feelings with her, and made love to her for hours. Joe had known of Helen's other affairs and remained indifferent to them, but he did not know she was now in love.

Despite the excitement of her affair, Helen still wanted her marriage to Joe, wishing she could have him back as he was during their courtship. She was also perceptive enough to see that her lover behaved toward *his* wife as Joe did toward her — which made her suspect that a new partner would not magically improve her life.

One night Helen told Joe everything; she was still thinking of leaving him and wanted him to know why. She told him all about her affair, how it made her feel important and loved, and that she had never felt that way before. *For the first time* she told him how much she resented the poverty of their sex life. She claimed that she had never told him before because she had never wanted to "hurt his feelings," although she had actually been unwilling to bring it up because she was afraid of his anger or (worse) indifference.

Now Joe was frightened instead of indifferent; he abruptly became aware that he really loved Helen and did not want to lose her, which suddenly made him more open to understanding his own protections. Of course, Joe's protections did not drop away immediately, following his new awareness. But as he saw the shape of his protections and the ways they blocked his new desire to revive his and Helen's commitment to each other, Joe began to break through the barriers. From that point on they were able to better understand each other and meet each other's needs.

It takes courage to explore another's behavior when that behavior may be painful to us. But as exploration reveals the "why" of a couple's interaction, a coherent pattern emerges instead of a maze of difficulties. As each partner comes to understand his or her equal share in creating the problems, blame, self-doubt, and discord give way to personal responsibility, mutual respect, and intimacy.

·4·

Explorations: The Process Applied

We shall not cease from exploration
And the end of all our exploring
Will be to arrive where we started
And know the place for the first time.
T. S. ELIOT

At this point you may be convinced of the value of explorations yet lack a clear picture of them — how they progress. This chapter looks at actual explorations in progress. As you watch others trying to break through their barriers, you may occasionally glimpse your own situation and a brighter future for your relationship. We have included some of the wanderings typical of explorations — the distractions and shifts of attention from one person to another, the touching on many issues before finally focusing on one person and then the other. You will see the clarity emerge and watch the exploration reach a satisfying conclusion.

Exploring Protections

In this session, Jordan is the therapist and Maxine and Don, a couple who have been in therapy for only a few weeks, are his clients. They have been living together for nearly a year and are now planning to marry. They have come into therapy because she feels uncomfortable about getting married without first resolving some problems and understanding her reservations. Neither of them is completely comfortable; the central issue lies buried beneath protections on both sides. As the session unfolds, Don is hostile, mistrustful of the therapist and the process, and determined to resist what he considers an invasion of his privacy. He resembles a debater examining a proposition in the cold light of reason. Not until Maxine opens herself to her pain is the issue of control and resistance revealed.

Don enters the session obviously uptight. Holding his body rigid, he stares coldly into space somewhere between Maxine and Jordan. Jordan's observations are in parentheses.

MAXINE:
We've been hassling all morning over money.

JORDAN:
Is that what you'd like to talk about in this session?

DON:
Sure. (His answer comes through a clenched jaw, with a clipped and controlled tone of voice.)

JORDAN:
Okay, is either of you in a place to want to understand the other?

DON:
(Disgustedly) I don't even know what that means.

MAXINE:
Do you have any ideas how we could solve this problem?

DON:
No, not particularly.

JORDAN:
I'm not so concerned about finding a solution as I am
hoping to get into a deeper exploration of why you each
feel as you do. A solution will emerge from that process.

DON:
(To Maxine) Then you'd better begin, because I don't
know where to start.

JORDAN:
You don't seem to be really open for her to explore her
feelings.

DON:
Well, this goes back to the first session. You're asking if
I want to explore her feelings and I don't know what that
means. Of course I want to explore her feelings, but
I don't know the first thing about going into this deeper
thing you're talking about. It all sounds like a crock to
me.

   (Don is even harder now and vibrations of hostility fill
the room.)

JORDAN:
It's not that you don't know how to go about knowing
another person's feelings. When you're really open to
learning, the questions will come fast enough. It's quite
simple; you'd say something like "I want to know more
about your feelings." But I don't experience you as
wanting to learn and that's where you're stuck.

DON:
You're full of shit!

JORDAN:
So far in this session I've seen no indication that you
want to know anything more about Maxine's feelings.

DON:
I thought she was going to explore mine. (Using his

73

debating tactic here when feeling attacked, Don suddenly shifts the premise of the talk.)

JORDAN:

If you want her to explore your feelings, we can start that way. You can do it any way you want.

MAXINE:

(To Don) What are you feeling right now?

DON:

I'm feeling . . . uh, like I'm being put on the spot.

MAXINE:

(She's angry with him now and puts him down.) Well, what's wrong with that? You put me on the spot lots of times.

(Since neither of them is open to learning and both just want to prove the other wrong, they get into an argument about who's on the spot and about her willingness to be on the spot and the argument wanders for about five minutes.)

JORDAN:

We're obviously not going to get anywhere near your issue until you find out what's going on right here and now. You're both very protected and I'd like you to try to explore those protections. Maxine, what happens when you come up against Don's defensiveness?

MAXINE:

I feel scared. We have a difference of opinion and he comes on so strong on his side that it's impossible for me to disagree.

JORDAN:

Well, not impossible, but it sure is difficult.

DON: (Still hard and quite defensive in his tone)

I think *that* exploration is pretty simple. I have a history of being very stubborn and definitive about my beliefs, and I tend to be a debater.

MAXINE: (Blaming)
Yeah, I guess I feel I'm not as strong as you verbally and I'd like you to get off your soap box and not debate with me about every little thing. I'd like a little more room to get close and to open up.

JORDAN:
But something closes you up in the face of his strong position.

MAXINE: (Introspective)
That's true, I do hold back. I guess I always have, since I was a kid. Maybe that accounts for my holding back with you, (Don). I'd sure like to get out of that pattern and be able to express my thoughts and feelings more openly.

JORDAN:
What both of you can explore right now is his debater's posture. There's something about that that scares you, so you withdraw from it. Can we go farther into that, why it scares you, what it taps into, what goes on inside you when you experience him that way?

MAXINE:
I've been experiencing him that way this whole session, and it's made me very nervous.

DON: (With her willingness to look inward, his hostility and hardness have lessened a bit.)
Why are you nervous?

MAXINE:
Because I feel you're hostile.

DON:
Toward you?

MAXINE:
Or just in general, not just targeted toward me necessarily, but a kind of aura.

JORDAN:
Do you know what she means?

DON:
Yes, I do, because I think I feel a little hostile. Not necessarily targeted but I sort of feel like I'm in enemy territory.

(As he says that he laughs uncomfortably and it seems to relieve his tension. The level of strain in the room drops noticeably.)

JORDAN:
When you experience his hostility, what does that do to you?

MAXINE: (Softer)
Well, I don't really know how to combat that. I get scared. I close up and I say to myself, "What's the use?" I'm not willing to fight that.

DON:
When you say scared, what does that mean? I mean, to me fear is something concrete, like when you have to go to your boss and ask for a raise, or a dog growls at you or something like that. Is that the same kind of fear you feel when you're afraid of me?

MAXINE:
The fear I'm talking about? I don't know. I suddenly protect myself.

(Maxine has become more physically withdrawn, curled in a ball. She seems very scared and on the verge of tears.)

JORDAN:
If you were not to protect yourself, what would be going on inside of you?

MAXINE:
If I stopped protecting myself? Oh, I suppose I would

come out with what I was feeling and I'd approach him instead of withdrawing.

JORDAN:

His hostility scares you and you protect yourself. If you didn't shut off what you feel inside you, and if you let yourself feel deeply, what would come out?

MAXINE:

I'm not sure. Anger, maybe?

JORDAN:

Anger would be just another protection. See if right now you can feel what it's like to be at the other end of Don's hostility, his making you wrong, his putting up a wall of ice between you.

MAXINE:

I want to cry and curl up like a little kid. That's it — I feel like a little kid.

DON:

You feel that way now? (He is really open, soft and genuinely caring toward her.)

MAXINE:

Yeah, and I don't want to explore it either.

DON:

Why not?

MAXINE:

Because I get tired of feeling like a little kid. I guess I feel that way an awful lot.

DON:

In this kind of a situation?

MAXINE:

Yes.

JORDAN:

You're judging that feeling. Do you believe there's something wrong with feeling that way?

(Don is touched by Maxine's openness and
vulnerability and moves from the opposite end of the
couch to put his arm around her.)

MAXINE:

It's about time I grew up. (Her tone is clearly self-critical.)

DON:

What do you mean grow up?

MAXINE:

Not feeling vulnerable, not feeling childlike, not feeling
little, not feeling stupid, small, and weak.

DON:

When I get angry, you feel that way?

MAXINE:

Yes, but *you* don't make me feel that way.

JORDAN:

Right. He does something that makes you feel afraid and
you equate feeling afraid with all those other feelings
you've judged as negative.

MAXINE:

Yes, I do.

JORDAN:

I think it's very important to help you respect those
feelings. It's appropriate to feel the way you do when
you're at the other end of another person's hostility,
closedness, hardness. I don't judge it as childish. If you
didn't protect yourself, you would feel just plain terrible.
It's scary. It feels bad. What you're saying is that you
don't want to feel those feelings, because you judge them
as childish. They are childish in the sense that when you
were a child you often felt that way. Before we learned to
protect ourselves we all felt hurt and afraid. So now we
are protected from those feelings and many people
believe they've gotten rid of them or that an adult

wouldn't feel them. But in reality, if we weren't protective we would all feel those same feelings when someone disapproves of us.

MAXINE:
But I want to fight back or develop more protections so I don't feel this way.

DON:
Why would you want that?

MAXINE:
Because I'd rather feel strong than weak.

JORDAN:
But it's important for you to realize that you only feel weak because you judge this feeling as childish. It's your belief that makes you feel weak. I've come to believe that my protections are my weakness. They come up when I'm afraid to be who I really am. I feel strong and best about myself when I'm willing to be fully me.

MAXINE:
Well, actually, ideally, I'd like to be who I am, no matter what.

JORDAN:
And who you are when Don is hostile is a frightened person.

MAXINE:
Right.

JORDAN:
I'd like to share something with you now that I was unwilling to share earlier. This is really hard for me to admit, but I still react exactly the same as you when other people act hostile to me. In the beginning of the session when you, Don, were angry and I felt your hostility directed at me, it scared me. Your silent anger is very powerful and I had a strong reaction in my gut. I felt my

stomach start to throb and I had to do something to shut
that feeling off. So I sat back and took some deep breaths
so you wouldn't see how I was affected. Sometimes that
judge in me still comes up to say, "What's the matter
with you? You're successful, you feel good about yourself
and you should be done with that stuff by now." But the
reality is, sometimes I'm scared and it feels like being two
years old. It feels like being a child because I'm not
supposed to feel those feelings at this time in my life. I'm
supposed to be done with feeling scared and threatened.

MAXINE:
Me too.

JORDAN:
The reality is that I'm not done with it and sometimes
I get frightened by another's anger at me. Even anger in
the room is unsettling. I want to get away, I don't want to
be in the same room with hostility.

MAXINE:
I have those same feelings.

DON:
I guess sometimes I do too.

MAXINE:
I felt afraid all my childhood.

JORDAN:
There must have been some very good reasons why you
were afraid all those years.

DON:
Were you afraid people wouldn't like you and put you
down?

MAXINE:
Maybe. I always tried to be perfect.

JORDAN:
And if you weren't perfect, then people would
disapprove of you?

MAXINE:
Yeah, then I wouldn't be right or smart enough or fast enough. I think that's part of it.

DON:
So that was a constant fear? If you weren't right up there at 100 percent, then you were going to get it, to be disapproved of? You always had to be perfect?

MAXINE:
Or I wouldn't be loved.

DON:
That must be a lot of what you feel when I get entrenched in being right. I can understand that in light of the talks we've had concerning your dad. You must see me, at those times, as being like him. And I also see your parents pushing you. I feel it every time we're with your folks. It's awesome.

MAXINE:
"My kid can be president of the United States."

DON:
And anything less than that is unacceptable.

MAXINE:
Eventually even that wouldn't be enough.

JORDAN:
So you believed that in your parents' eyes you were lovable only when you were functioning at 100 percent.

DON:
Are you aware of what they do that makes you feel their disapproval?

MAXINE:
It's a withdrawal of love. From my dad more than my mom. My mother has gotten that way too, but she wasn't always like that. I just remembered . . . I can still cry about it. (She starts to cry.) It's so strange to cry after all

these years. I remember messing up in a ballet recital and feeling humiliated, just, you know, awful. My mom didn't think it was so awful and thought it was ridiculous for me to feel so badly, but I felt terrible.

DON:

How does that relate to your father?

MAXINE:

I knew she could be accepting but that didn't matter because I knew he wouldn't be.

JORDAN:

That's what gets tapped into when Don gets angry. You know that Don is not like your father, in having that kind of expectation. But when he's angry, or hard in some way, that's where you go.

MAXINE:

Yes, it seems crazy that here I am considering marrying someone like my father.

JORDAN:

Well, he's not as disapproving as your father, but even a slight harshness still taps into this deep well of feelings that you've grown up with.

MAXINE:

I suppose so. (Considering) Yes.

DON:

It's like living your whole life waiting for the other shoe to drop.

MAXINE:

Kind of weird, isn't it?

DON:

That's a tension or a fear that must be in you all the time.

MAXINE:

Well, I guess so. I do feel somewhat driven every day.

I do continue to achieve and no matter what I achieve it doesn't take away my tension.

JORDAN:

How are you feeling about Don right now?

MAXINE:

Much better.

JORDAN:

What are you getting right now that's different?

MAXINE:

Just receptivity to how I feel. I guess a lot more openness. And I feel really cared about.

JORDAN:

The hardness or anger you reacted to is sometimes very subtle. He looks pretty much the same now as he did at first, but the hardness is gone. It seems like such an intangible thing, but it's very real. It's a vibration and you can definitely feel it. This is the kind of exploration that I've been talking about. You've just scratched the surface for now. There's a lot more you can explore with Don about your reactions, your sensitivity to his anger. You have a lot to learn about your protections and Don has a lot to learn about his. Don, you can learn a lot about why you get so hard when someone doesn't agree with you. I think the two of you could really get into exploring your money issue right now and come up with some important new awareness about that.

This almost-verbatim transcript of one session illustrates how one protection, identified and at least partly explained, opens many roads to further explorations. Had these two people been exploring by themselves, it might have taken them weeks to reach these awarenesses, but with persistence they certainly could have reached them on their own. All the answers were already inside, waiting to be discovered. The therapist has only helped in the discovery process, shortening the time between conflict and awareness.

Exploring an Issue

Peggy and Milt, married for ten years, have three small children under the age of seven. Peggy, a nurse, works nights and Milt, formerly a teacher, now works days in his dad's new store. He also conducts teacher workshops to generate extra much-needed income. Despite the pressures of three babies and severe financial problems, they have built a basically sound relationship. Right now, they are planning some workshops in which Peggy and Milt will be co-leaders, so we gave them a copy of an early draft of our book. They have become enthusiastic enough about exploring to tape their discussions so they can learn from listening to themselves. They readily agreed to let us include excerpts from one of their discussions (this one actually took place in bed).

Peggy and Milt, more aware of their own protections than Don and Maxine, can recognize a surface issue and probe it fairly openly. In this condensed version of their discussion they move, circuitously, from a conflict over Milt's spontaneity and Peggy's sense of economic reality through issues of how they spend money and time, to behavior that keeps a much deeper issue at bay.

The first part of their talk wanders around feelings and issues that come up when Milt, who feels that he is carrying the greater share of the burden of achieving intimacy, hits on two issues so closely connected they are hard to unsnarl.

MILT:
Whenever I suggest a night out, or a vacation, or going into therapy, you pour cold water on it. "We can't afford

it." "We have to get these notes (for the workshop) straightened out." "You know I can't get a babysitter on such short notice."

PEGGY:

Can we talk about specifics — a time when you wanted to do something and I talked you out of it?

MILT:

Well, like taking a vacation or going into therapy. Initially, we went into therapy on my insistence. You asked "How much is it going to cost?" and "Where will we find the time?" It's like, I didn't give a damn, we needed some help. It was real important. I felt like I really had to struggle to make that happen, that I was in it alone. And all the time I was wondering what really goes on inside you. What are you afraid of? Being broke or something else?

PEGGY:

(This is the beginning level of exploration, her initial thought. It is all she is consciously aware of.) I think there are logical reasons why I feel that way. My biggest thing is just the money. I've been doing the bills for a long time and you haven't. I worry a lot. You weren't getting any money from the store at first and my work was the only place we were getting our money. And every week I'd be doing the bills and trying to figure out how to meet them, based on whether I work five days a week or four. If I work five days every week we still don't have enough to live on without any other income, so the thought of spending money on therapy or a vacation just scared me to death. I couldn't enjoy a vacation or concentrate on therapy worrying about the mortgage and all that other stuff.

MILT:

Okay. I understand that. But when we were talking about

going on vacation and *that* was the issue, I seemed to feel
something going on between us that is bigger than the
issue or the reasons you gave to talk me out of the
vacation. Why, when I make a suggestion, do I mostly get
a negative response from you? You seem to me to be
taking the role of the parent, the responsible one and
that's what I'd really like to talk about, to understand.

PEGGY:

Okay, maybe I do feel like I'm more responsible and
you're like the kid who says, "Forget the money, we'll
get it somehow." We'll go on vacation and when the
mortgage comes due or any bills, you're not usually the
one who deals with crises. You know I can think of the
consequences of things more clearly than you do. Like
when you say, "Let's go out to supper and spend five
hours alone," immediately I start to plan: we leave at 4:00
and the kids will be coming home from school;
somebody will have to pick up Lainey and someone's
going to have to pick up Hilary; someone's going to have
to feed them supper and put them to bed; which
babysitter can do those things? You don't think of the
consequences, you just want it your way. Like a little kid,
you don't think about what that means, how we'll
manage to do that. (Her tone of voice is not angry or
accusing, just factual, trying to reconstruct the sequence
as it happens.)

MILT:

Is that something you feel consistently in our relationship,
in a lot of things or just — ?

PEGGY:

I don't think so, not in all things. You take responsibility
for supper and for a lot of things, but it's more. Just when
you make up your mind you want to do something,
you're more spontaneous and you want to do it right

away. Maybe, well, like at Disneyland when you want to go or stop and we're with the kids, you just want to do it as soon as you think of it. And I'm thinking "Whoa! The kids need more time to be prepared before we can just stop or start a different activity." You don't think of the consequences, just want to do it spontaneously and I value that, but I have to think of the results of what you want to do.

MILT: (Surprised rather than defensive)
Do you resent that?

PEGGY:
Sometimes I wish you'd think about how it affects me or the kids — how it would affect all of us.

MILT:
You resent that I put you in that spot, that I have a spontaneous impulse and that you have to play the heavy? Is that something you feel?

PEGGY:
Yeah. You make me look more like the bad guy. "Mom doesn't want to go. Peggy doesn't want to do this."

MILT:
Do we ever get into the reverse role? Do I ever take that responsible posture and you take the more irresponsible posture? Or do you think we both act consistently the way you describe?

PEGGY:
When we were talking outside about what we could do to the house to give us more room and I tried to think of what we could do to the garage or the inside, you said, like "Oh, it doesn't matter, we don't have any money. Let's not even talk about it." Then I stopped talking about it. So I guess you do sometimes.

MILT:
So are you saying that you feel you're in that role a lot?

Do you feel it's a burden all the time or just from time to time? Or do you feel it's very characteristic of our decision-making and a source of a lot of hassle between us?

PEGGY:
Well, I would say it comes up frequently, although I can't think of other examples right now.

MILT:
All right, I'd like to get back to the original issue I brought up, the intimacy issue, and see if we can connect it to this thing about responsibility. To me it seems you want intimacy as much as I do, but it's not something you drive for or that you feel any great loss from not having. I feel I take more responsibility, be it irresponsible responsibility, to try to create intimacy. I make suggestions about doing things, whether it's a trip or a dinner out or a time to do something, whether it is finding a sitter for the kids or whatever it happens to be. I feel I'm usually put down or made wrong or made to feel irresponsible for wanting things or for suggesting them.

PEGGY:
You say that you want to go places and get a babysitter and do this and that, but at home you're the one who wants to sit in front of the TV at night more than I do.

MILT:
Sounds like you're saying, "You're really not all that spontaneous, or you don't want intimacy as much as you say you do. Because on the one hand you're saying you want intimacy, but on the other hand you're the one who wants to watch TV." Is that what you're saying?

PEGGY:
It's not that I don't watch TV. Just yesterday I said I would like to get rid of the TV because I get sucked into

it too when it's turned on. I'd feel better if we just got rid of it, if we just didn't have it, because I think it gets in the way of intimacy. We waste a lot of time on it.

MILT:
So you feel that you want more intimacy too and you're feeling . . .

PEGGY:
But I don't need to just go out for supper to feel intimate. I'd like to be able to share close time in the house too.

MILT:
And you think that perhaps if the TV was gone . . . ? What's your fantasy about that? What does our time together look like to you?

PEGGY: (Musing)
That thing wouldn't be on after supper. Until the kids went to bed it would be pretty much the same, but then we could spend time together for a couple of hours at night before I went to work. That would be a *lot* of time. Then we wouldn't have to go some place away from the house, because that's what you're saying we have to do to have that time. I guess I don't like that thought. I would like to be able to be intimate in our own home, rather than have to go some place. I'm saying you have some responsibility too, when we're in the house. It isn't just me that doesn't want closeness or doesn't do anything to try to get it just because I don't want to go out for supper or get a babysitter or whatever it is.

MILT:
Are you saying that you see those things as superficial and feel that I could participate more by making things around the house more intimate?

PEGGY:
Well, that both of us could do that, not just you. This

whole discussion is because you feel that you're the one
wanting it more than I do. That I am the one who is
always squashing it and not wanting to get close.

MILT:

Does that make you feel bad when I say or imply that?

PEGGY:

Yes.

MILT:

Because it doesn't feel right, because that's really not the
way you feel?

PEGGY:

Right. That's not the way I feel.

MILT:

How do you feel? I'd like to know how much intimacy
you think we really have.

PEGGY:

We don't have enough of it. When you come home from
work, there's a lot of confusion initially when the kids
and the dog meet you at the door, and then lots of
activity around supper and then after supper you go in
and watch TV and the kids are around and then one or
both of us puts the kids to bed and the TV's on. You
collapse on the couch and you're gone.

MILT:

What you've been saying to me is that there are a lot of
things about what I do. And I think you're right that I do
these things and these things are important for me to take
a look at. But you also have a part in all of this. Are you at
all interested in exploring your part? Because what I start
to feel is that even though I do these things, somehow
you've gone along and I haven't heard very strongly, until
now, that you want to do something to have more
intimacy. So it still feels that I make the suggestions and
you reject them, but I don't feel you taking part in

making it happen. Is that something you feel you could
take a look at and we could explore?

PEGGY:

Sure, I guess the only thing I've ever said is that I don't
like the TV on so much, that I want to watch TV less.
That's all I've ever done about it.

MILT:

Why don't you say anything at the time or just turn off
the TV?

PEGGY:

I couldn't do that! That'd be too scary. Lots of times
I really want to do it, but . . . . Okay, so I turn off the TV
and then you say, "What do you want to talk about?"

MILT: (Surprised, with dawning understanding)
You think I'd say, "What do you want to talk about?"

PEGGY:

I guess I don't *really* think you'd say *that*. You might just
say, "I don't feel like talking tonight. I'm too tired."
I mean, the way you feel after the kids get to sleep, you
don't want to put any energy into anything. Oh, I don't
know, there must be something else I'm afraid of, but
I'm not sure what it is.

MILT:

Let's talk about your fear of turning off the TV and not
knowing what to talk about. Are you afraid of something
if we talk about ourselves?

PEGGY:

Well . . . I think I'm afraid of the unknown — what's
going to happen, what I'll find out. You know, that you
might be unhappy about something. I guess I'm always
afraid you might be unhappy with something that's going
on between us. Hmmm, I also think I'm not as skilled in
expressing my feelings as you are, like when I get so
emotional and I cry, I can't express my feelings.

MILT:
Are you saying you're afraid of discovering that I don't love you as much . . . ?

PEGGY:
I don't think that's it. I think you love me. More just finding out that you might be unhappy about something with me or unhappy with something in our relationship.

MILT:
What do you think I might be unhappy about?

PEGGY:
One thing all this might be related to is the workshop, dealing with the workshop. (Her tone suggests a sudden insight.) You've taken much of the responsibility for that, come up with most of the ideas for it. I see you as more skilled in identifying exactly what we're going to do in it. I think I'm a little scared about that. Maybe I don't want you to find out that I'm not going to be a help or that I'm not going to have much to contribute.

MILT:
You're afraid I'll disapprove of you?

PEGGY:
More that you'll be disappointed in me. That I won't be able to help as much and have as good ideas as you do.

MILT:
Then what would happen — I'd think less of you or . . . ?

PEGGY:
Yes, you'd think less of me.

MILT:
You're afraid as I find out more about you I won't like what I find out?

PEGGY:
Or that I just don't have ideas . . . I don't know.

MILT:
Are you afraid you're not good enough?

PEGGY:

Yes. (Starting to cry)

MILT: (Softly and gently)

What do you feel about that? (Peggy is crying quite hard now and Milt, moved by her pain is somewhat choked up himself. They cry together for a few minutes.) Do you have any sense of connecting this to the past at all? Did you have these feelings as a kid?

PEGGY:

I never felt insecure before. I feel I've gotten less secure as I've gotten older. When I was in college I felt more secure. In the past years I've felt more inadequate. Maybe since I stopped working regularly I've felt more inadequate. I think maybe I got good feelings from work. Since I stopped working days, I haven't gotten that good feedback. When you started doing the business and I was much more into the housewife-mother role and also when we — our whole life changed, when you started the new business . . . everything.

MILT:

So your feelings of inadequacy are related to my approval or just more about yourself? That's what I don't understand.

PEGGY:

I think it's more about myself — that I haven't had as much positive feedback since I stopped working. But that just happened to occur simultaneously with when you started the business. Your whole focus was on something else and then my whole focus was with the house and the kids and then I stopped getting a lot of positive feedback I used to get from my job.

MILT:

Are you saying that because we're starting on this workshop thing together . . . I'm confused. That my approval . . . ?

PEGGY:

No, I'm not saying that not getting your approval is causing my feelings of inadequacy. Because I don't feel as adequate as I used to feel. Now, when we're starting on this whole thing together, I just don't feel good about myself. And as a result of that I guess I *am* afraid you'll see me as inadequate. You always say and have told people how good I was at my job (crying again) and I think you're going to see whether that's really true. You've always *said* that, but I don't know how you knew it. How did you know it? Did I tell you?

MILT:

No. I knew though, from what other people said and just from knowing you. Just knowing how you would tell me about what happened at work and stuff like that. I just have a sense of your confidence, and your competence, and your sense of adequacy.

PEGGY:

So maybe it's related to that. That this is the first time you'll see me on the job. Maybe I'm afraid I won't live up to your expectations.

MILT:

Do you think my expectations are high?

PEGGY:

They're not too high. *I* think they *should* be high. I feel good that they're high. I'm just not sure I can meet them.

MILT:

Do you think that is true in other things too in our relationship? Is that any of the scariness of the intimacy, my expectations of you or your expectations of yourself, how you'll perform when we're intimate? Is that what frightens you? I'm just fishing. We started off talking about what you might be scared of in terms of being in control — being less in control — being spontaneous, and then we moved from that to the feeling of not being able to meet expectations, mostly with the workshop. In terms of the intimacy, is that what you were frightened of, is that the same thing? That you won't live up to my expectations for being what you think I want from an intimate partner?

PEGGY:

Maybe. It seems just generally that I won't be able to meet your expectations. I think it's just a general feeling of inadequacy.

MILT:

Are you feeling that right now as you are opening up to me? Do you have any fear that I won't like you or disapprove or be disappointed?

PEGGY: (Sobbing)

No. Knowing you, it doesn't make any sense that you'd be judgmental or angry at me or anything. I know you're not like that, so I don't know what I'm afraid of.

MILT:

Was there anyone in your childhood who was very disapproving?

PEGGY: (With a startled awareness)

Oh yes! My sister! She was always putting me down, always saying I wasn't good enough. I could never meet her expectations. (She's crying quite hard as this insight releases a heavy burden and deep pain.)

MILT: (Caringly)

Come here, hon. So you're afraid I'll act like your sister?

PEGGY:

Yes, but now that we talk about it, I know you're not like that at all.

Sometime in the future Peggy will need to explore further her early childhood relationships and their influence on her present behavior. But for the present she feels released, having explored until she could fully express her feelings and get Milt's understanding. Milt, however, was not feeling finished and needed to talk some more. They explored why he always wanted to go out to be intimate, why he always turned on the TV, and how he felt when Peggy resisted. When he was able to get into his soft feelings and get her understanding, he was released and they felt very much in love. The problem didn't just magically go away, but for the moment their intimacy was very intense; they reported that beautiful lovemaking followed. While they hadn't solved either issue, they were now feeling friendly and loving toward each other, and the door was opened to deeper explorations.

From Conflict to Resolution — Our Own Awareness

It sometimes takes years to untangle the subtle web of issues contained in some conflicts. We would like to share a summary of the back-and-forth awarenesses we gained from exploring an important issue of our own.

The Issue

Jordan wanted to make love and Margie rarely felt like it. Each time this issue arose both would immediately become protective. For many years, to avoid Jordan's withdrawal Margie would make love even though she was not feeling very loving or sexy. This never quieted Jordan's complaints. When Margie decided that she wouldn't make love if she didn't feel like it, she began to refuse more and more often but always with hardness and irritation. When Jordan either received or sensed a rejection, he would turn away in a huff rather than want to find out why she felt the way she did. Margie would then get angry at Jordan for his turning away, unwilling to see that his reaction might have resulted from hurt feelings. Jordan would then get angry in response to Margie's anger. Neither could start to explore the issue until their protections were examined.

The Protections

MARGIE:

When Jordan snubbed me, I would get instantly angry — that is, when I didn't want to look inside and experience how hurt and afraid I felt. I didn't want Jordan to know he'd hurt me, nor did I want to explore why I was feeling the way I was. I just wanted him to feel he had done something wrong, so he would change. When I saw my anger as a protective device, however, I could see that I felt very unloved when Jordan withdrew from me, and I connected this to deep pockets of pain from my past. When Jordan shut me out and I allowed myself to experience the present hurt and fear, I would sometimes recall events of my childhood and even infancy.

Once I suddenly remembered moving away from our farm at thirteen months old; I cried off and on for two weeks with Jordan after recalling the pain of never seeing my grandfather again. I realized that when Jordan spurned me I often felt like that small abandoned child. When I felt my pain, instead of covering it with anger, I got to know myself more and more deeply, which made me better able to handle Jordan's withdrawal. That doesn't mean I am unaffected by it; it always makes me very sad, but now I usually pursue finding out why he is withdrawn rather than blaming him for it. When I want to know him rather than criticize him, he is usually willing to explore his own hurt and fear.

JORDAN:

Earlier in our marriage, when Margie was irritated and critical, I would either lash out at her or withdraw to punish her. Then I became aware that my angry withdrawal was a defense against feeling hurt. But I never actually *felt* hurt. I would say things like "What you just said really hurt me." Margie often replied with "I don't feel you being hurt." The truth was I didn't feel anything in my body — no pain, hurt, or fear. "Then how do you know you're hurt?" she would ask. I was stumped. "I guess I'm not willing to allow myself to feel it." "When you *tell* me you're hurt rather than *feel* it, I feel you're blaming me and I get defensive," she would reply. I felt stuck.

In the middle of one of these arguments, Margie began to cry. When she described the pain she felt when I shut her out, I realized with dismay how I had probably hurt many people in my life, children, parents, friends, and especially Margie. I shared my sad thoughts with Margie, who was deep in her own thoughts. As I talked, tears were welling up and were about to burst out when Margie said, coldly and critically, "See, even now you're just talking about it and not willing to feel your feelings." All the rising feelings immediately drained, and I felt nothing.

A few minutes went by and she finally said to me, "What's going on?" I answered, "Normally I would be furious with you for putting me down. Now, I can accept it, but it really hurt me. I feel dead right now. It's amazing to me that I could be feeling so much one minute and so completely cut off the next." As I told her what was going on, without blaming, my sad feelings returned, and with them a

flood of thoughts about not wanting to be so
vulnerable. I didn't like her having the power to
hurt me; it felt stupid that a man of my age should
be so easily hurt. When Margie seemed accusatory,
I would instantly feel like a naughty child. I imagined her staying angry at me forever while I was
helpless. This scared me, and I would get distant or
defensive. All this happened in seconds, before
I even realized I was afraid.

The Consequences of Our Protections

MARGIE:

What I want most is for Jordan to want to know
me deeply. However, when I get mad, my anger
makes him feel wrong, and then he certainly doesn't
want to stick around to find out what *else* he's done
wrong. By making him wrong for not wanting to
know me, I actually play a part in his doing that.

I have also realized that to be a fully sexual person
I need to feel loved and not give myself up. If I give
myself up even a little bit, my sex drive and my
responsiveness both diminish. I need to like myself
to feel sexual, and I don't like myself when I give
myself up. Passion occurs only when I feel loved
and feel good about me at the same time.

JORDAN:

As we explored, I realized that what I was
unhappy about — Margie's lack of interest in sex —
was the very thing I was helping to bring about.
When Margie feels loved, she is very sexual. Of
course, I would like her to feel sexual even when
I'm protected — and sometimes, when she is feeling
very good about herself, she does — but I had to
accept at that point in our lives that my protections

still set off hers.

As we explored the issue still further, we found the answers to many questions about ourselves.

The Values, Beliefs, Fears, and Expectations Surrounding the Issue

JORDAN:

My values were "A woman should always attempt to please her husband," and "She should put herself aside rather than upset me." I wondered how I got these beliefs and if they still applied. I recalled hearing other men say, "A man must be boss in his house. Never let your wife get away with anything. It's her job to please you." I had never articulated these values and beliefs to myself before; now I had the choice of redefining them or leaving them as they were, though whatever the choice, it was mine, not Margie's. My expectations were "If Margie really cared about me, she would be turned on whenever I wanted to make love," and "If she really cared about me, she would do what I want, as long as my requests were reasonable." Behind these values, beliefs, and expectations were deep doubts that I had avoided for years by deciding to take in stride Margie's lack of desire for me.

One evening I allowed myself to feel the pain of her rejections. Memories came tumbling though my mind. I recalled my teen years, when I so badly wanted and needed sexual experiences. I recalled the humiliation of masturbating, feeling inadequate not to be having sex with a woman. I believed then that being desired would have made me feel worthwhile, adequate, and manly — but that never happened. Oh, the pain of feeling vulnerable! As I shared my feelings with Margie, I realized that I had always been afraid that I was physically unattractive. My image of myself was stuck as the skinny teenager I used to be; I recalled feeling inadequate in the boy's gym, when I feared that my penis was too small. As I experienced these past pains, crying and talking with Margie, I began to release myself from those old images and see myself as I really am today.

Because of my insecurities about my body and my lovability, I had always been afraid of losing Margie, which led to my attempts to keep her from feeling too good, which then made *her* feel unloved. In trying to protect myself from losing her, I was actually bringing about the thing I was most afraid of.

MARGIE:

My explorations of this issue have been similarly powerful. I recalled that day from my childhood when my grandmother opened the closet door and caught my cousin and me playing doctor. She glared down at us coldly, threatening to tell my parents if she ever caught me again (not him — I was the only wrong one). I got the message loud and clear: for girls, looking and touching were *wrong*. My childish sexuality was in reality very innocent; I was just curious. But I was told in so many different ways that this was wrong that I put great effort into shutting out all desire. I never touched myself, never masturbated, and slowly but surely repudiated curiosity and desire. Later, when I was a teenager, my relatives saw me very inaccurately. They were always worried that I would get into trouble (i.e., be promiscuous, get pregnant). If they had really seen me, they needn't have worried; I was too frightened of my sexuality to get into trouble. I couldn't

understand what they were afraid of. Didn't they
know I had learned my lessons well, not only from
them but from movies, TV, books, and peers?

As I was growing up, my sexuality and my
personal worth were defined by men. All the books
that told me how I should respond sexually were
written by men; the doctors who embarrassed me
with their examinations were men. It was men who
had to be pleased, somehow. They wanted sex and
they wanted virgins. How could I give them both? It
seemed that no matter what I did I was wrong. I was
in a no-win position. Because I didn't "put out" the
boys got angry, but those girls who did were
sneered at. Why was it okay for the boys to want
sex and not okay for the girls?

As I grew older, my sexual feelings got stuck
somewhere between desire and fear. When I met
Jordan, fear was by far the winner. Although
I wanted to be close to him, I was very out of touch
with my own desire, so when Jordan wanted sex,
I felt as if I were doing it for him. Slowly, because of
his love and patience, desire began to creep in, and
with it came even more fears. Would he want sex
when I did? Would he continue to respect me if
I became a highly sexual woman? What if I became
too sexual — would he be able to handle it or
would it threaten his masculinity? I feared that his
definition of good sex would not be the same as
mine. (He could enjoy just a physical experience,
while my enjoyment seemed much more tied to
emotional satisfaction.) I feared that he would
dominate me sexually, so I thought I should keep
sex from becoming too important. To protect myself
from all these fears, I just reacted to his wants rather
than allowing myself to want. But this, of course,

was not meeting his needs; he wanted to be desired. It's taken a long time to find out who *I* am sexually, rather than conform to external standards. But the more we explore, and the more I understand and respect myself, the more sexual and sensual I become.

We are always surprised when we are asked, "What do you talk about in an exploration anyway?" Those who ask this question have become so accustomed to protecting themselves against being deeply known by another that they literally cannot imagine frank exploration. The answer to their question is, of course, "Anything at all" — anything that engages the attention of one or both partners, or causes conflict for one or both.

The Goal of Explorations — Acceptance and Intimacy

When we explore until we understand each other we finally reach the most cherished state — feeling accepted and accepting, deeply respectful of self and of partner. This is the doorway to intimacy.

Acceptance is not the same thing as tolerance. Perhaps you've made statements like "You're entitled to your feelings," or "Yes, I accept your behavior." If you uttered those words while ever-so-slightly shaking your head disapprovingly or pursing your lips condescendingly, if behind your words were thoughts like "That's really dumb," or "There's no excuse for that," then you were tolerating the behavior while pretending to accept it.

When we do not understand and respect another's behavior, but are willing to go along with it, then we are tolerating the other — which will never allow him or her to feel accepted. We feel truly accepted when we behave spontaneously and receive approval. Real acceptance is not easy, especially when we feel personally responsible for another and when we are personally affected by his or her choices. It is often easier to be more accepting of friends and other people's children than to accept our mates and our own children. Grandparents are often more accepting of their grandchildren than they were of their own children.

Coming to acceptance does not mean that we will always *like* our own or another's feelings and behaviors, *but that we will not judge them as wrong.* "But," you may be thinking, "sometimes my partner's (or my own) behavior just doesn't make sense." That statement always means that you do not have a full awareness of all the important reasons each of you has for behaving or feeling as you do. Your exploration is not yet complete. Coming to accept ourselves and others occurs through a process, not by a decision, since we cannot accept something when in our gut we feel it is wrong or bad. Feelings and behavior that seem dumb, crazy, bizarre, or inappropriate to us are being judged through the filter of our values and beliefs, fears, hurts and expectations. Only as we explore them can we respectfully understand them and only then will we come to true acceptance.

The Atmosphere of an Exploration

The ideal time to explore a conflict is while it is happening. But a conflict often occurs at an inconvenient time — at a party, just before an appointment, or when you are involved with something else. Or, you may not even be aware that something has upset you until later.

One of our rules of thumb is to try to make time every day to clean the slate. Often when we get into bed, we spend time together unwinding and connecting. Most times we talk about events of general interest, but talking allows us to bring up issues that need discussing or to become aware of a distance between us. A lack of responsiveness prompts us to try to understand what has happened to block our usual warmth and affection.

When we get defensive and fight, the atmosphere is chilly. When we are willing to be affected by each other, we open up. When we feel understood and respected, our affectionate feelings return. When we are feeling vulnerable, we usually want to be held. When we are exploring our pain, we snuggle up next to the other's warm body. The safer we feel, the deeper into our feelings we allow ourselves to go.

We spend a lot of time doing this because we've found from experience that our relationship suffers when we don't. Each time we discover new things about our protections and about the fears, values, expectations, and pain that lie beneath, we feel closer and more affirming of ourselves and each other. As the years go on, we have less need for our protections and are more willing to open to each other. The less we protect, the stronger our love.

Since so many basic issues have now been resolved between us, we are much more able to remain loving. In the past, our intimacy usually lasted for only minutes or hours, occasionally for as much as two or three weeks at a time. But it was very fragile, since the slightest protection blocked it. We used to struggle toward intimacy, but be there for only a short time before tumbling back. Now, when this occurs we can get through the distance in a few minutes or a few hours and reconnect deeply, where it used to take days, weeks, or even months to reach that intense high again. The aliveness of our relationship used to be generated mainly by our conflicts; now it comes from our openness to each other, so we enjoy longer peaceful periods with only occasional conflict.

Many people believe that the way to maintain excitement and interest is to remain mysterious, fearing their partners will become bored if they reveal too much about themselves. That's impossible, since we are all complex, fascinating, and infinite beings; there will always be mysteries. For any couple, working through the inevitable battles and exploring each other deeply can be a satisfying and infinitely interesting process; each is always discovering new things about the other, which keeps the relationship fascinating to both.

·5·

Intimate Love: The Reward of Explorations

Love is like the moon.
When it does not increase
It decreases.
SEQUR

Although explorations are not the only way to reach intimacy, exploration opens the path to intimacy whenever there is a block. When two people share freely with each other what they are really thinking and feeling and receive acceptance in return, intimacy flourishes. Explorations lead to a special kind of love we call Intimate Love. Intimate Love is not the infatuation of new love nor the emotional evenness of respectful, nonpassionate relationships; it combines the best characteristics of both — a deep respect and caring, together with the intense feelings of new love.

Feeling Loved

Intimate Love gives to each partner what each needs to feel loved. We can express our love in many ways and give a great deal to our partner; however, if we are not giving what the other person needs to feel loved, the gift is ultimately meaningless.

Imagine yourself as a plant which needs a special kind of sun and water. Your partner gives you lots of sun, and you love the wonderfully warm feelings that you get, but he or she offers you little water. Although you can get water from other sources, this relationship limits you because it lacks a vital nutrient. You do not feel loved and understandably do not feel loving toward your partner nor appreciative of what is given you.

The key questions to be answered are "Do I feel loved?" and "Do you feel loved?" rather than "Do you love me?" or "Do I love you?" For both partners to feel loved, each may be asked to give to the other in ways that are very difficult. We often have to confront and resolve some deeply ingrained fears before we can give our partner what he or she needs. Whenever we, as therapists, see this sort of problem in our clients' lives, we feel great empathy, since we have faced exactly the same thing ourselves.

JORDAN:

Margie lets me know in many ways that she's interested in knowing me. She's eager to hear my feelings and what I have to say. But for a long time, despite her obvious interest in me, I often did not feel loved.

MARGIE:

There has never been a doubt in my mind about Jordan's desire for me sexually; he lets me know in many ways how much he loves to see and touch my body. I know how important lovemaking is to him. I always knew Jordan loved me very much, but often I didn't feel loved. It took me a long time to figure out what was missing. Finally, after I admitted my intense pain at feeling unloved   even though anyone would have said Jordan did love me, and my feelings were "crazy" — I realized what I wasn't getting. Although Jordan was very intense sexually, I hardly ever experienced that intensity anywhere else. He rarely let me in on his own intense joy or pain, and he was rarely involved with or deeply affected by my feelings or spontaneous enthusiasms. Through the years, as we've explored this issue, I discovered that what I most wanted was his intense interest in how I felt and thought *as well* as his sexual interest. Unless he valued my intensity and shared his own intensity with me, I knew I would never feel really loved, no matter how much he desired me.

JORDAN:

When Margie told me she didn't feel loved, I was crushed — and perplexed. I was a therapist, ostensibly interested in how people thought and behaved. But as we talked, I realized that my interest in Margie was restricted. Getting into feelings (hers and my own) made me vulnerable; when she brought up something she was unhappy about, I would often feel judged, wrong, or inadequate, believing that I was responsible for her unhappiness. With my clients I didn't feel that way; after all, I knew I wasn't responsible for their feelings. I began to appreciate how much easier it was to be a therapist than to be a husband. My childhood training had convinced me that feelings were "weak," and I must cut them off to be "strong." So I had always avoided my feelings and hers, and now she was asking for more. What she needed to feel loved was the hardest thing of all for me to give,

since it came from my greatest vulnerability. It sure
would have been easier if she could have settled for
some good lovemaking.

Our discussions did, however, lead me to discover
what was missing for me. My major dissatisfaction
was her lack of intense interest in sex. She was
responsive to me and enjoyed sex, but since she
rarely initiated it, I never felt that she desired and
needed me as I did her. When Margie loves touching
and seeing my body and wants to make love, I feel
most loved.

MARGIE:

It was hard for me to understand why Jordan
didn't feel loved; I was giving him everything that
would have made *me* feel loved. Finally, he told me
that he needed me to be more sexually aggressive.
The area in which I felt most unsure and vulnerable,
he needed! Whenever I feel in the least threatened,
I always pull back in the area of my greatest
vulnerability: my sexuality. It sure would have been
easier if he could have settled for a good discussion.

JORDAN:

It was an interesting dilemma. I need from Margie
the thing that is hardest for her to give, and vice
versa. We gave each other the thing that was easiest
for us to give, but both of us pulled back in the area
where we felt most vulnerable. I realized that if
I was getting her sexual interest in me but I wasn't
getting her interest in how I feel and think,
I wouldn't feel loved after a while, either. As each of
us becomes more complete, each of us has more
love to give the other — so in one sense both of us
are more loved than before.

Knowing Our Partner

To feel loved we need our partner's willingness to be
known. We need him or her to share deep feelings with

us *and* be affected by us. This makes us feel important. Sharing superficial thoughts or reactions to daily events (what the children did, what happened at the office) does not give us this feeling; exploring how our partner is affected by daily events gives us some of it, and exploring how he or she is affected by us gives us more.

When your mate is upset by anxiety-producing situations, does he or she share the emotional turmoil with you or keep it inside? Fred was a happy-go-lucky person — agreeable and eager to please. He loved his wife Linda very much and was a good husband and provider. He was very thoughtful, never forgot her on special occasions, even bringing her presents for no special reason. During the ups and downs of sixteen years of marriage, Fred had always been Linda's protector and comforter. In his effort to be acceptable, a "nice guy," Fred had completely turned off his deeper emotions.

During a particularly difficult period in his professional life, Fred broke down one evening. As Linda held him while he cried, she saw him differently than ever before. Fred had always showered her with material things, but Linda had felt shut out of his life. He had given her presents but she needed his presence. As he shared himself with her, she felt needed and felt loved for the first time.

Many people deny their mate's importance by remaining unaffected by and uninterested in their mates' activities or feelings. For example, when you're excited over a project you're working on, is your bubbly enthusiasm met with a cool, perfunctory response or shared enthusiasm? When you're feeling frightened or distressed over something in your life, does your mate talk about what is upsetting you or just tune you out?

Most of us hide our hurt, fear, or disappointment when our partner has done something that upsets us: we have learned not to let others see they have the power to hurt us. When you've had an argument, does your mate seem unaffected or want to resolve the conflict and get back to good feelings? When you've hurt your mate's feelings, does he or she let you in on the pain — or get angry or become indifferent? *If your partner is not affected by you, you will probably conclude that you are unimportant.*

Being openly affected is important, not only to allow our partner to feel loved but also for our own development. It lets us discover the parts of our personality we have always protected — the sensitive, insecure, easily frightened parts. Our protective strategies also hide the free and fun-loving parts that generate great joy and intense passion, which, though we have hidden them because we fear they are unacceptable, are the parts of us that ultimately make us lovable. *We are most lovable when soft, open and vulnerable, and least lovable when we are tough, hard, and protected.*

Being Known — Seen, Understood, and Valued

Knowing our partner is essential, but by itself will not leave us feeling loved. We also need our partner to know us — to see who we really are and to understand why we are that way.

We all doubt whether we will be loved for our feelings, thoughts, desires, or dreams. Will you be loved if you fail or are afraid or are deeply affected by things? You may be loved when you are being "nice," but what have you had to repress in order to act like that? If your husband just values your body and your skills as a wife, mother, and dinner party hostess, you may not feel deeply loved. If your wife just values your salary, the importance of your position, or your skills as a handyman, you probably don't feel deeply loved either. Will you be equally loved for your "wrong" or "inadequate" parts?

Until you expose your innermost self to your partner and receive understanding in return, you will always fear being found out and rejected. *The more of your personality you expose and feel accepted for, the more deeply loved you will feel.*

We need to be seen accurately. This is not as easy as it may seem, especially for those who have been together a long time. Edie married Rick when both were in their early twenties, not realizing how sexually inexperienced he was. Early in their marriage she became unresponsive to him sexually. In therapy she said, "Rick is just not a very sexual person. He wasn't sexual before we met and he isn't now. In fact, I don't think he ever will be." She did not respond to Rick because of an image of him that she couldn't or wouldn't change. Because Edie saw him that way, Rick continued to think himself unattractive.

Then Rick and Edie separated. Although Rick was afraid to date at first, much to his surprise he found that women sought him out. In fact, they had always been attracted to him, but his poor self-concept had kept him unaware of that. Soon he became involved in a passionate affair. Now, of course, Rick sees himself entirely different-ly. He needed another woman to see him as being sexy before he could see himself that way. People occasionally need to separate because they get stuck behaving the way the other expects them to behave. Only as they meet new people who see them differently can they appreciate the real person hidden inside.

One of our clients expressed what it means to be seen this way:

> I want Sam to see me as I *really* am, not as he *thinks* I am
> or *wants* me to be. I want him to see how strong I am
> rather than how strong he wants me to be, and how
> sexual I am, rather than how sexual he wants me to be.
> When he acts as if I should fit into *his* image, I don't feel

seen or loved. If I say that I feel hassled and tired and then he asks me to run an errand for him, I feel he hasn't seen or heard me. I feel violated when he asks me to do something that I'm obviously not ready to do; for instance, when he approaches me sexually or affectionately when I'm withdrawn, rather than wanting to explore with me what I'm feeling.

Once our partner gains a deep enough understanding to truly accept us, we feel valued and loved. The power of feeling loved is forcefully demonstrated in some of the stories of miraculous changes you may have read about. Perhaps you recall times when you personally changed as a result of feeling truly loved. The intoxication of feeling seen, understood, and valued releases us from protecting and opens us to learning and evolving.

Caring for Your Partner without Losing Yourself

One of the most important components of Intimate Love is the individual integrity of each partner. As Fromm observes in *The Art of Loving,* "In contrast to symbiotic union, mature love is union under the condition of preserving one's integrity, one's individuality."

You cannot become truly intimate with another if you lose yourself. A deep, loving connection occurs only between two people who are not defensive, who are not threatened by each other's feelings, who can flow together without feeling overwhelmed by the other person. The less you fear being engulfed by the other, and the more you know you can survive the loss of the other, the more you can be open. But when you are deeply afraid of losing the other or of losing yourself, you are going to hold something back.

For many individuals, "taking care of me" has meant not caring about his or her partner. This is as detrimental to Intimate Love as giving up one's self.

In Intimate Love each partner enjoys taking care of the other. Our client Phyllis said, "I love thinking of Hal and giving him what makes him happy. When I think of Hal's needs and he thinks of mine, things between us are lovely, especially when each of us gets joy out of giving. But when I'm thinking of his needs and he's only thinking of his needs, then I end up feeling unloved." Phyllis and Hal have learned that people who think that intimacy "should" consist only of breathless, ecstatic moments and "doing your own thing" have a limited view of love. Peter Cady wrote in *The Findhorn Garden* that the love the gardeners were asked to provide their plants "rather than a sentimental emotion, was the ability to be truly sensitive to the plant's needs." If we recognize that plants need this kind of understanding, surely we humans have an equal need to attend similarly to each other.

Attention and caring are totally different from self-sacrifice and martyrdom. The former come from desire, while the latter are a result of fear, obligation, or guilt.

Freedom and Intimacy

Doing what we want and need for ourselves while continuing to care deeply for our partner isn't always easy. We must cherish our individual freedom and be willing to deal with our partner's reaction to it — which is often pain, anger, or indifference. And we must not restrict our partner's freedom. As Clint Weyand writes in *Thank You for Being*: "My love must be willing to let you grow in directions I haven't traveled. If I don't give you this freedom, my love is only a thinly disguised method for controlling you." When we care deeply enough for our partner to explore how he or she is affected by our behavior and to help him or her understand the fears that arise in the face of our freedom, intimacy deepens. When we respect the other's freedom and accept our own reactions to it, our relationship will remain at least as intense and exciting as when we first fell in love.

To have an intimate relationship, both partners need to feel the freedom to live their lives in ways that satisfy each of them and still meet the other's needs. While each of us has needs that can only be met by the other, we each also have needs that we must meet separately, such as a desire for a competitive racketball partner or a need for artistic expression. However, unless our need to explore and express our feelings about all the different sides of ourselves is met within our relationship, our intimacy suffers. In contrast, the highs of our lives happen when we both say or do exactly what we want and get the other's love and respect in return.

Intimate Love encourages us to feel and share our natural spontaneous feelings. As we feel loved, we are more willing to lower our protections and expose more of our hidden selves. The most frustrating aspect of the search for Intimate Love may be that we cannot pursue it as a direct goal; we reach it only as the by-product of our willingness to be open with each other. But we cannot always wait until we feel loved to express our feelings, and being open with each other leaves us very, very vulnerable.

Safety and Intimate Love Are Mutually Exclusive

A seemingly ideal situation would be to feel all the wonderful feelings of intimacy with total safety. Although we would love to experience the intense "highs" of sex and joy without the "lows" of pain, such perfect safety is simply impossible. We may be rejected for expressing our feelings, but unless we are *willing* to risk rejection and possible pain, and then share it rather than protect against it, we cannot maintain our intensity and intimacy. Each time we go through this process — *conflict-resolution-intimacy* — our mutual love and our self-love grow. The choice is usually hard. Either we can be protected from feelings in an attempt to be safe or we can express feelings and be open to the joy and the pain they create. Since protecting from pain frustrates all intimate possibilities, the sharing of pain is the key to releasing us to Intimate Love.

Intimate Pain

When we do not share our pain, we invite two distinctly negative consequences. Holding back both blocks the full and passionate expression of sex and joy and by-passes the opportunity to create the wonderful intimacy and healing of sharing pain together. You can't care deeply for someone without being in pain some of the time. In fact, you can't open to life in general without a capacity for deep emotion. Openly sharing our painful feelings and receiving the warmth and acceptance of another is profoundly intimate. When our pain opens our partner to his or her own pain, we both connect to the common fears and hurts that affect us all. Paradoxically, sharing pain with someone who loves us and accepts our pain actually feels good. It does not feel good to be in pain, of course, but it feels wonderful to "let go" to it with someone who accepts it, like releasing a hidden secret. People are often more intimate with each other in affairs than in marriages because they risk expressing their pain to the other, and receive warmth and caring in return. In fact, many affairs originate in two people sharing with each other the pain of their respective marriages.

Pain As a Healing Experience

All of us have repressed thousands of major and minor painful past experiences. The pain registered (usually subconsciously) every time we were slighted or disapproved of by parents, teachers, siblings, or friends now forms our personal pool of self-doubt. Present painful experiences reactivate the pain of those past events. Thus a seemingly minor criticism or disappointment may have a searing effect, bringing up painful high school years, the death of a loved one, parents' disapproval, or some other trauma.

Truly experiencing pain is a cycle — we go down to the bottom, where the pain is deepest, cry or scream it out, then slowly rise feeling lighter and released. The pain is not unending — it always has its own limits. We may have to feel the painful feelings several times before the deep pain of a particular event is released, but eventually, when fully experienced, that pain weighs us down no more. Because feeling loved is so nurturing, expressing the pain with the support of a loved one actually heals the old wound. Once it is healed we are freer, since we no longer need to protect against it.

It's hard to be there for a partner in pain if we are afraid to tap too deeply into our own pain, or if we fear that the other will expect us to solve his or her problem. Feeling incapable of making the trouble go away, we tend to withdraw to a safe distance. But what is in fact needed in such intense pain is comfort and caring. As Spider Robinson points out in *Callahan's Crosstime Saloon,* "There's nothing in the human heart or mind, no place, no matter how twisted or secret, that can't be endured — if you have someone to share it with."

We have been taught to avoid pain, but *before we can really get over it, we need to get into it.* We need to feel our pain enough to gain new information about our deepest feelings if we are to lay to rest the situation that caused the pain. We evolve when we can re-experience past pain with an adult's insights and awareness.

MARGIE:

Sometimes, when Jordan and I are exploring I start to cry, recalling a painful experience from my past I didn't let myself cry about at the time. When I'm crying I don't want Jordan to take responsibility for my pain. If he tries to make me feel better and stop crying, I feel manipulated and interfered with. I just want him to hold me and be available to talk about my feelings when I finally stop crying. When I do this, I feel as if a pocket of fear and pain has been cleared out. I feel renewed and very much loved.

In the continuum of human experience, alienation is at one end and Intimate Love is at the other. The touching of hearts that occurs when we share pain lifts us out of the essential solitude that is a condition of existence. Because the modern world provides so many alienating experiences, we need to share our pain to restore ourselves to wholeness. During a weekend workshop for couples we conducted, one man wrote: "The pain I may feel by being vulnerable is joyous compared to the agony of aloneness when you are separate from me and unavailable."

Intimate Pain Opens the Door to the Passion of Intimate Love

As we share pain, the weight of our protections is lifted and we feel lighter and clearer. We see our partner with a heart that is so full of love it wants to burst. We want to be as close as possible, to be one with, to be inside of. Our entire being comes alive with the intensity of our passion. Letting go to these feelings is wonderful; it feels orgasmic — whether it brings sex, laughter, joy, or even tears.

We rarely experience this passion because most of us have been so busy protecting ourselves that we have lost touch with our natural selves. Everyone has the warmth and passionate intensity of a small child underneath his or her protections.

Intimate Love releases us to freely give and receive affection. It is not true that affection is something only children need and that adults outgrow. Our need to give and get affection is always with us and can best be satisfied by our loved one.

If the major purpose of being affectionate is to get some sex, to make the other think you are a good lover, to fulfill a sense of obligation, or to avoid disapproval, then it is a manipulation — and *manipulations are not intimate.* Affection is genuine when it is a gift — and a gift is given freely, not merely to get something back.

JORDAN:

For many years my being affectionate with Margie was a way to turn her on so we could have sex. But I freely gave affection only to my children. I knew that children needed lots of affection, so I was delighted to do something that gave me pleasure and made me a good parent. To my chagrin my children let me know that they were sometimes annoyed by my hugging, squeezing and touching. Sheepishly I admitted to myself that I wasn't really doing it for them — *I* loved to touch. But if my kids didn't need it as much as I did, who else was there? Margie! Why hadn't I ever thought of her before? Touching was so associated with sex I'd lost sight of my own need for it. Margie and I began to discover the pleasures of simple affection, giving and receiving.

The more all of us discover the pleasures of affection the more we open to the sensual joy available from our own and our partner's body. Sensual feelings are those highly pleasurable sensations that come from our senses.

Allowing these feelings to permeate our bodies and flowing with the movements and sounds that accompany them feels wonderful. Expressing our sensuality — holding, caressing, hearing, kissing, tasting, smelling — with our loved one adds a profound dimension to a relationship. As Helen Colton points out in *Sex After the Sexual Revolution,* "Knowing the difference between *sensual* need — for touching, stroking, caressing — and *sexual* need — for orgasmic experience — is an important part of sexual maturity."

Intimate Sex

When Intimate Love and affection flow freely outside the bedroom, then they also flow easily during sex, creating Intimate Sex. When relationships are not open and loving, sex is not a genuine expression of love. Many people today look for "instant intimacy" through sexual encounters with people they hardly know. For many, it is far easier to create the illusion of intimacy with sex (often augmented with alcohol or drugs) than to be vulnerable enough to be truly intimate. As Jess Lair says in *Sex, If I Didn't Laugh, I'd Cry,* "Sex is opening our hearts to one another and then opening our bodies. When we open our bodies to each other in sex and won't open our hearts, sex becomes a terrible pain."

When sex is used for releasing tension, proving adequacy, masking difficulties, or creating the illusion of intimacy, it eventually becomes boring and routine. You may then think you have to *learn* how to respond, what buttons to push, or how to talk to each other. But, in this case, techniques can only lead to unsatisfying, routine experience, and the search will continue for new techniques or new partners to ignite passion. You may read books, have therapy, attend classes, or talk to friends, trying to learn how to respond sexually or how to get another to respond sexually. You can learn to be orgasmic, *but you cannot learn how to be turned on to each other.* Most sex books or sex therapy teach you only how to be a better sexual technician.

Becoming educated sexually is important, but you can never learn to create passion through the skillful manipulations of your own or your partner's body. Continuing passion and desire result from intimacy, not from genital stimulation or intercourse. The frequency and intensity with which a couple makes love is primarily determined by how much each partner feels loved. Trying to manipulate another to feel desire is denying the fact that there are very good reasons why one or both of you is not turned on. To try to arouse yourself or your partner in the face of not feeling sexual is to demean and violate yourselves. The alternative is to explore why one or both of you are not feeling sexual, then resolve the underlying issues rather than try to force yourselves to behave hypocritically. When a person truly feels loved, sexual responsiveness flows. We have often seen a client, after many years of sexual unresponsiveness, become intensely sexual during an affair in which he or she feels free, special, and loved.

Most new relationships begin with intensity; feeling loved, lovers spontaneously express feelings they have rarely experienced. They are open, discovering new things about each other; they have fun and feel excited about their relationship. Sex reflects their delicious feelings.

Not every sexual experience can be profound, but whenever we are willing to be vulnerable with each other, Intimate Sex is possible. In a long-term relationship intense sexuality will endure only if partners continue to share and explore. When each person begins to pull back to protect, loving feelings and passion fade. The physical aspect of sex alone cannot keep it exciting, no matter how practiced the techniques, how beautiful the partners or how perfect the bodies. Without emotional intimacy sex eventually becomes boring and infrequent (or nonexistent).

Unlike routine, goal-oriented sex, directed toward intercourse or orgasm, Intimate Sex has no end goal. To express loving, creative feelings through sex is exciting and satisfying *in itself*. Intercourse and orgasm will most likely occur, but not in any prescribed way — not necessarily at the same time or in the same way each time. Whatever happens is the result of each person's being tuned in to what each wants. In the blending of their needs and wants the partners' experience will be unique each time they make love.

It is the difference between approaching sex as a race or as a dance. If it's a race, your goal is the finish line (intercourse or orgasm). Each runner is in his or her own lane focused on the finish line. Barely noticing each other, you race forward, anxiously striving to accomplish your goal. You may both reach your goal and experience pleasure, but only momentarily.

For dancers it will be entirely different. You begin by facing each other, seeing and appreciating each other. The pleasure is *now*; you are not concerned with the ending at all. As you dance you are acutely aware of your partner. You wind along slowly and in a relaxed way; you may stop, talk, have fun. Eventually you will arrive at a finish, but — as happens when people are creative — this point is not predetermined. The finish is usually ecstatic and always satisfying, a combined loving effort. Together you have created something that neither of you could have accomplished alone or with a person who did not share your deep commitment to the loving process. At the end, you feel satisfied both physically and emotionally.

Although we personally do not always reach the ecstasy of the two dancers, when we are in an open and intimate state our sexual experiences are incredible. Sometimes we are light and playful and sometimes deeply passionate. We can't believe that our lovemaking can still be so intense and exciting after nineteen years of marriage. We have these experiences *only* when we are both completely open and deeply connected, only when we both feel very, very loved.

Intimate Joy

When intimacy is expressed as uninhibited, freewheeling joy, it is that rare childlike state of having fun and feeling good, light, and happy. Smiles or laughter are not contrived or held back and we feel them through our entire body. Without the spirit of intimacy, we have at best only a forced pseudo-intimacy that may look like the real thing but does not feel like it. Trying to have fun without being deeply connected is putting the cart before the horse; the fun follows naturally from the love and intimacy, rather than the other way around. The joyful spirit of intimacy seems almost to add another dimension to life — the way a flat picture would be transformed if it were seen in three dimensions. Intimate Love is fun, sexy, romantic, inspiring. Whether you have it in your relationship has little to do with how many years you have been together, but depends instead on how often and how deeply you share yourselves with each other.

JORDAN:

When Margie and I are open, deeply connected, everything changes. Everything lightens up, becomes less serious; we find ourselves laughing and playing together a lot, feeling freer and more playful with our children. Everything we do is fun, from simple chores to lavish evenings. Swinging on the swings at the park can be either delightful and hilarious or self-conscious and stilted depending upon whether or not we are intimately connected. When I'm protected, I often find it hard to smile broadly and laugh deeply, but when Margie and I are open and intimate, I feel myself smiling easily and laughing with great abandon. Things strike me funnier when we are connected intimately. I know that Margie is in that high joyful place when she starts cracking jokes. Margie only cracks jokes when she's feeling terrific.

MARGIE:

My intimate connection with Jordan is like the center of a wheel. From that center the spokes go in all directions, but each is connected to the center. When we feel distant, every other aspect of my life loses some of its clarity and joy. But when we connect deeply, I feel love in a divine sense; I feel connected with God, with life and all that is beautiful. The world becomes clear and bright. I have the sense that if I died at that moment I would have known everything there is to know. I feel strong, powerful, creative, one with myself. I can feel my energy flowing into Jordan and his flowing into me in a continuous circle, with no barriers between us. We feel a sense of total freedom — we can say and do anything without fear. We feel as if we are flying.

Section Two

Explorations on the Path of Evolution

·6·

Childhood — Why We Became Protected

*Without . . . a safe place to stand, no
energy can be utilized to explore possibility . . . and the stress of the unknown-
unpredictable becomes a chronic threat.
We then spend our lives trying to avoid
this threat.*

JOSEPH CHILTON PEARCE
The Magical Child

Because so many of the beliefs, fears, and protections that
shape our lives originated in childhood, we must revisit
those early years to see the protective process as it began,
not to find excuses or assign blame, but to respect the
important reasons behind our protections. Many of our
most pressing issues, which seem to be the product of
present circumstances, actually derive their power from
childhood events. Our responses and our feelings reflect
our earlier self-doubts and sensitivities. For example, if one
partner innocently comments that an outfit looks a little
tight, the other may respond with seemingly inappropriate
hurt or anger if he or she were a chubby child.

Conflicts are automatically easier to work through when both partners understand the extra-sensitive issues and their origins. We cannot understand and accept our own and our partner's fears, values, expectations, and protections until we have clearly focused on the connection between the present and the past.

One of the most significant factors in our adult relationships is how we were loved as children. The more loved and more secure we felt as children, the less protective we are in our adult relationships. However, many of us carry the burden of being inadequately loved as a child, and so did our parents and their parents before them. Our protective responses to this immensely painful fact were fixed in us long before we met our partner.

Another factor for most of us is that our early years were peppered with real and persistent assaults on our individuality. If we hadn't developed protective mechanisms then, we would surely have suffered more pain than we did, perhaps an unbearable amount. For many, protecting was the lifeline to sanity.

Habits learned in childhood are never the only reason to explain adult behavior. No one behaves solely out of habit. *Present behavior must serve an important, continuing purpose.* Behavior is repeated because it works, protecting us from confronting present fears that have haunted us since childhood. When we perceive the connection between present behavior and past experiences, we can begin to move beyond behavior that was appropriate and necessary in childhood but may no longer be needed.

As some ideas about childhood are presented here, hopefully you can identify with and explore sensitive issues from your own past. Protecting yourself from this childhood pain by blaming your parents or yourself only frustrates the growth process. People are not basically bad, deliberately setting out to create problems for themselves or foster insecurity in their children. On the contrary, we do what we believe to be in our own best interests or in the best interests of our children. We are simply unconscious of being motivated by our fears, and the wish to protect ourselves from them.

We have limited our comments in this chapter to parent-child relationships, but parents are certainly not totally responsible for a person's development. Siblings, relatives, friends, teachers have all influenced our personalities. However, the most influential factor in our personality development is our relationship with our parents.

The Seeds of Self-doubt

All children need approval from the important people in their world to feel lovable and worthy: a child's self-esteem comes from such approval. As children, we were approved of when we did what was "right": we were not noisy in restaurants; we said "thank you"; we were well-mannered at the dinner table and at other people's houses. We may have been approved of for our achievements — walking or talking early, or making friends easily. As we reached school age, we may have been approved of for behaving well in class and getting good grades. Our client Barry recalled his parents' home movies, in which he starred. One memorable sequence showed him, at the age of three, playing in a park wearing a white shirt, white pants, white shoes and socks, and a white beret. His mother invariably commented, "He was such a good little boy. I could dress him like that in the morning and he would stay clean all day," which always brought approval from those assembled for what a good job she had done. *By age three*, Barry had become so fearful of disapproval that he had given up much of his natural curiosity and spontaneity to be a "good boy."

When we didn't behave according to the values of our parents (or others) we got disapproval, in many forms — the silent treatment, yelling, irritated looks, scoldings, threats of and/or actual physical punishment. The message was always the same: "You are not lovable the way you are. You are behaving badly and you will get my love only when you do things the right way — my way."

Very early in our lives our self-doubts began as our feelings were disapproved of. We were not born with self-doubt; at birth we were open, trusting, curious, interested, spontaneous, highly sensual, and capable of feeling intensely and deeply. (Genetic factors, prenatal and birth experiences influence these capacities.) As infants, we had no values or beliefs; we acted spontaneously, guided entirely by our emotions and desires. When we were comfortable, we were alert, responsive, happy, and open to the world. When we were frightened, uncomfortable, hungry, frustrated, or physically hurt, we cried. But when our natural responses — pain (fear, sadness, frustration), joy, sensuality, and sexuality — were criticized, we learned to repress them to avoid the sting of disapproval.

A small child's inner sense of self is not strong enough to tolerate much disapproval. When not approved of for ourselves as we are — especially for our feelings — we begin to mistrust the rightness of the feelings themselves. For example, neither Marilyn nor Barry really liked Barry's mother because she was hard, angry, and judgmental, but they catered to her out of fear of her disapproval as well as a sense of obligation and guilt. Their daughter Lisa sensed her grandmother's hardness and did not like her. When the grandmother would hug Lisa, Lisa would pull away. Alone with Lisa, Marilyn would say accusingly, "Why didn't you hug your grandmother?" Lisa would reply, "I don't like her. She's mean!"

Marilyn would respond with, "Don't be silly. That's a terrible thing to say. She loves you. Next time you be nicer and hug her." Inside, Lisa knew that she did not like her grandmother, but she was confused by her mother's attempts to change her feelings, and in time began to distrust her own perceptions and feelings.

When your father or mother said, "Put on a jacket. It's cold outside," did he or she respect you when you said you weren't cold, or were you forced to dress according to your parent's metabolism? Were you allowed to follow your own inner sense of how much to eat, or were you told to finish everything on your plate? The "mother or father knows best" messages we all received finally convinced us that we didn't know how to act, think, or feel. The more we stopped trusting our own inner signals, the more we lost touch with our inner experience and intuitive sense of what was right for us. We began to look outside ourselves for the right way to be, hoping to avoid rejection. The more we gave up trusting our own inner experience the more available we became to being controlled.

The natural reaction to disapproval is sadness and often, tears — but tears brought more disapproval. Most parents don't want to see their children in pain, and they certainly don't want to acknowledge that they have hurt their child's feelings. When parents feel responsible for a child's unhappiness, they usually attempt to stop its expression by disapproving:

"Big boys don't cry."

"Come on, don't be such a baby."

"Now, now, be a big girl."

"Don't be so sensitive."

"Don't wear your heart on your sleeve."

"That's nothing to make such a big deal about."

"Stop crying or I'll give you something to cry about."

Eventually children learn to shut off pain, lest they be wrong and unlovable. Rather than try to understand a child in pain, most parents attempt to get the child to *stop* being in pain, or to shield him or her from painful situations.

Parents, conditioned by *their* parents, have usually grown so far away from their own spontaneous, childlike, sensitive inner selves that they can no longer remember the special properties of children. Having shut off all memories of how much the slights they felt in childhood hurt them, they criticize with impunity. When a parent stops a child's crying, the child is denied a natural outlet that discharges hurt. The child then needs to wall off the pain inside, to keep from wanting to cry.

Parents hurt their children like this when they don't recognize their own pain. When they allow themselves to feel *their* buried feelings fully, they're more comfortable with their children's feelings. Children will be hurt now and then in the process of growing up, but sympathetic parents can guide them kindly through the inevitable slights and rejections, or even through major traumas such as loss of a parent or close relative, making the difficulties much easier to bear. Nurturing a hurting child will eventually heal the pain.

As a child grows up, his or her difficulties are seen as further evidence that he or she is wrong and inadequate. School problems, social problems, and family difficulties are thought of as the fault of the child, who is then labeled maladjusted, underachiever, stubborn, selfish, lazy, shy, silly, childish, immature, disrespectful, or uncouth. Some children are taken to therapists to be made better, right, or normal. If the therapist participates in this attempt to change the child, his or her self-doubts deepen. Children encounter many people who are quite willing to tell them what is wrong with them.

Searching for approval, we naturally accepted those values and imitated those behaviors our parents considered right. But we learned from acts even more than from speeches. If our parents yelled or hit when they were angry or frustrated, we learned to yell or hit when upset. Our parents may have disapproved of us for doing it, but their *actions* toward us and others provided the most telling instruction. Some children go to the other extreme, becoming the opposite of what their parents were or wanted them to be. Either way, in conformity or rebellion, the child's behavior is not in harmony with his or her own unique personality.

All of us survived cultural conditioning by creating an image we hoped would be right. Many of us were left with a powerful subconscious fear that our natural selves are not lovable, maybe even ugly, and not to be seen by anyone, including ourselves.

When we examine the conditioning process with hindsight and awareness, most of us feel like uttering an anguished "Why? Why was it all necessary?" Our parents were unaware of the ramifications of their disapproval, which came from their own fear — that if they didn't control us we might humiliate or embarrass them. They wanted to avoid their friends' disapproval, having grown up themselves without a deep sense of inner worth. They were afraid that people would think, "What's the matter with those people? Can't they control their children better than that?"

They also feared that if they didn't control us and impose their values on us, we would grow up to be socially unacceptable. Because of our cultural wisdom that children do not innately possess the natural resources to become responsible and loving on their own, most parents believe they must teach their children these qualities. This process is called "socialization" or "acculturation." The parents' job is to change the child's natural responses (which are assumed to be unacceptable) so the child will fit the cultural definitions of what is right or normal.

Many parents today are far more aware than their parents were. Many of them understand that children learn from example and that to feel loved and attain self-respect, children need solid evidence of their parents' respect and love. But parenthood is still a struggle to overcome the limitations of too little knowledge about ourselves and our children's feelings. Most of us born before 1945 grew up in authoritarian households, where we either gave ourselves up or resisted parental domination. Then child-raising went through a permissive era, which sometimes produced children with little sense of responsibility. The former style of child-rearing had little concern for the child's feelings, only with the parents' demands, the latter gave freedom but didn't teach responsibility. Most people believe in one extreme or the other, or flip-flop from one to the other. *But both approaches deny the most crucial element a child needs to feel cared for — involvement with the child's needs.* What children need in order to grow into self-respecting, responsible adults is their parents' interest and help in understanding themselves and the effects of their behavior on others, rather than strict control *or* unlimited freedom. A parent's *intent to learn and understand* in a parent-child conflict is what gives the child the feeling of being loved and fosters his or her personal evolution.

Parents who are trying to feel, express, and understand their own feelings can generally communicate with their children. Some of us were lucky enough to have loving and enlightened parents. But most of us had fearful and insecure parents whose need to protect themselves set in motion many of the self-doubts we struggle with today.

The Beginning of Power Struggles

Between the ages of one and three, most children begin to feel a sense of personal power and independence, and begin to establish a separate identity. Wanting the freedom to make their own decisions, they start to rebel. Thus begin the "terrible twos," when children want to become autonomous yet still keep their parents' love. Parents want to control the child without losing his or her love. Both parents and children face the question: "Do I have to give up me to be loved by you?" In most households the answer is "Yes." But because neither parent nor child wants to give up and both want to control the other, power struggles are set in motion that will continue throughout the years.

Power struggles between parent and child erupt wherever the parent wants something from the child and the child can resist: feeding, toilet training, taking baths, brushing teeth, dressing, going to bed at night. For example, Lisa wanted to decide for herself what to wear to nursery school. Marilyn, her mother, wanted Lisa to look pretty and well dressed so other mothers would see what a good mother she was. Lisa and Marilyn fought and screamed over clothes every morning. Lisa went to school crying and Marilyn collapsed in exhaustion, never realizing that clothes were not the problem. A power struggle was the problem.

A child's behavior can seem ridiculous or bizarre when it's not recognized as primarily a power struggle. On a warm summer night, Josh's father suggested that he would be more comfortable sleeping without his pajama top. Josh said, "No!" His father tried to explain why Josh would be more comfortable the other way. Josh still balked. When logic did not work, dad got angry, but Josh was adamant. Dad finally left shaking his head, bewildered over his son's irrational behavior. When Josh's resistance is understood as his need to take a stand, the scene makes perfect sense. He wanted to keep his integrity. If he compromised, he would be giving himself up.

Childhood power struggles usually abate until adolescence brings a more trying version of the toddler's fight for independence. Parents who are perplexed by a teenager's mindless conformity to the taste of his or her peers in clothes, music, and recreation miss the inner logic of the mystifying behavior. Maturity requires a shift from parental values to one's own value system. Teenagers, not having developed a strong enough sense of self-confidence to make their own decisions without looking for approval, merely shift the authority from parents to peers. Parents fiercely resist inroads on their authority, but the teenager's need for outside acceptance and a separate identity is absolute. Family conflict with adolescents can only be modulated when one or both sides adopt an intent to learn rather than to continue blaming, resisting, and controlling.

Power Struggles: Then and Now

We carry into our marriages an almost uncanny recapitulation of our early relationships with our parents — which is no surprise, actually, for it was at home that we learned our basic strategies for survival. Adult relationships feature power struggles transferred almost unchanged from the parent-child encounters of each partner's early years.

Child-raising is most often the mother's responsibility, as she is more deeply involved than the father in establishing control on a day-to-day basis. Both boys and girls may resist their mothers' attempts at control. As adults, women may assume a role like their mothers'. Men, on the other hand, often transfer this resistance to their mates. Dan's fear of Jane's control was based not only on Jane's wanting control, but also on Dan's ingrained resistance to women. Whenever Jane was at all parental — critical, angry, directive — Dan felt like a scolded child and automatically rebelled, withdrawing and shutting her out.

Jane, on the other hand, was particularly sensitive to being shut out and ignored. Her father had been a very busy man and usually did not have time for her. When Dan shut her out, she felt hurt and frightened. She did the only thing she knew how to do — the thing her mother (her role model) had done when frightened or hurt: she vascillated between giving herself up in the hope of getting Dan's love and yelling at him accusingly when he continued to shut her out.

Both Jane and Dan came into their relationship believing that you are either "one up" or "one down." Both wanted to be the winner rather than the loser; both wanted to be in control so they couldn't be controlled or feel the pain of being disapproved of or shut out.

The heritage of protections often means couples are doomed to repeat the ineffective maneuvers of their own childhoods. The first break in the cycle may happen accidentally, as in a serious crisis, but the most fruitful and long-lasting way out is the way of the adventurer in every culture: haunted by dangers (sometimes imaginary) handed down from the past, a brave individual steps outside the familiar and begins a voyage of discovery — made more exciting and rewarding when a partner shares the risks and the rewards. Integral to the voyage is an excursion into the dark corners of the past and the willingness to re-experience the feelings associated with those memories.

·7·

Fears of Learning

All of us carry fears and insecurities into our adult relationships. Although some people have become less fearful by confronting their fears, those who often seem fearless have merely become successful at hiding their fears. But we all try to arrange our lives to avoid what threatens us, hoping vainly that what we don't know won't hurt us.

If a roving reporter were to ask people what they were most afraid of, the immediate answers would range from "I don't like spiders" to "I'm afraid of flying." Everyone can identify at least a few relatively minor fears like these. But this chapter concerns the fears that we deny — those that lie buried, unconscious, and unacknowledged. *These fears* — or the shadow of them projected into our consciousness — *dominate our lives.*

The following is merely a small selection of the most prevalent situations we fear:

rejection
failure
success
being wrong
not having control over our loved ones
others having control over us
being shut out
becoming sexually uninhibited
wanting what we want, feeling what we feel
losing ourselves
losing face
being spontaneous
feeling and expressing our deepest feelings
being vulnerable
knowing another well
knowing about ourselves
loving another deeply

We remain ignorant of our worst fears because we think it's wrong and weak to be afraid. Fearful of being rejected if we admit to being afraid, we deny it. But the first step in overcoming our fears is being willing to face them and understand them. As David Viscott wrote in *Risking*, "Understanding feelings, even fear, is strength."

In our relationships, what we fear is the emotional pain that some situations might create. The key to facing that fear, which raises our protections and blocks our intent to learn, is seeing pain in a new light and overcoming our fear of it.

Pain As a Learning Experience

Natural emotional pain is any unpleasant feeling — grief, fear, rage, anxiety, disappointment, or sadness — felt without blaming anyone else. Nonblaming pain leaves us unprotected, totally open and vulnerable and is so unusual that most of us have rarely experienced it. We learned to protect against emotional pain at about two years old, and in fact, when in natural pain, often feel as if we *are* two years old.

Each of us feels the bodily sensation of emotional pain in different ways: a stinging sensation in the eyes, a heaviness in the chest, an ache in the stomach, a tightness in the forehead, a quiver in the chin, or a lump in the throat. If not repressed, these sensations emerge as tears, for just as laughter is the natural expression of joy, tears are the natural expression of pain.

Although pain is unpleasant, and understandably something we would like to avoid, *opening to pain is the only way we have to learn what it has to teach us.* Frederick S. Perls writes in *Gestalt Therapy* that pain is "nature's way of calling attention to what needs attention." Though we may have learned to recognize physical pain as a signal of trouble, we seldom extend the analogy to emotional pain. We're not required to like being in pain. What's to like? But because exploring ourselves and our partner might bring up something painful, we must at least be *willing* to be in pain before we can learn about ourselves.

A child unwilling to risk being in physical pain would never learn to walk, let alone rollerskate or ride a bike. Children just roll with the punches — getting hurt, crying over it, getting up again, and starting over. Just as bodily pain accompanies the learning of physical skills, emotional pain is the price of acquiring genuine self-knowledge. Everyone's daily life has its share of disappointments and sadnesses: your best friend forgets your birthday; an acquaintance slights you; you're bored with your work; your boss is upset with you; your biggest client threatens to leave you; you discover a suspicious lump in your body; your child is injured or falls ill. When you refuse to experience the pain that goes with a given difficulty, much of your energy goes into protecting against the pain, which robs you of the energy you need to deal decisively with the problem.

Most people prefer to stay bogged down in low-grade misery from which they can see no escape rather than use their pain as a catalyst to learn and change. As William Glasser says in *The Identity Society:*

> Failures, suffering in many ways for long periods, seldom learn from their pain to behave more responsibly. Millions of unhappily married couples, for example, respond to each other with irritation and anger because they do not know how to do otherwise. Starving for love, they give each other only pain. Frustrated in their locked-in relationship and pushed by painful feelings, they either act quickly and thoughtlessly or do nothing except wallow in their own suffering.

Our difficulty in dealing constructively with pain begins in childhood. Parents' efforts to protect children against any harsh reality — a conflict in the family, the death of a pet — deprives them of practice in handling pain. When parents don't allow for open expression of pain, whether it's minor (such as a disappointment or a failure) or major (such as the loss of a parent or grandparent) children never learn that they *can* experience pain, be deeply affected, and still survive. This is how we learn that we have to be, or seem to be, unaffected.

Stanley grew up in an "ideal" family. He was the oldest of three children with two loving parents. They had enough money and lived in a nice house in a good neighborhood with lots of other children. When Stanley was ten, his father was killed in a train accident. For the next three days he was shunted off to a relative's house and not even told about the accident. Coming home to a house full of strange people, he was told, "Your father is dead." He was not allowed to attend the funeral, and nothing more was ever said about the event or its personal consequences. The family moved to another, much smaller house in a neighborhood without other children, and Stanley took over as head of the family. Stanley's mother withdrew; the only way she knew to deal with tragedy was to be stoic. She implicitly made the children understand that to cry was weak and they had to be strong. Stanley shut down his feelings, and they have been shut down ever since. Now, at the age of thirty-one, he is attempting to regain contact with his feelings. He has just begun to cry over the loss of his father and the pain of never having had an opportunity to say goodbye.

A child's larger-than-life fears of pain are still part of the program of the inner child within each adult. As Dorothy Briggs observes in *Celebrate Your Self*, "The Inner Child's fear is greater than the adult experience of that same fear. But you don't discover this fact until you face the hurt." We have experienced this again and again in our practice. When asked, "Why are you afraid of your pain right now, today?" most people answer, "I'm afraid if I let go, I'll go crazy." They are afraid of being overwhelmed by the pain, stuck in it forever. *But the truth is that all of us are able to tolerate much more emotional pain than we think we can.* People are unable to tolerate pain only when they vainly attempt to keep from feeling it — when it builds and builds until they finally crack under the strain.

Avoiding Pain Limits Awareness

When we shut out pain, we shut out awareness. In *Gestalt Therapy*, Frederick S. Perls contrasts two automobile drivers: neither of them is particularly aware of the sound of the car's engine when it is running well, but the first is highly sensitive to any sign of malfunction and investigates the problem immediately. The other, either because he or she does not hear the sound or is afraid of what will be found if the hood is lifted, drives on anyway and later is stranded, the victim of a problem ignored until it became unmanageable.

We have all expended a great deal of effort not to feel or be aware of our feelings. We have dulled our sensitivities and become toughened and thick-skinned; our sensitivity is the price we've paid for becoming "normal." Some people have become so protected that they are not aware of feeling *anything* in their bodies. When asked "What do you feel?" they answer, "Nothing," and they really mean it. Shutting off inner responses to avoid feeling pain has shut down all other feelings, too. When protected against pain, we have no way to find out what is going on inside our body; we must determine intellectually what we feel, rather than *feel* what we feel. As Claude Steiner says in *Scripts People Live,*

> I believe that we are able to know what is good for us if we can experience how it feels. When we listen to our bodies we find that cigarettes feel bad, that clean air feels good . . . We can listen to our bodies and tell when we want to be alone and when we want to be with someone, when we want to sleep, when we want to talk, or sit or lie down.

Edward came to us for therapy because he was impotent with his wife Sharon. Separated from her, he discovered that he wasn't impotent with other women and told us he "couldn't figure out" why he couldn't respond with his wife. Had Edward been tuned in to his body, he would have *felt* the anxiety and fear that surfaced when he was with Sharon; he would have recognized that he was frightened of being controlled by a woman as strong as she was. He would have also felt the pain when Sharon disapproved of him, and the anger her disapproval ignited in him. With women who weren't important to him, Edward wasn't afraid, but because Sharon was important to him and he was afraid of her, he shut down sexually to protect himself. As Edward tuned in to his body, feeling his anxiety and fear *directly,* he could connect his impotence with his anger and fear. When he was actually willing to feel these feelings, he was then able to express them which helped him to resolve his difficulty. When he was no longer afraid, angry, and holding back, his impotence disappeared.

Repressing Pain Leads to Physical and Emotional Problems

Repressed painful feelings do not go away just because they are denied; they simply fester out of sight or erupt elsewhere, as when an angry man comes home and kicks the dog. When such feelings are most thoroughly repressed, they erupt nowhere at all, but undermine the physical and psychological health of the individual. Dennis Jaffe in *Healing from Within,* observed that chronic physical ailments are often repressed pain in disguise.

Pain is stored in the body and not eliminated until expressed. Filled with strong unexpressed negative emotions, a person may sink into a feeling of deadness which he or she thinks of as normal but is actually a state of depression. As uncomfortable as it feels, depression is a way of insulating oneself against an even greater pain.

For all of us, unexpressed emotions associated with painful memories are like open wounds hidden deep within. We try to keep these wounds from being touched, simply because they hurt so much. We protect ourselves against anything that even reminds us of this pain, but *until we are brave enough to re-experience it, the wound will remain.*

This does not mean simply acknowledging verbally that such pain exists but *re-experiencing the emotion itself.* Explorations (whether in therapy or between a couple) that only discuss a person's painful issues do not get to the heart of the problem. Talking can become another protective mechanism keeping distance between the person and the pain. Protections work like a screen or filter imposed between a person and reality. Real catharsis occurs at the level of emotions, which must flow for genuine healing to take place.

Clara, one of our clients, had been married to Dean for twelve years when he left her. As the result of a wounding childhood, Clara had always been insecure, particularly terrified of losing her husband and ending up alone (though these very fears had made her excessively demanding and accusing with Dean, hastening his departure). When Dean was gone, Clara was left face to face with her worst fears: being alone, having to be independent, having to find a career, meeting men, having to establish a new relationship. Clara had always been a "good girl" who denied her true feelings, and she didn't know how to let out the storm of feelings that now raged within her. She went through severe depression, the result of repressing her real feelings, but finally broke through to her genuine anger and pain. The eruption was intense: Clara needed to pound, flail, and yell to experience the full reality of her fears and her anger. She needed to do this a number of times, each time with guidance and support. She emerged still frightened, but stronger and more determined.

The next few months were difficult and lonely. Clara had always feared that she was unattractive to men, a belief strengthened by Dean's lack of sexual interest in her. When she began dating, however, some men were attracted to her, and knowing this helped her get over a persistent and deep-seated fear. Clara became much stronger as she encountered and mastered her inner demons. When Dean finally returned, they began to put their relationship back together on a new and much more satisfying basis.

Fear of Loss of Love and Loss of Self

The situation we all fear the most because it hurts the most is the loss of love. For some, this fear creates such constant anxiety they are always protecting against it. Even though we want intimacy, many people would rather not risk loving and being intimate than suffer the pain of losing love. Although the fear of losing a loved one through death brings shudders, rejection looms as a greater probability in most people's minds. *Rejection is any form of disapproval,* from a transitory indifference or criticism to abandonment, the ultimate rejection. It is one of the worst blows anyone ever has to sustain; most of us are so deeply frightened of rejection that we will do almost anything to avoid it. Consequently, most of us are sensitive even to the smallest slight, a disgusted look or a disapproving shake of the head.

When we fear disapproval and rejection, we are available to losing ourselves. Many fear they will give in to their lovers' demands, becoming consumed rather than risking rejection. Most of us vascillate between the fears of loss of other and loss of self, depending upon the dynamics of the relationship. If the partner is demanding and controlling, the fear of loss of self predominates; if the partner is resistant, indifferent, promiscuous, or somewhat of a loner, the fear of loss of love predominates. Both fears are rooted in the doubts and insecurities concerning our adequacy and lovability.

Fear of Being Unlovable — Wrong, Inadequate, Foolish, Weak

Most of us believe that if we are wrong, we are by definition unlovable. We often fear that it is wrong to want what we want, feel what we feel, or do what we do. So we give ourselves up, tailor our behavior to avoid rejection, repress our fears, and avoid conflict. We have all learned to play it safe by refusing to think about our areas of greatest self-doubt although we all secretly suspect that one or more of the following labels applies to us:

> foolish, immature, helpless, sick, outrageous, hopeless, neurotic, crazy, bad, unmasculine, unfeminine, stupid, slow, humorless, boring, oversexed, undersexed, too aggressive, passive, too sensitive, insensitive, unattractive, judgmental, defensive, frightened, selfish,unloving, rigid, controlling, manipulative, insecure, henpecked, too quiet, too talkative, too intense, childish, disorganized, irresponsible, dependent, needy, rebellious, angry, stingy, extravagant, incompetent, unsuccessful, out of control, a jerk, weird.

We work to become more competent in our areas of strength and avoid our areas of vulnerability. A person who believes he or she is intellectually competent but socially inadequate may seek out intellectual challenges, but avoid social situations. A person who feels unsure sexually may avoid sexual contact, while the person whose greatest self-doubts lie in his or her emotional adequacy may seek out sex but avoid emotional intimacy. No matter how competent, successful, or self-assured a person is in certain areas, avoiding areas of insecurity does not resolve the gnawing doubts.

As Theodore Roszak says in *Person/Planet:*

> The individual may be filled with lavish self-importance, but never with a sense of inherent personal worth,

because as individuals we are measured — and we measure ourselves — only by externals: by acquisition and conquest, by *having*, never by *being*. And this is the very opposite of self-discovery; it entails subordination to an exterior, competitive standard. This is the heart of the matter. Self-discovery makes the person . . .

Self-doubt may reside in any one of the areas that make up our entire being: intellectual, emotional (including sexual), physical, social, spiritual, and creative. In many relationships, sex is the hardest area of conflict to resolve, primarily because of fears of sexual inadequacy. Sexual issues connect with a tangle of many deep fears, including, among others, the fear of emotional vulnerability, the fear of getting carried away by one's feelings, and the fear of inadequate performance. Many women fear disapproval if they don't have an orgasm or don't have one during intercourse, or if they are inhibited and fearful during sex; many men fear they're inadequate if their mates don't have orgasm, if they don't have an erection, if they lose an erection, if they ejaculate quickly, or if their sexual desire isn't as great as their mates'. Often a man who believes he wants a highly sexual woman becomes passive and uninterested when his mate becomes more sexual. Afraid that he's inadequate, he withdraws to protect himself from the disapproval he fears would follow a poor performance.

Almost everyone fears looking foolish. Everyone has refrained at least once from asking questions out of fear that someone would say, "You mean you don't know that?" We've all held back emotions — whether laughter or tears — for fear of being thought a fool, losing face, being humiliated, losing respect and position. The highest card in the Tarot deck is the Fool. There is an important message in that: until we can feel secure enough to be judged a fool and not feel wrong, we will not let go to expressing our feelings.

JORDAN:

When I received the anxiously awaited call from our agent telling us that a publisher had agreed to publish *Free to Love,* I was thrilled. Wow! A fantasy come true! I found Margie on the front lawn with our children and told her the news calmly. She started shrieking and jumping, then grabbed my arms and wanted to dance around. I winced, hastily glancing to see if any neighbors were looking, then hesitantly joined her happy dance. Talking with her later about what had happened, I realized how worried I was that the neighbors would think I was acting silly. I have screamed, cried, and jumped up and down at sporting events, but I couldn't let go and express my joy over one of the most exciting things that had ever happened to me because I wasn't willing to risk the disapproval of near strangers.

In a culture such as ours which values scientific, objective, rational people above all, many fear being rejected for expressing their softer sides. One of our clients whose relationship was in turmoil at the time expressed his fears in this poem:

Hold on, don't let go.
Hold on, don't let anyone know.

They didn't hurt you if it doesn't show.
They can't hurt you if you say it isn't so.

Will they laugh if you cry?
Will it hurt if you try?
Will you die?

They will laugh if you cry.
It will hurt if you try.
You will die.

This client expresses concisely the age-old dilemma between the free-wheeling Id and the conforming, stifling

Superego, with the weight of cultural expectations solidly behind the latter. A common fear is that our feelings will carry us into forbidden areas. Many people fear that once they open to feelings they will not be able to control them and will find themselves being too affected. We have often heard, especially from men, revealing questions: "If I become a feeling person, will I be carried away by my feelings? Will I be overwhelmed by them and have no control over them? Will I become so soft in business that people will be able to take advantage of me?"

The answer, of course, is "No." Even if you open to experiencing and expressing your feelings, you still always have the choice to be tough and unaffected instead. In some situations you will want to protect yourself and not let others know you are affected. Just because you choose to be deeply affected in your primary relationships does not mean that you must do that in your business or social relationships. Becoming a more feeling person doesn't mean you're at the mercy of your feelings; it means only that you have a choice of whether to be affected or protected in each particular situation.

A strong person is generally thought of as being in control of himself or herself and of others. Strength is equated with being tough, hard, angry; weakness with being soft. But the two are not exact opposites. When people need to be in control for fear of being controlled or run over by others, they are weak. In contrast, when they are willing to be open, they are strong. We can be soft, open, and vulnerable when we know that we are not wrong to want what we want or to feel or behave as we do.

In *A Fresh Start,* Leviton and Hill make this distinction between a dominant person and a dominating person:

> We have previously defined a dominant person as one who takes complete responsibility for his own life; a "take

charge" individual who sees what needs to be done and does it; independent, strong, capable and assured. This has no connection with a need to dominate or control others, which is generally associated with insecurity, jealousy, fear and lack of self-esteem. Both persons may appear strong and be successful but their inner selves are worlds apart.

The stronger and more secure we become, the more we are willing to be ourselves while encouraging our loved ones to do the same.

Fear of Knowing Our Partner

Exploring our partner's feelings may seem like opening Pandora's Box — who knows what might be hidden inside?

• Susan doesn't want to know that her husband Craig might not love her for her "natural self" — the intensity and spontaneity she generally subdues — and she doesn't want to know that she may not love Craig's real self, either, the loner who would rather tinker in the garage than go to a party. She wants to believe she can make him into what she wants him to be — fun-loving and social. She isn't willing to face one of life's most difficult realities: none of us can control another unless that other is open to being controlled. We are ultimately powerless to make another change, obey us, love us, or stay with us.

• Peter doesn't want to know about the pain he has caused Alice by his daily sexual demands on her and frequent criticism of her "prudish and inhibited" sexuality, because he doesn't even want to know that she's unhappy. As long as she continues to give in to him at least half the time, he's reasonably well satisfied, and if the two of them start looking inward, Alice might start to change in ways Peter finds unacceptable, — i.e., Alice might stop giving herself up. He also doesn't want to explore *her* fears of rejection, because doing so might touch off *his* fears of rejection if he's not in control.

• Bonnie doesn't want to know that Marty is upset by her intense preoccupation with her new job in advertising, because if she knows about it she'll feel guilty and wrong. The implication, as she sees it, is that to make things all right again *she* ought to change. She ought to work less and spend more time with Marty, even though she has no intention of doing so.

The most paralyzing fear of all is that the partners will discover they are unhappy with each other in ways they never knew existed, such as finding mutually intolerable traits or areas of irreconcilable conflict. Each may fear that if the partner disapproves of some specific act or behavior, separation or desertion must follow.

Fear of Conflict

Many people grew up in homes where conflict meant fights that left each person wounded and out for revenge. Witnessing the angry, hurtful battles or the coldness, tension, and distance created by such arguments often led to the conclusion that conflicts are too painful and must be avoided. When a person believes that conflict will lead to one or both people feeling like losers, it's understandable that he or she tries to avoid it.

Those who grew up in homes without overt fighting but with an air of tension from many unresolved conflicts may fear that conflict will open up areas that couldn't be resolved and would therefore eventually lead to the end of the relationship. Duane, one of our clients, who has always avoided conflict either by giving himself up or by lying, recently said, "I heard my parents fight only once. I was nine years old and I woke at three in the morning to yelling and screaming coming from the living room. I got up and listened. My parents were having a terrible battle. The next day they separated. To me, conflict has always meant the end of the relationship."

The emotions one feels in a conflict are painful in the extreme. An exchange of shouts with another driver, a heated discussion with an uncooperative salesperson — all these leave a feeling in the pit of the stomach, as if a bodyblow has landed. If such random and fairly meaningless encounters can change the whole day, obviously the implications of conflict with one's mate — the person whose approval is most necessary of all — are indeed threatening. When we live with another person, the possibility of conflicts that touch off our fears of rejection lurks around every corner.

- His desire to read a book may touch off her fear of not being important to him.
- Her refusal to have sex may touch off his fear of inadequacy.
- Her wish to go out with her friends may touch off his fears of losing her.
- His criticism may touch off her fears of being wrong.
- Her desire to do things her way may touch off his fears of not being in control.

However, only by exploring our conflicts can we uncover, deal with, and resolve these deep-seated fears. A person who habitually gives in may feel relieved when the shouting stops, but will feel a loss of self-respect, even if only subconsciously, for giving in. A habitually angry person may even seek out arguments with others, not understanding that staying angry is a way of not having to feel weak and powerless, emotions he or she fears most of all.

Fear of Knowing Our Protective Intent

Bhagwan Rajneesh says in *The Mustard Seed,* "Consciously you may think 'I would like to know myself,' but in the unconscious, which is bigger, stronger, more powerful than the conscious, you will avoid self-knowledge." It is perfectly natural to want to protect ourselves emotionally, and it is equally natural to *deny* that this is our intent, since most of us judge the protective behavior (anger, withdrawal, jealousy, selfishness, silence) as wrong.

Often in therapy we point out a client's protective behavior: "You seem very angry"; "You seem withdrawn, shut down"; "You seem to have a wall up"; "You seem very hard today"; "You seem defensive." When we do, we often get back more hardness, more anger, or more defensiveness — an indication that the client is either condemning himself or herself or feeling judged. If we try to discover why the person is behaving the way he or she is ("You seem very angry, and you must have some good reasons for feeling that way; I'd like to understand it.") the person usually relaxes, tears may spring up, the hardness falls away, and admissions tumble out. These feelings can be admitted only when they are not thought to be wrong. The expression of the feeling permits learning about the important reasons behind it.

All of us are, to some degree, not only afraid of knowing, but afraid of knowing that we are afraid of knowing. *In other words, we are protective but do not want to know and admit our intent.* However, when we deny that we are choosing to protect we are stuck.

Inspired by R. D. Laing's *Knots,* we made up a knotted verse on this theme:

Stuck.
I think I want to know and
I don't want to know that I don't want to.
Since I don't want to know, I don't even know
    that I'm stuck.
When I know that I don't want to know, I open
    to knowing what it is I'm afraid of knowing.
Unstuck.

Most of us are stuck in one or more of the following ways:

• We don't want to know that we believe staying protected from fear is more important than anything else in the world — more important than intimacy, than feeling free and happy.

• We don't want to know that our fear of being unlovable is so great that we can't risk being truly vulnerable to another, and that this has created all the misery in our lives.

• We don't want to know that we are fully in charge of our own choices and responsible for their consequences.

Existential writers have termed this kind of denial — the denial of one's intent — "bad faith." As William Ofman writes in *Affirmation and Reality,* "Bad faith . . . is a lie to oneself: it is from me, from myself, that I intend to hide the truth."

Acknowledging Fear and Intent Changes a Relationship

For this book to have an impact on your life, you must be able to acknowledge one thing, if only to yourself: in most conflicts with your mate or even in situations that might lead to conflict, your tendency is to protect yourself and keep from learning, and you're afraid to know that you are this way.

As soon as we acknowledge our fears and protective intent, we have given up blaming others and playing the victim. Even without changing any of the behavior that may be creating unhappiness, the relationship will immediately become more loving and intimate, since many changes have already occurred as the result of the single acknowledgment. Fears have stopped *being* the person and are now merely *part* of the person. When we can step outside our fear and look at it, the irrational strength of its hold over us has been weakened, if only a little. We don't have to vow to give up our fears and protections, or "try" to be rid of them: all that is needed is to call them by their true names and look at them squarely.

The more we become secure enough to risk rejection rather than deny our inner selves, the more we will be able to stay open even in conflict.

Overcoming Fear

Overcoming fear is a long-term process that involves becoming aware of the fear, talking about it to understand and respect it, and testing the fear.

Imagine yourself living in a swamp. You know that swamp inch by inch, every safe path, every danger spot. All your life you pick your way around the swamp eking out a bare existence. You can just make out, along the borders of the swamp, a cleaner, brighter, shinier world, but you do not venture into it. Passersby make fun of you; friends urge you to get out of your rut and taste the better life that is possible. You see the logic of their arguments and the ridiculousness of your choice, but you fail every time you try to leave.

Becoming more and more depressed, you sink lower and lower into the muck and gloom of your world. Then one day, someone new stops to chat and says to you, "Living this way seems stupid, but there must be something very important keeping you here."

"Oh, no," you protest, "I'm just a jerk."

Your new-found friend persists, "What is there outside of this place that you're afraid of?"

"Well, I don't know, but I imagine there's a big hole with demons in it that I might step into."

"What makes you think so?"

"I fell in holes as a child and got hurt a lot."

"Oh, now it begins to make sense."

"Yes, it does. Maybe I'm not such a jerk after all."

With greater self-respect you may become strong enough to risk confronting the demons that you fear. This is the necessary step to overcoming your fear — your willingness to face it. No amount of thinking and talking will get you to the point where you can step out of your swamp without fear; *you will have to make the first step while still afraid.*

In therapy, a client may have been helped to greater understanding and self-respect, yet remain unwilling to take the step (become thinner and more attractive, feel more sexual, leave an unhappy relationship, leave an old job or take a new job, open to new relationships and the like). At that point, the therapy may be over. We tell the client that we're willing to continue to help explore his or her fears further, but the most productive meaningful action will be to take the step of facing those fears — then we can help them through whatever difficulties may follow.

Confronting Fear — A Personal Example

A personal example will illustrate how fear can be overcome with the help of one's partner.

JORDAN:

Margie had been a skier before we met and had said several times that she wanted to ski again, but I always came up with reasons why we couldn't go. We couldn't afford it; our children were too small; and so forth. Finally we could afford it and all the children were old enough. "Let's go skiing," she said one day. I was irritated with her for wanting to go and shifted to stronger tactics, including my silent withdrawal. But Margie wasn't scared off. She confronted me with my attempts to manipulate her and I denied them. She finally said, "Look, I really want to go and I don't like being made wrong for it. I also don't want to talk you into something you don't want to do. If you really don't want to go, I'll go with the kids. But I sure would like to understand why you're so dead set against it."

When I realized that nothing was going to dissuade her, I dropped my protections and was willing to look into myself. I began to recognize the fears behind my resistance to skiing. As we talked the fears began to surface one by one: fear of not being able to afford taking five people skiing, fear of not being able to learn to ski, and fear of getting hurt. Over the next few days other causes for alarm popped into my head: fear of mountain driving, fear of being cold, fear of getting stuck in the snow. But as each fear arose, we discussed it until I felt better about it. We finally reached the point where, although still nervous, I was willing to risk the trip.

My first day was a DISASTER! It was one of the worst days of my life. I have always prided myself on being a very good athlete, but I couldn't get control of my skis. (I could see dramatically why I always fight so hard to be in control of things.) I was the worst one in my class. I felt humiliated as the class kept having to wait for Jordan to struggle to his feet after one of his twenty-five falls and ten collisions. One of my worst fears was coming true — I was inadequate and a failure. Finally, an hour before class ended, I mumbled some excuse to the instructor about not feeling well and trudged off to wait for Margie and the kids. Maybe they had had as miserable a day as I did.

When they floated into the lodge, I knew I was really in trouble. I sulked through my hot chocolate, and as we talked more fears tumbled out. I feared they would all love skiing and I would either have to accompany them on ski trips and sit all day in the lodge by myself or else stay home alone. And even if I did try again the next day, since they were all better than I was, they would be off together and I would be alone struggling with the mountain. We kept talking; by the end of the evening I had uncovered eleven different fears, only a couple of which I had been aware of when Margie first said, "Let's go skiing." (On the way home, at night, on a two-lane stretch of crowded highway, I fantasized a car pulling out to pass another and coming into my lane, and the number mounted to an even dozen.)

As we talked during that first evening, Margie assured me she didn't want to ski without me, and we came up with some new ideas for teaching me

how to ski. Once more my fears lessened, and
I decided to try again. Having expressed my fears
and been comforted, I felt hopeful and went to sleep
curled up under Margie's wing.

Going up on the chair lift the next morning, my
knees were knocking from more than the cold;
I shared my apprehensions with Margie and scored
my first major victory by managing to get off the
chair without falling. By lunchtime we had made a
few runs, and I was starting to get the hang of this
crazy sport. By the end of the day, I knew I could
master it if I stuck with it, and I even began to have
some fun.

Hiding from my fears would only have
perpetuated them. *Talking did not make my fears
go away; understanding them with Margie's
support helped me to confront them.* Overcoming
them made me feel terrific.

The skiing issue was just like all the personal or
marital conflicts our clients (or we) have ever had to face:
fears predominate at first, but lessen as they are examined
carefully. Fears dissipate only as we feel more confident,
and confidence grows with successfully meeting challenge.
While the fear may never go away completely, meeting
the challenge not only makes us feel great, it also gives us
the courage to confront other fears in the future.

·8·

Protections

What often happens in a "marriage,"
legal or otherwise, is that each partner
unconsciously manipulates the other's
behavior . . . Each can move the other like
a marionette, yet neither one is aware of
the strings.

MEIRS AND VALDENS
People-Reading

Recognizing protective behavior is an important stage of exploration. Protections are strategies we use to keep our unconscious fears from consciousness.

Most of us can't see how we have become protective. We prefer to see ourselves as open and gentle; it may be shocking to hear that others — especially those closest to us — may see us as hard, critical, and closed. While reading this chapter, you will easily be able to see your partner's protections; it is your own you will have trouble recognizing, although your partner will probably be glad to tell you all about them.

To paraphrase the poet: "How do I protect myself? Let me count the ways." The nearly infinite variety of methods people use to protect themselves from pain can be reduced to the three general categories we defined in Chapter One — Compliance, Control, and Indifference/ Resistance. We explained compliant behavior as giving oneself up and going along with what another wants out of fear, obligation, or guilt. This chapter shows the specific behaviors attached to Control and Indifference/Resistance.

Control — Protecting Me by Changing You

In *Man the Manipulator*, Everett Shostrom describes manipulators as "people who exploit, use, and control themselves and others as 'things'." He goes on to list the staggering variations on this theme: dictators, Mother Superiors, rank pullers, bosses, bullies, weaklings, worriers, nags, whiners, parasites, weepers, perpetual children, hypochondriacs, attention demanders, tough guys, nice guys, pleasers, know-it-alls, blamers, resentment collectors, shamers, comparers, sufferers for others, martyrs, calculators, addicts, clinging vines.

Most of us learned manipulation at an early age. We grew up believing that our only choice was to be either selfish or selfless, exploiter or exploited. Most people would say that it's wrong to manipulate others — though everyone tries to do so much of the time. We hope you can drop your negative judgments as you read this chapter, for if you think a certain behavior is wrong, you won't be able to admit how much of it you actually do.

If given our choice, naturally we prefer to have another person do what we want, rather than not do what we want. We usually try to get that person to do what we want with disapproval, followed by more drastic methods if that doesn't work. Approval is so important to most people that often the mere threat of disapproval is enough to get the other person to change. All forms of disapproval are accusations that say, "You're wrong for what you are thinking, feeling, or doing," underwritten by the belief that "my way is the only right way."

Blame is often implied: "It is your fault that I'm hurt (scared, disappointed, annoyed)." The partner trying to control is hoping to take advantage of the other's *fear or guilt*: fear of disapproval or guilt over having done something wrong.

Disapproval also entails a punishment: "This is what you're going to get when you disappoint or upset me." To try to control someone is to *demand* rather than to ask or influence. Although a request may hope to change the other person, it is not an attempt to control if the partner is free to say "No" without disapproval, and free to say "Yes" without feeling a loss of integrity. Often a demand may *sound* like a request, as in "Honey, would you take out the garbage?" If the response "No, I'm busy right now" gets back a congenial "Okay," then the question has been a request. But if the retort is a sarcastic "Thanks a lot," or silent anger, then the question has been an attempt to control.

Symptomatic Body Language

Our bodies are powerful agents of manipulation. When we disapprove of someone, our voice has a hard edge; our body is tense. We look and sound like an authoritarian parent. We sometimes use anger to intimidate our partner into behaving the way we want. We speak loudly, shout, scream, stomp around, slam doors, pound or shake our fist, throw things. We have narrowed eyes, a clenched jaw, hunched shoulders, furrowed brows, tight mouth, or disgusted looks.

Many people who have worked hard at learning how to express anger have been disappointed and puzzled when this did nothing to help their relationship. When the intent of anger is merely to blame, it will almost always be met with a defensive, protective response. The often misunderstood difference between anger and assertiveness is that the latter is going after what we want firmly without considering the other person wrong. The anger we have described is always an accusation. A wife's "Dammit, do you have to be such a slob! Who do you think I am — your mother?" is rarely met with "You're right, honey. From now on I'll put my clothes in the hamper." A more common retort would be, "Get off my back and stop acting like my mother. You're always uptight over something!"

Threats

Threats are very effective when they tap into the partner's guilt or fear. The person making the threat hopes that if the consequences seem dire enough, the other will give in and change. Here are some common examples:

- Physical violence — "If you don't get over here, I'm gonna whack you." "Shut up or I'll belt you one."

- Becoming ill — "Don't get me upset — my heart can't take it." "I'm getting a (headache, stomachache, etc.) from all this."

- Mental illness — "You're driving me crazy." "I can't handle this any more. I'm going to have a nervous breakdown."

- Suicide — "I feel like killing myself when you say that to me." "I can't go on living like this."

- Emotional withdrawal — "I don't want to be around you when you behave like that." "I can't stand the sight of you."

- Sexual withdrawal — "If you think you're going to get in bed with me tonight, forget it."

"Don't expect me to be turned on if you keep on watching TV."

- Financial withdrawal — "Pull that number again and I'll cancel your credit cards." "If you go to school instead of staying home to take care of the house, don't expect me to support you."

- Physical withdrawal — "I'm not going to stay around if you keep pulling that stuff." "Why don't we just call it quits? This is hopeless."

- Exposure — "Wait till your boss (father, friends) hears about this."

- Invoking higher authority — "God will punish you for that."

Criticism

Criticism means any unasked for, often hostile comments that make the other wrong. These can be fairly subtle: raised eyebrows, "tsk, tsk," sighing, shrugging shoulders, or shaking the head disapprovingly. Or a direct verbal attack: "What the hell's wrong with you?" "How could you be so stupid?" Sarcasm and ridicule wound deeply, though the critic can deny a hostile motive: "I'm only kidding — can't you take a joke?" "You're too sensitive. Don't you know when someone's joking?"

Criticizing one's partner is a way of life in many relationships. When one partner believes there is a right and a wrong way to be, it probably seems self-evident that the other should change if he or she is believed to be wrong. Many people sincerely feel their partners would improve by changing, so they criticize out of the misguided belief that criticism is helpful. But trying to help others change by putting them in the wrong never helps.

Meaningful change occurs only with the understanding that enhances self-esteem, not through criticism.

Explanations and Lectures

Criticism may be followed by outwardly calm and rational explanations. But these explanations often are not what they seem. The explainer, unable to deal with the partner's feelings or non-compliance hopes that a litany of logical reasons will bring about the change. The following interchange will illustrate:

Sue wanted to go to a movie on Friday night, but Ray forgot about this commitment and got home too late. She complained and he answered, "You know I had to prepare for my Monday meeting, and then the freeway was all jammed up." When she expressed her disappointment again, Ray rejoined, "Look, I said I couldn't help it. We'll go next week. And besides, there's nothing good playing anyway." Ray felt guilty whenever Sue was upset, so rather than comfort her, he attempted to talk her out of her feelings with his logical explanation, thereby relieving himself of discomfort.

Lengthy explanations become lectures. With an overwhelming barrage of facts the lecturer hopes to change the other's mind. But even when explanations and lectures are given in a calm, intellectual, and logical (though parental) tone of voice, the intent is not to understand, but merely to gain control by convincing the other person that he or she is wrong.

Crying or Being Hurt: "Poor Me"

Those who cry when they hurt may see themselves as pitiable, but frequently they are accusing and critical instead. Our women clients often say, "I'm a very open and emotional person. Not like my husband — he doesn't know what it means to feel. I express my feelings often, but my husband is just put off by them. When I cry, he doesn't seem to care and sometimes gets mad." But often the husband is just defending against concealed accusations. She is not saying, "I'm hurt and I need your help in exploring my part in creating the situation leading up to these feelings." Nor is she wanting to understand her husband's behavior. The message is actually, "You've hurt me. I am the helpless victim of your wrongdoing. Maybe if you see how miserable you're making me, you'll change and be the way I want you to be." Receiving this message, the husband shuts her out even more firmly, protecting himself from her attempts to control him. Feeling uncared for, she then becomes more hurt and more critical.

In the course of her marriage to Ralph, Barbara became interested in understanding herself; she went into therapy, read books, and attended classes. She wanted Ralph to go with her, but he wasn't interested. As Barbara came to know herself better, she wanted to connect with Ralph, to share her inner feelings and to know his. But Ralph remained protected and unavailable. After a number of years, Barbara decided to leave Ralph and seek out a relationship with a more sensitive, understanding man. When Barbara left, Ralph was in a great deal of pain, feeling the victim of Barbara's decision to leave. He tearfully appealed to her whenever he had the chance, hoping she would feel sorry for him, see that she was wrong, and come back. However, this kind of "poor me" pain only pushed Barbara farther away. Had Ralph taken responsibility for his end of the relationship, his pain would have been from *his* protective choices throughout their marriage; after some re-evaluating, perhaps there would have been a reconciliation.

The Silent Treatment

The Silent Treatment — withdrawal into silence while inwardly seething — is a non-verbal form of disapproval.

The message is the same as for all other forms: "You have done something wrong." In addition, it says, "I will not be involved with you until you do things my way." Total unavailability is always awesome and frightening to the other person.

JORDAN:

For years Margie and I battled over whose form of
protection was worse. "Your yelling is terrible,"
I would say. "If only you weren't so critical
I wouldn't withdraw." She would counter with,
"I can't stand your withdrawal. If you wouldn't
withdraw, I wouldn't get so angry." Finally, after
many years, we realized that overt anger and silent
anger are two sides of the same coin, just different
ways to protect.

But then, one day, Margie got angry and instead of
yelling at me she turned to stone. The more I tried
to break through, the harder she became. Never
have I felt so helpless and terrified. Even though we
understood that our protective devices were
basically the same, I discovered my own chief
protection was the most threatening to me. I would
much rather deal with a person's overt anger than
have to knock on a wall of ice.

Set-ups for Control

Set-ups are the behaviors that precede attempts to control
— expectations, manipulative questions, and being nice.

Expectations are how we believe our partner should behave if he or she really cares. "If you really loved me you would . . . " Expectations are set-ups: you expect a particular response, then disapprove of your partner when you don't get it.

A manipulative question is a demand or accusation clothed as a question. It is often a question whose answer is already known and judged to be wrong. Knowing that Barry had lunch with his secretary, Marilyn asked him with whom he had had lunch. When he told her a "business associate," she blew up at him. He was now doubly accused: both of having lunch with the secretary and trying to mislead Marilyn. But even if Barry had told her the truth in full detail, Marilyn would have been angry. She did not really want to know the truth about why Barry wanted to have lunch with his secretary; she only wanted Barry to admit he was wrong.

Asking a question to which only one answer is acceptable is also a trap. Wanting to make love, Barry said to Marilyn, "What do you want to do tonight?" When Marilyn said, "Gee, I'm kinda tired. I'd like to go to sleep," Barry blew up. The question was dishonest. He did not really want to know what Marilyn wanted to do; his question had only one acceptable answer. He was fishing for Marilyn's love and approval and was angry when he did not get it, interpreting her lack of interest in sex as disinterest in him.

Being nice can be a subtle form of control. Of course, not all kindness is an attempt at control, but when we are nice to get someone else to do our will in return, then the behavior is actually a set-up. Even giving gifts can be a means of control. The message hidden inside many gifts is "I'm giving you this so that you'll give me something in return."

Protecting Me by Becoming Indifferent

To protect ourselves from rejection or control, some of us give up wanting anything from the other person. We become indifferent. We deny our vulnerability, convincing ourselves we don't need anything. For example, we fear that if we intensely desired sex, our partner would be able to withhold it until we became the way he or she demanded. To protect ourselves from this potential pain we retreat. Note that shutting another out is different from the Silent Treatment. With the latter, we are angry; with the former, we feel nothing. Paradoxically, to avoid giving ourselves up to our partner, we voluntarily give up our own aliveness.

Sexual Withdrawal

In many primary relationships at least one partner has become sexually unresponsive. Although people can become completely unresponsive sexually, more often they find themselves devoid of sexual feelings only with their partners, which provides an excellent excuse for infidelities. When sexual feelings do not flow freely between mates, there is usually a power struggle going on, and one or both partners feel afraid of losing themselves — a fear that is never more apparent than in sex. A "sex" problem is often not strictly about sex, but can be the result of giving up oneself in other areas of the relationship. When we withdraw sexually, the message is "I don't want you to have that power over me, so I'll protect myself from really loving you and from encountering my worst fears — that if I really love you and want you, I will put my own needs aside rather than risk losing you."

Emotional Withdrawal

When emotionally withdrawn, partners are not moved or touched by the other; they are not saddened by their pain or excited by their enthusiasm. They may be physically present or even sexually aroused, but not affected on a feeling level. Stoic and impassive, they neither cry nor laugh deeply. When they make love, it may be just a physical experience without passion or tenderness — or they may allow themselves to feel deeply *only* when making love.

Paradoxically, many people who may be moved to tears by a sad movie remain completely untouched by the real sadness and pain in their own lives and the lives of their loved ones. They are afraid that if they soften, they will be controlled. For some men remaining hard and unmoved is the only way they know to be "masculine."

Today some women are in a similar predicament. After years of catering to their husbands' demands, they realize that they have been putting aside their own needs. They have made love when they weren't turned on, smiled when angry, hidden their dissatisfactions, put aside work or creative projects, or spent more time with their children than they wanted to — all to keep the peace, avoiding guilt feelings and their husbands' disapproval. When they finally see how much of themselves they have lost, they do an about-face; they stop giving themselves up, but they harden to do it. They shut their husbands out completely, either by becoming distant and uninvolved or leaving the relationship. They are afraid that the only way of dealing with their husbands' negative reactions will be to give themselves up again. They can be soft and caring only when they feel stronger inside, able to get what they need assertively without letting their guilt and fear dominate them.

Physical Withdrawal

When we choose to work long hours, then spend the remaining time in a solitary pastime like watching television, we are physically withdrawn. (We may, of course, also be sexually and/or emotionally withdrawn at the same time). For years Dan had spent all of his time building his business. When Jane complained that he was never around, he put her off by explaining that he was doing it "for you and the kids," and that in a couple of years the business would be on its feet and he could spend more time at home.

In a couple of years the business was on its feet, but suddenly Dan had a new love: jogging. At first it was only for an hour a day, but after a few months Dan joined a gym and was spending another hour or two there. Before therapy, Jane had felt totally shut out of Dan's life. When she got angry about it, he said he loved her but continued to shut her out. Dan did love Jane; that was why he was afraid to be involved with her. If she had not been important to him, he would not have worried about giving himself up. But because he feared her disapproval, he believed that spending time with her would let her control him. Only through explorations in therapy and with Jane did he come to understand the reasons behind his behavior.

Symptoms of Indifference

Our world is full of pastimes and devices that help us withdraw and shut out pain. Almost anything we do can be used to avoid feeling pain; *it depends on the intent of the behavior.*

Television

For millions, television helps turn off the mind and shut out the world. It is, in fact, a daily tranquilizer with few obvious dangers, unless we consider the dissolution of a relationship a harmful side-effect. How often do we walk into the den or bedroom and automatically turn on the set? At bedtime, is it our mate or Johnny Carson who interests us? A TV set in the bedroom is such an easy way to avoid talking, making love, or facing each other — and the unpleasant possibilities that might come up. "But I work hard all day and I need to relax," you might say. "What's wrong with unwinding in front of the TV?"

There's really nothing wrong but you may also be using TV to avoid something that needs attention — your mate in particular.

Overeating

Overweight usually serves some very important functions in a person's life. It may, for example, be an effective way to keep from having to test oneself in the world. What frightening things would a person have to confront if thin? Relationships? Sexuality? Success? Being attractive to the opposite sex? Being intimate and thus vulnerable to rejection? As one of our clients said when we discussed her fears of an intimate relationship: "This all ties into being forty pounds overweight. What guy is going to look at me?" As long as she can feel sexually unattractive, she doesn't have to face her fears.

Sometimes people remain heavy to protect their marriages. They subconsciously fear that if they were thin, they might have an affair; being heavy will keep them from this temptation and from having to confront their marital difficulties. Often the act of eating is a way to avoid upsetting feelings such as boredom, loneliness, or sadness. Food can be a way to dull the pain of those unhappy feelings.

Overeating sometimes results from a power struggle — with a parent, a mate, or even oneself. Many people find that the moment they tell themselves not to eat, they immediately go ahead and do it. It's exactly the same situation as when one person tries to change another through criticism. One part of the overweight person says, "You're so fat and ugly! Go on a diet!" while the disowned and criticized self rebels and eats anyway out of spite.

Alcohol and Drugs

Alcohol and drugs can shut out the truth. A spaced-out mind doesn't have to encounter loneliness, anxiety, or fear. The following dramatic example occurred in our office. Paul was an alcoholic who had been in therapy with a variety of different therapists for years. He had not had a drink in two years and had decided it was time to explore the difficulties between his wife and himself. As we talked about their relationship, the question of sex came up. They had not had sex in two years — in fact, since Paul quit drinking. As we began to explore the topic, Paul broke out in a sweat and said that he was craving a drink for the first time since he had been sober. Sex was so frightening to Paul that he avoided it entirely or sought it only when intoxicated. For Paul, drinking was the way to avoid knowing his fears of sexual failure and rejection.

Illness

Since we are not medical doctors, we cannot discuss here all the factors that make certain people particularly illness-prone. We will focus on the emotional factors only. Illness takes up a lot of time and energy. If we are ill a good deal, our illness may be serving some purpose. It may, for example, be a strategy for avoiding knowing about something difficult — such as an unhappy marriage — or it can be a way of not having to test our potential for personal accomplishment. And it can certainly help to avoid threatening activities such as sex, work, or social events. Usually, a person does not consciously want to be ill. But the stress that occurs when we protect ourselves from pain, the tension that accumulates when we don't want to confront our fears, can create such difficulties for the body that it eventually succumbs to illness.

Nancy and Frank had been married for twenty-five years. Nancy was a virgin when she married, and soon after the wedding she developed a severe vaginal infection, resistant to treatment, that prevented intercourse for a number of years. She continually sought out different doctors for various ailments and would go into the hospital periodically for tests. Nancy was uncertain about her attractiveness; rather than subject herself to the possibility of Frank's rejections she remained ill. Frustrated by Nancy's illness, Frank shut her out by watching television every night until he fell asleep, further reinforcing Nancy's insecurities. No solution, hard or easy, could be reached until Nancy began to understand her history and *her present intent.* She only began to examine other possibilities when she was able to see that her life was being frozen in dissatisfaction through her own choices.

Pursuing Wealth and Material Possessions

In our culture, working hard and making more and more money are acceptable ways of avoiding the unhappiness in our lives. Joseph Chilton Pearce, in *Exploring the Crack in the Cosmic Egg,* says:

> We fool ourselves into believing that: "If I had a million, then everything would by okay" . . . The pursuit acts as entertainment of the mind, staving off despair. When the pursuit finally crashes in ruins, or when the pursuit is overwhelmingly successful, the buffer effect is no longer operable, and one has no insulation against his despair.

Many people, primarily men, spend their lives working in the hope that when they "make it," they will finally feel secure. But those who do make it often find that joy and peace of mind actually lie somewhere else. Women often go on spending binges in the vain hope of filling their days with activities and their lives with desirable possessions, only temporarily warding off their fear and loneliness.

Resisting and Rebelling

Resistance and rebellion are the very effective counterparts of the control strategies we've already discussed. Perhaps more clearly than any of the other types, these protective strategies have their sources in early family conflicts. They once were the child's desperate attempt to sustain personal integrity in the face of constant family pressure to change or conform. The one who resists lets his or her mate make decisions, then rebels against what has been decided to keep from being controlled. Doing this, however, limits the person to reacting rather than acting. The following are typical examples of resistance:

- Consistently forgetting to pay the bills, then getting upset and refusing to do it when reminded.

- Telling your mate that you wish he or she would make plans to do things more often, then not wanting to do whatever is planned.

- Objecting when someone, especially your mate, requests something from you.

- Telling your mate you want him or her to initiate sex more often, but finding you are not in the mood when this happens.

- Saying you will water the plants every week, forgetting to do it, and then calling your mate a nag for reminding you.

- Telling your mate to get off your back and stop nagging you, then being irritated when he or she fails to remind you of an appointment.

Ironically, when the resist-and-rebel strategy is well entrenched, it can prevent a person from doing things he or she would truly enjoy. We may want to make love, or go on a picnic, but find ourselves turning to something else as soon as our partner suggests either activity. *We may be so intent on not doing what our partner wants that we fail to look and decide for ourselves what we really want to do.* As John O. Stevens observes in *Awareness: Exploring, Experimenting, Experiencing,* "The extremes of compliance are the conformist who always complies and the rebel who never complies. Both are equally trapped in a rigid response to ... outside demands."

Christine's husband Al is a classic example. He let Christine make all the decisions, then either went along reluctantly or pulled back completely. Early in their marriage, Christine was not very interested in sex. Consequently, Al was full of desire. But as soon as Christine became more sexual, Al turned off completely. Eventually Al felt totally dead; he left the marriage thinking he just did not love Christine. The day she decided to file for divorce, however, he suddenly felt madly in love with her. He spent the evening crying and declaring his adoration. They decided to get back together. But that night when Christine wanted to make love, Al again pulled back. Until he is willing to take responsibility for what *he* wants, no matter what Christine wants, Al will have difficulty with any relationship.

Being a Victim

Whenever we refuse to discover how we contribute to our own distress, we are acting like victims. The victim is saying, "I am innocent and helpless, a reactor, totally dependent on what you do." When we admit that we are not totally blameless, but still believe the other is more to blame, we just give lip service to the principle of personal responsibility.

You may be thinking, "If I'm unhappy, why should I be the one who has to do something about it? Shouldn't my partner stop doing what's making me unhappy?" It may seem unfair, but the one who's unhappy is the one who needs to begin to understand himself or herself.

Should your partner become unhappy as a result of what you do, then it becomes his or her responsibility to work toward understanding his or her own behavior.

We all want a guarantee that things will go the way we want them to go, and we try to avoid knowing how things really are. We stick to our old protections because we *hope* they will work for us even with all the evidence to the contrary. But whatever diminishes our pain must also diminish our consciousness. The more we cling to our personal anesthetics, the less able we are to regard conflict-induced feelings as a gift of information, a starting point on a journey toward greater self-awareness.

·9·

Consequences of Protection

> *Whatever choices we make, there will be consequences.*
>
> NATHANIEL BRANDEN
> *The Psychology of Romantic Love*

The Paradox of Protection

The Problem

We all need to be loved. The more we love someone, the more important his or her love is to us, and the more frightened we are of losing it. We fear that if we don't act the way our partner wants us to, we'll be rejected.

The Common Solution

We protect ourselves either by giving ourselves up, attempting to control the other, or becoming indifferent.

The Paradoxes

1. Although almost everything we do is to protect us from pain, much of the pain we feel results from our protective behavior.

2. By trying to protect against losing ourselves to another person, we actually end up losing touch with our natural selves.

3. The more we either give ourselves up or are disapproved of, the more inadequate and unlovable we feel. As our fear of rejection grows, we look for more and more effective ways to protect ourselves.

4. When we put up our protections, we are estranged from our partner. Thus our own protections often lead directly to our partner's rejecting us, which is what we originally wanted to avoid.

Protective circles are not perpetuated by mean, sick, bad people. You and I, basically good people, hungering for love, unwittingly bring about the opposite of what we so desperately need. What people do to themselves and to each other because they want to protect themselves is the saddest thing we encounter in our work. Day after day in our office we are involved with people who long to be understood, cared about, nurtured, and loved — yet they will not open, reach out, and embrace each other. Sometimes one is willing, but the other isn't; then the one who was rejected retreats to lick his or her wounds and waits to get even. We often weep from the pain of witnessing two wonderful, hurting souls so protected that they can't give each other the only thing that could heal them, which is love.

Types of Protective Circles

Protective circles lead to relationships that run the gamut from noisy relationships with lots of fighting to "civilized," hushed relationships whose partners lead uninvolved, parallel lives.

No one, including the partners, can judge the quality of a relationship by external appearances only; a knowledge of intent is necessary too. For example, Judy announces to her husband Harvey that she is going back to school. Harvey feels threatened by the idea and bellows at her, "Dammit, what do you want to do that for? What's going to happen to me and the kids? I don't want you gone all day." Harvey is aware of fearing that he won't be as well taken care of if Judy is preoccupied with school, but he is not consciously aware of his vague and uncomfortable suspicion that she will meet men on campus and may fall in love with one of them.

When Doreen tells her husband Ben that she has found an interesting job, he just mumbles something from behind his newspaper. Doreen isn't exactly encouraged to carry out her plans, but not forbidden, either. It's tempting to judge Harvey's male-chauvinist intimidation tactics more harshly than Ben's lukewarm reaction, but each husband's internal feelings are the same. At the level of intention, both marriages are in exactly the same situation: neither husband attempts to understand either his wife's desires or his own fears.

Frequently repeated protections make deeply ingrained protective circles as formal and predictable as a minuet. Four protective circles recur in most primary relationships: *Control-Compliance, Indifference-Indifference, Control-Control,* and *Control-Indifference.* (See the Paths through Conflict chart, page 29.) Most couples spend time and energy in all four, since individual strategies vary depending on the issue and the feelings of the moment. You will, however, probably recognize one circle as your own pattern, as familiar and as recognizable as your handwriting.

The first two strategies — *Control-Compliance* and *Indifference-Indifference* — make for a deceptive calm. The partners are not truly intimate; they have worked out an acceptable but routine (and sometimes finally intolerable) design for parallel living. They move carefully, like dancers who dance either far apart or in fixed patterns to keep from colliding. In the latter two — *Control-Control* and *Control-Indifference* — there is overt turmoil stemming from deeply ingrained power struggles.

Control-Compliance

In this circle, one person is in control and the other has given himself or herself up to avoid conflict and disapproval. Although there is peace, the person who has capitulated feels distant. He or she generally feels more relaxed and spontaneous when the mate isn't around. Such partners will not generally seek therapy: As long as both agree (subconsciously) on their mutual course of action, the relationship is stable. But if the one who has been capitulating resists or attempts to gain control, the relationship goes into turmoil. Failing that, the controlling partner may simply become bored with or lose respect for his or her mate.

In some relationships control shifts between the partners depending on the issue. When this occurs, each partner is at times in control, and at times capitulating.

Indifference-Indifference

In this pattern, both partners have withdrawn and become indifferent. The relationship is relatively even and peaceful, with few lows and few highs. The two people live side by side, respecting each other but not feeling in love. They have given up wanting much from each other and have settled for peace. In the early twentieth century, this was the accepted strategy used to keep a marriage from splitting up. A recent study of couples married more than fifty years revealed that the vast majority put the survival of the marriage first, their happiness second.

This type of couple rarely seeks marriage counseling. In a sense, they have already "cut their losses" and decided to settle for safety. The very peacefulness of their choice makes it hard to sense that anything is missing. Their marriage may seem to others to be made in heaven. But this is exactly the type of "perfect" marriage that shocks everyone by suddenly coming apart after twenty-five or so impeccable years. Even after many years, the partners may feel that they don't really know each other. By avoiding conflict, they have never opened up the issues that would let them explore and understand each other. When the partners do talk to a counselor or therapist, their remarks tend to sound like these:

> "We don't seem to have much to say to each other."
>
> "My partner doesn't share his or her feelings with me."
>
> "All we talk about are the kids, work, sports, other people."
>
> "My partner seems withdrawn much of the time."
>
> "We never fight, but our talk is so superficial."
>
> "There's a wall between us."
>
> "We're bored with each other."

Control-Control

When each person wants to change the other, a power struggle ensues. This circle brings on bitter fighting or covert anger and tension when both are using the Silent Treatment. Some of the remarks we hear from people in this kind of relationship are:

> "We can't talk without getting into an argument."

"We fight over trivial things."

"My partner isn't on my side."

"We compete with each other a lot."

"Our differences are much bigger now
than when we first met."

"I don't feel as if we're friends."

It is impossible for both partners to be satisfied, since each
is trying to win at the other's expense. They are stuck in a
fight, so intent on winning that they fail even to listen to
what the other is saying. No real resolution is possible as
long as the two parties are locked into fighting, as shown
by the brief skit below. We have often done this skit in
workshops and on TV shows. The quoted remarks in the
parentheses are directed toward the audience.

A man and a woman sit in chairs a few inches apart.
He looks uptight. His body is stiff. There is a sense
of icy tension about him. His eyes are narrowed, his
jaw set.

SHE:

"What's the matter?" (Wary.)

HE:

"Nothing." (Denies, while being cold and distant.)

SHE:

("Something's going on; I know that uptight
look.")

"Come on, you seem really upset. What's going
on?"

HE:

"Look, you're just going to get mad, so forget it."
(Predicts and withdraws.)

SHE:

("This drives me up a wall.")

"I won't get mad; just tell me what's the matter."
(She promises and denies as well.)
HE:
("Okay, you asked for it.")
"I can't believe you're not even aware that we're
late again." (His tone is accusing, expecting her to
feel just as he does, to see her acts in the same light.)
SHE:
(Irritated and accusing as well.)
"You're so upset just because we're a little late?"
HE:
(Accusing, hoping to make her feel guilty.)
"You said you wouldn't get mad."
SHE:
(Irritation escalating.)
"I'm not mad!" (Denies.) "I just want to know
why you're so hung up about being on time!"
(Blames.)
HE:
("Attack me, will you! — I won't even respond.")
(He looks straight ahead, silent and withdrawn,
protecting himself and punishing her.)
SHE:
("Okay, great — now I get the silent treatment.")
(Her anger is now building as she is demanding and
hard.)
"I asked you a question. What's the big deal about
being fifteen minutes late?"
HE:
(Calm and distant in the face of her mounting
agitation, he is now condescending and putting her
down.)
"Look, I can't talk to you when you're angry.
When you calm down, then we can talk."

SHE:

(Jumping out of her skin, her voice raised in high-pitched anger.)

"I *am* calm! I just want to know what the big deal is?"

HE:

(Steadfastly calm and removed.)

"You're yelling." (Denies involvement by refusing to be affected.)

SHE:

(Face reddening and voice many decibels above normal.)

"I'm not yelling! I just want you to answer me one thing! Why are you so uptight?" (Continues to deny and blame. The fight is now focused on the protections rather than on the issue of being late.)

HE:

(Remains silent and withdrawn.)

SHE:

(Cold, hard, and completely frustrated.)

"Hey look, you're the one who started this!"

(Collapses in utter frustration.)

They now turn away from each other to pout and console themselves. Each feeling justified, they prepare their next moves.

Fights are a series of attacks and defenses that go on until one or both people succumb. The exchanges are like those in a courtroom. Each tries to win, i.e., get the other to change. The atmosphere is competitive, not cooperative. Neither is really listening to the other; as one is speaking, the other is either readying a defense or preparing to use what the other has just said to counterattack. Since they both believe that every conflict must end with a winner and a loser and since neither wants to lose, their intent is to be "one up" and put the other person "one down."

This process may work in a court of law, but it can never leave the participants feeling respected, understood, or loved. There are no real winners in a lover's quarrel. Even the one who wins can never feel good; if the adversary totally gives in, he or she is not worthy of respect; if the adversary has only temporarily given in, then it is necessary to be constantly on guard for the next encounter. The loser must harden to protect against any further loss of integrity and will probably try to get even. This type of relationship brings to mind the Schopenhauer parable about the two porcupines: They huddle together for warmth on a freezing day, but their quills hurt each other and they move apart, only to find they are freezing again. Their ultimate solution is to move back and forth, alternately freezing and hurting, until they find the right distance to keep between them.

Control-Indifference

In this circle, one partner is trying to control the other while the other is indifferent or resistant. The Control-Indifference circle is also a power struggle, although different from the Control-Control circle. Here one person is valiantly trying to change the other, who just as valiantly resists being changed. In this circle partners may switch roles, depending on the issue. He may push for sex while she resists; she may push for sharing of feelings while he resists.

When you are the resisting/indifferent partner you often:

• Feel pulled at or feel on guard and afraid to let go and be yourself.

• Agree with your partner or do something for him or her, feeling as if you're giving in or losing.

• React to your mate rather than act spontaneously. You don't make your own choice but wait to see what the other wants, then either go along reluctantly or rebel.

• Are irritated by simple requests.

• Feel loving and excited in anticipation of meeting your mate but are unable to be demonstrative when she or he shows up.

• Are able to express loving thoughts in letters or cards or on the telephone, but not in person.

• Feel guilty or defensive.

• Felt better about yourself before you met than you do now.

• Feel better about yourself and freer when with friends or alone than when with your partner.

• Feel that your integrity is constantly being threatened.

When you are the one trying to control, you generally feel:

• Frustrated and irritated much of the time.

• Critical of your partner.

• Righteous.

• Needing to know everything that's going on with your partner, especially whom he or she has spent time with.

- Needing recurrent proofs of your partner's love.

The power struggle in this circle devastates a relationship in a way that is difficult to grasp. The problems often seem to defy logical analysis. During their courtship, Sue cooked elaborate meals for Gary. Gary proposed to Sue with thoughts of a lifetime of culinary bliss filling his mind. Not too long after the wedding, however, Sue's cooking deteriorated markedly; at best, the meals were only so-so, and at worst Sue was "too tired" even to prepare a simple hamburger. Gary was genuinely puzzled; it didn't seem possible that Sue could *unlearn* her cooking ability. What had happened? Before they were married, Sue cooked for Gary out of a desire to do something loving for him and be creative. After the marriage, this gift could no longer be given freely, for it was now a *marital obligation* and Gary would be angry or dissatisfied if it were not fulfilled. With the freedom and joy gone, Sue couldn't summon enough energy even to be a merely adequate cook, let alone prepare the superlative meals she had once prepared with love. Until Gary and Sue resolved their power struggle, they were stuck with their anger and resistance.

Power Struggles

When you're having trouble communicating — talking about issues and finding mutually satisfying resolutions — you can consider the probability of a power struggle.

Almost every couple gets into power struggles, which occur when one person wants something from the partner, doesn't get it, but continues to try. When deeply entrenched, power struggles spread throughout the relationship.

Almost anything you want from your partner can become part of a power struggle — reading this book, for example. You like it and want your partner to read it; he or she resists. *Trying* to get your partner to read it begins a power struggle.

A power struggle is a tug of war, with each person at opposite ends of a rope. In the Control-Control circle, where both are attempting to be right and win, each is trying to pull the other onto his or her side. In the Control-Indifference circle, one person is trying to get the other onto his or her side, while the other resists. The more one partner pulls at the other for love, time, affirmation, sex, communication, money, neatness, or anything else, the more the other resists; the more one resists by shutting the other out, the more the other feels rejected and pulls.

For some couples, intense power struggles begin early in their relationship. For others, power struggles may not become serious until there is a major difference of opinion over an important issue. Once a power struggle takes hold, loving feelings begin to fade.

Sex is one of the most common areas for power struggles, either as the primary site or the area into which power struggles over other issues have spread. In the sexual power struggle one partner is usually the unhappy one, complaining that the other does not want sex or does not like a particular part of the sex act. The complaining partner assumes that something is wrong with the other partner, and that the trouble should be "fixed." Hal wished Lucy would be more sensual, freer, aggressive, and "not so uptight." Meanwhile, unknown to him, she was having an affair, aggressively enjoying many varieties of sex with her lover. Because Hal kept making her wrong for being as she was, to be free with him felt like doing it for him rather than for herself. In her affair, where she was not in a power struggle, and where she felt accepted, she could be free for herself *and* please her lover.

When Lucy was away from Hal, she often had very sexy thoughts about him. But as soon as she was with him and felt pressured for sex, she became resistant. She instantly *lost touch with her own desire for sex when her primary intent was to protect against being controlled.* The resistant one always loses touch with what he or she wants as soon as he or she resists the other, for the primary intent to protect blocks out all other desires.

When the power struggle between Lucy and Hal was broken she said at one point, "It's very hard for me to feel like saying 'Yes' to Hal unless I have the freedom to say 'No' without his getting angry with me. When I don't want to make love, and he is interested in finding out why not, then I usually feel loved and often want to make love."

While Lucy was struggling with her resistance, Hal was also in a very difficult position. If he was not to pressure Lucy, he had to decide what he needed to do for himself in the face of her resistance. Should he masturbate? Have an affair? Leave the relationship? For Hal, none of these alternatives was acceptable. He loved Lucy and wanted her. But until he became willing to understand her resistance and his own need to control, he was stuck.

When one partner rarely wants sex, a power struggle is almost always going on. Power struggles over sex rarely occur in casual relationships because lovers feel less need to control each other. You may have wondered whether Lucy would have been better off leaving Hal and marrying her lover who accepted her. We think not. Without understanding her resistance, Lucy would have a sex life like that in her marriage to Hal as soon as a power struggle began in her new relationship.

Sometimes power struggles so pervade a couple's interactions that even trivial issues turn into a hot or cold war. When two people become entrenched in their respective positions, a separation is sometimes the only way for each to obtain a different perspective on their problems. When couples separate and *continue to work on their relationship* — each understanding his or her part of the power struggle — they usually resolve their problems and eventually get back together.

Separation without insight into power struggles usually does not break them. Some couples separate, eventually divorce, and years later are still locked in power struggles. Other couples feel wonderful towards each other while separated — feeling alive and sexual in ways they had not felt since the beginning of their relationship — only to fall back into their old pattern when they move back together.

The request that initiates a power struggle is often reasonable, and your partner's refusal may make no sense to you. You may then attempt to explain logically why you feel as you do and want what you want. Your partner's continuing resistance may then bring out your heavy artillery — threats, crying, yelling. But nothing works. You become increasingly frustrated, hurt, and angry. You feel unloved. What's your option? Keep trying? Give up? Neither will work, unfortunately. You can't give up wanting what you want and to keep trying entrenches your partner in resisting; and the distance increases. The solution comes with an intent to learn.

Breaking power struggles is very difficult because they are often subtle and reactions have become automatic: You want, he or she resists, you pull harder, etc. But it's one thing to want your partner to be different and another thing to try to make him or her change. There is only one way that change comes about without creating a power struggle — to continue to want what you want, but when you don't get it, to explore why not. An exercise for breaking or preventing power struggles can be found on page 279.

Symptoms of the Protective Circles

While the patterns of the various protective circles are different, the resulting consequences are the same. The following problems are symptoms that indicate protective circles:

1. Conflicts Do Not Reach Satisfying Resolutions

Though some couples fight and some do not, the effect is the same: the basic conflicts — over sex, responsibilities, money, children, time, etc. — are never resolved. A primary symptom of protective circles is having the same conflict over and over again. Conflicts are never resolved by fighting *or* by avoidance.

2. Breakdown in Communication

No matter what the type of protective circle, we hear the same complaints from partners intent on protecting:

> "I hold back from telling certain things to my partner."
>
> "We don't communicate any more."
>
> "My partner doesn't seem interested in what I think and feel."
>
> "I sometimes lie to my partner."
>
> "I sometimes think my partner is lying to me."
>
> "I feel as if I don't know him or her very well."

Actually, there is not such thing as a breakdown in communication, only breakdowns in understanding. We're always communicating, but a great deal of communication takes place nonverbally; in fact, words are often used to cloud what a person is really communicating. Communication always reflects your intent. That is why you can take a course in learning "how to communicate," and yet get nowhere if you remain unaware of the *intent behind the communication.*

3. Little Joy, Boring Sex

> "The excitement has gone out of our relationship."
>
> "We never have fun together."
>
> "Sex between us has become routine and rather boring."
>
> "We hardly ever make love any more."
>
> "Our sex lacks romance and passion."
>
> "I don't often feel that my partner desires me."
>
> "We're not very affectionate any more."
>
> "Our affection seems routine and superficial."
>
> "It's hard to believe, but we haven't had sex in months."

Conventional wisdom says that sex becomes less satisfying in long-term relationships because of lack of novelty. We disagree. When sex becomes unsatisfying for one or both partners, it's because one or both are holding back. Since sex involves feelings as well as a physical drive, emotional involvement and openness are necessary if sex is to remain fulfilling. Routine ways outside the bedroom make for uninteresting sexual encounters, too.

The lack of joy and excitement in a long-term committed relationship is as common a complaint as dull sex. Most people believe they no longer play and have fun because of the pressure of responsibilities. Not true: fun is yet another victim of protections. Spontaneity — a necessary ingredient of fun — evaporates for the same reasons sexual feelings do. Joyful and sexual feelings, the spice of life, are the natural outgrowth of feeling in love. When we do not have them, we muddle through our lives without zest. The boredom in our relationship or in our lives in general is a result of attempts to be safe rather than to risk conflict. We cannot have excitement when safety is our primary goal.

4. Anxiety and Tension

It's impossible not to feel anxious when we are constantly trying to find a way to gain approval and avoid disapproval. On the other hand, wanting control also creates a great deal of tension. We must stay on top of every situation to make sure things stay the way we want them to be. Insecure, we fear that our partner is staying with us out of duty or fear. The controlling partner is often apprehensive when his or her partner is out with friends, especially those of the opposite sex. We can never trust or feel secure with our partner because if we can control and manipulate him or her, others can too — and that's scary. *Only when we believe our partner is with us because he or she wants to be — out of desire and caring, rather than out of fear, obligation, or guilt — will we feel secure.*

5. Loss of Self

We all protect; the level of protection is a matter of degree. Our protections may make it possible for us to *think* we are safe, but not to *feel* good. When we are angry, defensive, rebellious, withdrawn, uptight, tense, or anxious, we don't feel at peace. The greater our protections, the more out of touch with our natural selves we are. We find ourselves being the very adults we resolved not to be when we were children. We lose touch with the inner image we may once have had of ourselves — the gentle, open, and loving person who lies buried beneath layers of protections.

When we think only in terms of how another will react, "Do I want to go out to dinner?" may become confused with "Does my partner want to go? Is it okay to want to go out this often? Will my partner be upset with me for wanting to go?" That one is a relatively simple problem; it is much more difficult to discover our real feelings on such complex issues as sex, our own and our partner's family, spending money, child-rearing, work, how to spend one's time. When we act protectively, we never get to know what is uniquely right or wrong for us.

6. *Feeling Unloved and Unloving*

"I don't feel cared about much of the time."

"I know my partner loves me but I don't feel loved."

"I feel my partner doesn't respect me."

"I often think of getting involved with other people."

"Things like work, children, family obligations, hobbies, or sports seem to be more important to my partner than I am."

"I rarely feel the intense in-love feelings I once felt."

"My partner is angry and critical toward me a lot of the time."

"I feel lonely most of the time."

"I love him or her but I don't feel in love."

"Our relationship is a good one but something is missing."

We're often perplexed when we give what another seems to want, or get what we seem to want, and it's still not enough. We may be providing sex, fidelity, or material things, or be giving ourselves up in any number of ways, yet our partner may not feel desired or loved, and vice versa. But when our actions are motivated by fear, obligation, or guilt, our partner will sense this and never feel loved and satisfied. The only behavior that feels truly loving and satisfying is when we know that our partner is doing what he or she *wants* to do. We all need to feel loved for who we are, without feeling as though we had to manipulate to be loved. Ultimately we must recognize that *behavior can be manipulated, but loving feelings and feeling loved cannot.*

Safety Is an Illusion

Whether a relationship is peaceful or hostile, once loving feelings die, each person is a sitting duck for an affair. In today's society, with its relaxed attitudes about contact with the opposite sex and increased opportunities for it, everyone has a good chance to make an intimate contact with someone new. Often an affair is not consciously sought; it happens innocently, sometimes in a surprising way.

Ruth was a plain-looking woman who lived her life very formally, doing the right thing. She was always good, kind, courteous, and quiet. In her early thirties, she married a man very much like herself. Early in their relationship he began to criticize her and she began to withdraw to protect herself from his threatened rejection. Her sexual feelings, which had bloomed during their courtship, went dormant once more; their relationship settled into one that was "okay" but not very loving or sexual. Ruth felt that her husband was not really interested in her.

One day a co-worker, a casual acquaintance, asked her to have lunch with him. Their conversation was brisk, light, and interesting to both; they talked about themselves and the difficulties of their present relationships. Thoroughly enjoying themselves, they decided to meet again the following week. It is never a very long step from feeling someone's intense interest and respect to feeling loved and sexual. Soon thereafter Ruth was having her first affair. Her safe and protected marital relationship was suddenly threatened and in turmoil. The safety sought by both Ruth and her husband turned out to be an illusion.

People who think they have everything under control are sometimes shocked and devastated to find out their partners are leaving them or have been having affairs. Very often a client will say in a first visit, "We were married for twenty-five years. I thought we had a really great marriage. We never fought. Things were calm and peaceful. And then suddenly my husband (wife) walked out on me. Why?" These people thought they were safe, but *safety exists only as long as both partners collaborate to create it.* At any time one partner can decide he or she has had it, and then the "safe" relationship goes up in a puff of smoke.

The protective circle operates to some extent in all relationships. Some of you may be experiencing many of the dire consequences of protection and are looking for a way out of the difficulties you have created. Others may have established relatively satisfying relationships but hope to make your relationship better. Confronting your protections and the underlying fears is the only way we know to do this. A protective circle can be created in a moment, but it can also be broken at any moment, whenever one of the partners desires to know and learn rather than to protect.

·10·

Values, Beliefs, and Expectations

And what is good, Phaedrus,
And what is not good —
Need we ask anyone to tell us these?
ROBERT M. PIRSIG
Zen and the Art of
Motorcycle Maintenance

Exploration inevitably unearths the values, beliefs, and expectations that influence our behavior. All of us have a deeply ingrained value system absorbed from what our families and culture consider "right." We have learned to believe that there is a right way to do everything: to walk, talk, look, smell, eat, dress, make love. People not living by our values seem wrong, inadequate, or bad — or at least not as good as they would be if they lived our way.

The values we particularly cherish become the basis for expectations — how we believe people should behave if they care for each other. Each of us has fantasies about what it means to be really loved — subconscious scenarios that serve as unexpressed expectations. In our work with couples, we often hear the following: "If you really loved me, you'd . . ."

> include me in everything.
> want the same things I want.
> be on time.
> remember my birthday.
> help around the house/have the house
>   neat by the time I come home
>   from the office.
> be turned on to me most of the time.
> want to listen to my feelings.
> want to spend more time with me and less
>   time working or with the kids.
> work harder to make more money.
> spend less money.
> be interested in the things that interest me.
> never do anything that hurts or threatens me.

Unmet Expectations

When others don't live up to our expectations, we usually feel hurt or angry; when we don't behave according to our own standards, we feel guilty. The guilty conscience of the latter person is identical to the angry accusations of the former — one is venting disapproval outward, the other inward.

Here are some examples of conflicts that arise over differences in values and unmet expectations:

> *Value:* A house should be neat.
> *Expectation:* If you love me, you will keep the house neat.
> *Conflict:* You do not keep the house neat enough by my standards.

> *Value:* A loving spouse never does anything to hurt his or her mate.

Expectation: If you love me, you will never do anything that upsets me.
Conflict: You do things that hurt or upset me.

Value: Lying is wrong.
Expectation: If you respect me, you will never lie to me.
Conflict: You have not been honest with me.

Value: A (man/woman), (husband/wife/child) *should* . . . (Fill in the appropriate word or phrase.)
Expectation: If you love me, you will behave the way I think you should.
Conflict: You do not live up to my standards of behavior.

Value conflicts happen between any people who live together. Differences in values can easily become battles to win, to prove one's point, to control the other. When trouble occurs, your choice is, as always, to protect or to learn from the conflict. Conflicts actually provide important insights when the values and beliefs underneath them are explored rather than treated as each partner's own set of the Ten Commandments.

Many people behave as if programmed by their rigid values, quoting maxims like "A husband should spend his evenings at home with his family," or "A spouse should never say 'No' when the other wants to make love," or "If you love each other, you will never do anything that hurts or threatens the other." If you are the injured wife, you'll feel hurt or angry; if you are the errant husband, you'll feel guilty. The basic assumption is that at least one partner is wrong.

But, you may ask, isn't it better to be neat, and isn't something wrong with people who aren't? Isn't extramarital sex wrong? Isn't it right to be honest and wrong to lie? That discussion is ultimately fruitless. All of us have beliefs about the right way to live. Often these values are sound; living up to them would definitely be beneficial. *But when you are open to learning, the point is not to decide whose values and beliefs are right or wrong, but rather to understand the important reasons each of you has for believing as you do and why your actions sometimes contradict your beliefs.*

Still, you may wonder, are there *no* absolute values? We personally do believe there are absolute rights and wrongs, but when your primary intent is to learn about yourselves, that question just isn't relevant. Questions that do matter are ones like these: "Why do I get so upset when my partner doesn't agree with my values?" or "What happens when I attempt to impose my values and beliefs on my partner?" or "Is this value ultimate, God-given? How did I come to believe it?"

Does this mean that either of you has to give up your own values and beliefs because the other disagrees? Do I have to give up me to be loved by you? No. Respecting each other's values does not mean giving up your own. Your own may change as your self-understanding deepens but never because you were forced to give them up. *To give up your values and beliefs under pressure is to lose a sense of yourself; to change through awareness is to gain a deeper self-respect.*

We take a most important step when we realize fully that our disappointments are caused by *our* expectations. Everyone has expectations, of course, but as Dorothy Briggs points out in *Celebrate Your Self,* "There is nothing wrong with expectations in and of themselves, but there's turmoil in them if you expect that you can always control their being met. You cannot." Personal responsibility means learning that our partner is not wrong for failing to meet our expectations, since these come from within ourselves.

When not engaged in a power struggle, we can get great pleasure from doing what our partner wants us to do. We will give freely, however, only when we feel we can say, "No, I really don't want to do that for you," and not be punished. *We do not enjoy saying "Yes" unless we feel the freedom to say "No."* Only then can we give out of caring, rather than out of fear, duty, or guilt.

Questioning Our Values and Beliefs

It is one thing, of course, to see the need to modify the rigidity of our value systems, quite another to do it. There is no doubt about the difficulty of this task. But questioning our values rather than trying to convince another to believe our way lets us shed values and beliefs we have outgrown. For example, imagine yourself as a man with the following conflict: You believe that a woman's responsibility is for home and children and a man's for financial support, but your wife wants to work and wants you to share domestic responsibilities. You would explore your assumptions about men's and women's roles that have kept you from unrecognized dimensions of yourself. What would happen if you were freed of the burden of responsibility for your family's financial security? Would you work less, change jobs, go back to school? What would more free time do? What would more involvement with the children mean? The nurturing and affectionate parts of you would be called on which may be parts of you that were always stifled before. As you became more involved with your children, you might question your ideas about child-raising and explore your own childhood. As a result of explorations some of your values and beliefs would change; others would not. You would begin to establish a unique identity by *choosing* values rather than just absorbing them from your culture.

All of us think we're independent adults, but actually we're closer to that cartoon of the honeymoon couple unpacking their bags, inside each of which is a crouching parent. None of us grows up without years and years of absorbing what our parents and culture thought were the right ways to be a woman or a man. The following is a potpourri of some of the messages you may have received.

For little girls, the most important message may have been: Make yourself less in order to make a man more. Don't be too intelligent or too accomplished or too aggressive because men won't like you. Don't beat a man in ping-pong, tennis, or mathematics or his ego will be hurt. Don't be right about something when he's wrong. Don't want too much. Cater to his every desire and you will keep him. Be passive, compliant, beautiful or cute, or dependent. Don't worry about a career because you'll get married and your husband will take care of you. You can express sad feelings with tears and happy feelings with childlike enthusiasm, but control your sexual feelings. Don't be sexually aggressive; he wants to make the conquest. If you come on strong he may feel insecure about his ability to perform. Fake orgasm if you have to, but above all, don't bruise his ego. Do whatever you have to do to get your man and keep him, even if it means losing yourself.

Boys are told: You should be able to take charge in any situation and know what to do. Be independent and in control (especially of your woman) — serene, unruffled, and unemotional. Be cool; don't feel (let alone show) hurt, fear, or disappointment. Crying must be reserved for major crises such as a death or losing an important sporting event. Soft feelings are weak; you must be strong. Sex? Well, of course you need sex, but don't let that mushy love stuff get in the way. The chase and the conquest are all-important; that emotional stuff will keep you from accomplishing the important things in life, like being successful and making money. Enthusiasm is kid stuff; it doesn't fit the image of "cool." Playing and having fun are wasteful and immature; competition and winning are all that's worthwhile. So never let go, unless you are stoned or drunk; then it's okay.

As you can see, the mere volume of "shoulds" about ourselves and each other is enough to guarantee a lifetime of problems even under the best of circumstances. And as our society undergoes a major transition in values, value decisions are becoming more difficult. Some of the values listed above may still seem "right" to us, while others seem quaint remnants of the period before Women's Liberation. Social and moral values are changing so rapidly today, that the "right" masculine values drummed into a boy by his father might be scorned as "male chauvinism" by the time he's old enough to date.

The Belief That Devastates Relationships

One belief and one corresponding expectation is responsible for unnumerable difficulties in adult relationships: You are responsible for another's happiness or unhappiness. Therefore, when you love someone, you should never do anything that causes pain or upsets him or her. Barry Kaufman, in *To Love Is to Be Happy With*, says:

> Highlighted in the series of beliefs little people are taught is the one "you make me unhappy." The concept is that they are directly responsible for another person's feeling bad . . . that others aren't responding to their own beliefs, but the child is by some means mystically manipulating the strings and making them unhappy . . . as if he could, as if he had the power!

When we did something that irritated or upset our parents, we got the message that we were wrong and responsible for their reactions. When upset, parents rarely try to understand why their children are behaving as they are or try to see their own reaction as a product of their fears, values, or expectations. Instead parents get angry, thus blaming the children for causing their upset. Naturally parents want children to grow up believing they are wrong when they upset their parents. Instilling guilt and fear in children effectively maintains control over them. The more a child feels responsible for his or her parents' unhappiness, the less likely it is that the child will misbehave.

If we believed that we were responsible for our parents' feelings, we eventually adopted the corollary belief: Other people are responsible for our happiness or unhappiness. When in pain, we can blame others. Also, once we believe that we are responsible for another's feelings, we are imprisoned by guilt and blame, unaware that we can have the freedom born of personal responsibility for our own choices. Exploration helps each partner make that freedom a reality.

·11·

Freedom and Responsibility

> *I am free and responsible for all that I do,
> for all my acts, for all my commitments.
> Freedom and responsibility are one. And
> only then is it I who do it. A free man is
> responsible, and my freedom lies in the
> assumption of that responsibility.*
> WILLIAM OFMAN
> *Affirmation and Reality*

To have both freedom and intimacy we must understand what it is to be personally responsible to oneself *and* to others. If we don't, freedom is merely license. This chapter challenges some cherished beliefs about personal responsibility in human relationships. Yet we urge you to read on with an open mind. We have tried to anticipate and answer your objections, for we know that until your perfectly reasonable objections have been met, you will be unlikely to agree with our conclusions.

Responsibility is usually defined as adherence to a prescribed set of familial, religious, or cultural values. Responsibility is a moral issue: responsible people are those who behave "properly," and irresponsible people those who behave "improperly." In this chapter we focus on responsibility as a *personal* concern, a tool for individual awareness and growth.

Personal Responsibility

Each human being has freedom of choice over his or her own actions; all of us are accountable for our choices and their consequences. No other person can be responsible for the feelings that result from our choices, whether they be happy or sad.

When a person makes an honest attempt to see reality as clearly as possible, he or she also wants to understand how protections create problems. According to traditional wisdom, the behavior we call protective — anger, manipulation, withdrawal, bullying, laziness, and so forth — is bad and irresponsible. We claim that *the only irresponsible behavior would be the choice to protect and then blame others for the misery our protections have created.*

Let's take the case of a hypothetical self-centered person. Traditional morality condemns egocentricity because "it is wrong to be self-centered." Believing this, the self-centered person is unwilling to face the unappealing truth about himself or herself, which cuts off self-knowledge and the possibility of change. We believe that when a person has chosen (usually subconsciously) to be self-centered, he or she has respectable reasons for making this choice. Personal responsibility, then, means to admit the trait, see the purpose of the behavior, accept those reasons and look clear-sightedly at any negative results. Being personally irresponsible would be simply to remain oblivious of the self-centeredness, all the while blaming others whenever unhappiness arises.

Most people find it hard to take responsibility for themselves because the word "responsibility" always meant "blame" or "fault." When one's parent said accusingly, "Who's responsible for this?" what he or she really meant was "Whose fault is this?"

We Are Not Responsible for Each Other's Feelings

The guilt that drives people through a lifetime of unresolved misery arises from the parental injunction: "Thou shalt never cause anyone else any unhappiness." To let go of this notion is not easy, since it has been so deeply embedded. *But we can only be responsible for what we do, not for how others feel in reaction to what we do.* The converse is also true: *we are responsible for our own feelings and reactions about what others do.* Our happiness or unhappiness results from our freely chosen actions and the same is true for others.

When we believe our partner is responsible for our happiness, we feel angry when we do not get what we want. When we first saw Laura she had been married to Mitch for twenty years and had two teen-age children. From the earliest days of their marriage, Laura had always been furious when Mitch came home late from work. When he spent the evening in front of the TV, she accused him of not caring. At first Mitch was merely protecting himself against being intimate, but eventually his working even longer hours and watching more TV were an escape from Laura's harangues. Had Laura wanted to understand Mitch's behavior instead of criticize, they could have explored the issue. But she became more and more demanding as the years went on. She constantly nagged at her children for not eating right, not dressing right, or not doing well enough in school, and she was miserable because neither her husband nor her children behaved the way she wanted them to.

Laura is now alone. Her husband has left her and her children want little to do with her. For the first time in her life she is faced with the truth — that she alone is responsible for making herself happy, and that her attempts to dictate her family's lives only estranged them from her.

Control strategies like Laura's frequently backfire. When we attempt to *make* another conform to our definition of happiness, the other person may go to any extreme to protect from outside control.

In *Sex After the Sexual Revolution,* Helen Colton defines personal responsibility as she describes mature love.

> The mature love says: "I will do all I can to help you to grow to your optimum potentiality and capacity, even if that means you must sometimes be away from me and do things without me. Because I love you as a human being I want you to become all that you are capable of." The childlike, ego-centered love says: "You have to be here to do for me, for me to lean on so I can feed on you. If you are not here to hold me up I will collapse. You and I need togetherness so I can keep you responsible for what happens to me."

It's hard to believe that we aren't wrong for actions that upset another; we've been told so many times that doing what we want is selfish. But when we do something for ourselves that unintentionally offends another's sensibilities and/or frightens him or her, have we done wrong? If you believe that you should never do something for yourself if it hurts someone you care for — that is, you should give yourself up if your mate is hurt by something you want to do — then whenever you meet your own needs, you'll feel guilty. You can't win. If you don't do what you want, you lose yourself, and if you *do* what you want, you feel guilty. You're caught in a classic Catch-22.

Let's look at the case of Stanley and Lynn, a couple who own a business together. They both wanted the business to be a success, but Stanley wanted to spend more time at it than Lynn did. They worked hard all week; on the weekend Lynn wanted time alone with Stanley, but Stanley wanted to go into the office on Saturday. Lynn always felt hurt. If Stanley stayed home, he felt resentful, but when he went to the office he felt guilty. *As long as he felt responsible for her, he couldn't win.* Stanley had good reasons for wanting to work rather than be with Lynn. He didn't feel sure of himself with her and was afraid of losing himself in any shared activity, while at work he felt strong and important. Until he began to explore and understand those reasons he was stuck.

Lynn's complaint was, "If only he would spend more time with me, I could be happy." This attitude is very common — the complainer feels stymied because the partner will not "shape up," but that attitude itself denies personal responsibility.

Before therapy, Jane was constantly hurt because Dan rarely wanted to be with her. Although she thought that her only possible choices were to feel hurt and get angry, she did have another: wanting to learn about and understand Dan's feelings and behavior, as well as her own reactions. Who was responsible for her choice and her unhappiness? While Dan did do things that touched off her fears of rejection, the choice to blame was hers alone. You might say, "But she wasn't aware of learning instead of protecting, so how could she do anything else?" That's an important point. Although it is unfortunate that she never knew another choice, Dan is still not responsible for her reactions.

Since our feelings and responses always arise from our own values, beliefs, fears, and expectations, it is impossible to be responsible for another's reaction. Jennifer and Vic faced a touchy situation when they came to us for therapy. The conflict occurred because Jennifer wanted to have lunch with a man she had recently met in class. Believing Jennifer was responsible for upsetting him, Vic became angry, hoping (subconsciously) to activate her guilt and fear. The more he tried, the angrier she became and the more unloved he felt.

Exploring, Vic discovered that he greatly feared that another man — more attractive, wealthy, intelligent, and/or sexual than he — could sweep Jennifer off her feet and out of his life. He had had these insecure feelings long before he met Jennifer. His personal value system included the belief that it was wrong for a married woman to go out to lunch with another man. But this was his value, not Jennifer's. He also expected that if Jennifer really loved him, she would not do anything that upset him.

Who was responsible for Vic feeling unloved and hurt? Not Jennifer. If Vic hadn't had those fears, values, and expectations, Jennifer's actions wouldn't have upset him. Jennifer wasn't responsible for his insecurities; she merely activated them. In reality, Jennifer was giving Vic an opportunity to learn about himself and overcome those long-standing doubts. He had the choice to protect himself or to learn, but the choice was his alone. By stifling her own desires she would have denied him that opportunity, thus perpetuating his insecurities. (She would also have been unable to learn about the values and beliefs that had made her feel guilty and afraid of expressing her desires.)

Even the most hurtful situations can lead to extremely productive explorations when two people are willing to know themselves and each other better, rather than getting the other to stop doing whatever it is that's causing pain.

Caring without Taking Responsibility

When we meet our own needs, and in so doing, hurt another unintentionally we can care about the other, even feel sorry that we hurt him or her, *without* feeling responsible and guilty. We will feel guilty only when we feel *wrong* for doing whatever we did for ourselves. When we feel wrong, guilty, and responsible for another's feelings, we cannot care deeply about his or her pain. Instead, we'll feel defensive, maybe even deny that we did whatever we are accused of, or try to talk the other out of feeling hurt, rather than wanting to understand why he or she is hurt.

When we want to do something but believe we are wrong if our actions put another in pain, we are trapped. We either give ourselves up to avoid being wrong and wind up resenting our partner, or we harden ourselves into seemingly uncaring people in order to be able to do what we want. In that case, our partner feels, appropriately, uncared for and his or her pain is made even greater. For Vic, Jennifer's indifference hurt him more than her desire to go to lunch with someone else.

If we believe that our partner stays with us only because he or she could not get anyone better and will seek someone else when he or she feels more adequate, we will protect ourselves by stifling our partner. If both partners feel the same way, each would participate in keeping the other down rather than helping each other feel better about themselves.

We all need affirmation from others, most particularly from those we love. When we do not feel self-respect as children, we need to learn it as adults. Partners have the power to nourish or to deplete each other. Approval nourishes and disapproval depletes. Which we do is our own choice, and we are each responsible for that choice. However, while we can greatly *contribute* to our partner's self-esteem or self-doubts we are not the *cause* of either.

Sometimes a partner who subscribes to old notions of responsibility may be entirely unwilling to accept responsibility for creating his or her own feelings —

because he or she prefers being a victim. Even under these unfavorable conditions, you can still feel sorry for the other *without* feeling guilty, wrong, and responsible for his or her misery. If you refuse to be blamed or manipulated, your partner may eventually see that happiness is his or her own responsibility — and if not, will remain miserable. If you constantly bail a person out of the misery created by his or her own actions, that person will never learn to be responsible.

Problems Are Equally Created

When problems occur, one or both individuals usually take great comfort in believing that the other is *more* to blame:

> "My partner's anger, criticism, and withdrawal keep us from being closer."

> "I want intimacy and closeness; my partner is the one who's closed."

> "Sure, I do some things that create difficulties between us, but the things my partner does are worse."

When we fail to recognize our own protective behavior, we are constantly frustrated by our partner's failure at intimacy. Often one partner accuses the other of being the closed party, failing to realize that the accusation itself is a form of protection. Meredith always claimed to be the open one in their relationship; after all, she would say, "At least I cry or get angry when things upset me, but Tony just withdraws." They had both been taught that it is better to express your feelings than keep them inside, so they both agreed Meredith was open and Tony was closed. Actually both are equally closed and protected;

neither is open to learning; and they are both stuck, one blaming and the other feeling wrong.

Conflicts arise for any number of reasons when two partners attempt to meet their own needs, but conflicts *persist* only when two people choose to remain mutually protected. Protections are simply a way to shift responsibility from oneself onto another, remaining blind to the fact that we ourselves dictate the way our lives turn out. Since it always takes two people responding protectively for the protective circle to continue, any problem in a relationship is always *equally created.*

One of the ways of avoiding responsibility is to remain unaware or ignore the fact that all one's free choices have consequences. Jennifer was free to have lunch with another man, although there were consequences from both that desire and the way she presented her desire to Vic. How each of us feels in reaction to the other is *our* own problem. We can each protect against our hurt or fears, or we can want to learn about them — those are our choices. Denying that we have chosen to protect and that we are responsible for the resulting consequences is neither right nor wrong, but it is a dead end.

We Are Not Responsible for Each Other's Intent

When our partner's intent is to learn about himself or herself, we can help. But we cannot be responsible for our partner's intent. If our partner chooses to protect and refuses to explore, any attempt at change will likely fail. It is hard to face the reality that we are helpless to force another to look inward when he or she doesn't want to, but a person has control only over his or her own intent, not over his or her partner's. Before Barry joined Marilyn in therapy, Marilyn generally wanted to understand Barry's anger, but that didn't help much. He simply continued to yell at her. When she asked him why he didn't want to understand her feelings or his own, he wasn't interested in that issue, only in accusing and sulking. Until Barry wanted to understand Marilyn and himself, Marilyn could do nothing *about Barry.* She continued to explore her *own* feelings and work on raising her self-esteem so that she didn't have to be protective with her sexuality. (If Marilyn merely blamed her lack of sexual feelings on Barry's anger, she wouldn't be taking responsibility for herself.) Ultimately, if Barry had never shown any desire to explore, Marilyn would probably have left him.

When your partner will not participate in knowing himself or herself or in knowing you, taking personal responsibility would mean seeking self-knowledge elsewhere. Through therapy and other experiences you can stop taking your partner's behavior personally; then you can be interested in understanding your partner and helping him or her take down the protections little by little. First, of course, your partner must be available to being known. For a relationship to evolve, each partner must *take responsibility for reaching a point where he or she feels good enough to help the other to good feelings.*

When you take responsibility for your own good feelings, your partner may feel threatened. For example, suppose your partner is sexually withdrawn, and unavailable. Taking responsibility for this would mean that he or she would explore why. But if your partner refuses to seek ultimate resolution, either you are stuck being a victim or you can seek to get your own sexual needs met. You may begin by understanding your part in the relationship, exploring your contribution to the problem. Meeting your own needs responsibly may include masturbation or outside sexual experiences. The latter may be especially threatening to your partner. Doing what you need to do openly and honestly while staying soft and open to exploring your own and your partner's feelings, and dealing with the consequences, can lead to many new awarenesses for both. Doing it behind your partner's back bypasses learning, since it does not give your partner a chance to deal with the truth. If you are too afraid to be honest, then to be personally responsible is to do whatever you have to do to gradually *become* strong enough to be honest. Honesty means being honest about your *own* feelings and behavior and wanting to learn about your partner's — without blame or judgment.

If you have an affair because you feel bad about yourself and need affirmation from another and/or because not being sexually involved is very painful, then you are taking care of yourself and assuming responsibility for your own good feelings. But if you have an affair merely out of spite, to manipulate your partner, or as an attempt to *avoid* dealing with your part of the difficulties, your behavior is not responsible, since learning and growth were not its primary motive.

Personal Responsibility and Freedom — An Open Marriage?

People often ask us how the Evolving Relationship differs from similar notions of Liberated Marriage or Open Marriage. There is no doubt that when the question "Do I have to give up me to be loved by you?" is answered "No," each person has freedom of action, thoughts, and feelings. But that does not automatically mean an open marriage in the way most people understand the term — unlimited license (especially sexual) without concern for or involvement with one's partner. *That kind of open marriage means immediate gratification but not necessarily personal growth, and usually brings increased emotional distance between the partners.*

When two people go outside their relationship to meet an important need *before* thoroughly exploring how both contribute to the difficulty, they miss learning about themselves and their relationship; the chances are the couple's intimacy will suffer and the problems remain unsolved.

People learn and grow the most from outside sexual experiences when they share their experiences with their partner and are dedicated to working through the reasons, reactions, and consequences of their behavior. When openness and freedom lead to learning, the relationship will be enhanced rather than diminished by the experiences, sharings, and explorations.

Needless to say, sexual freedom profoundly affects relationships. One of the most challenging conflicts in a relationship is sexual fidelity since fears and values run very deep in this area. The fear of loss is never greater — of one's pride as well as one's partner. But partners who persevere through this discover what's right for each and fashion a unique relationship that meets each of their needs. Exploring and resolving issues of sexual exclusivity helps each person feel more secure and thus less intent on controlling each other and oneself.

Ann and Glenn are two people working through this issue. Glenn entered therapy furious with Ann. He had just found out she was having an affair and only wanted to prove her wrong for doing it. Although Ann did feel guilty, she was enjoying the relationship with her lover and was not about to give it up. After two sessions of Glenn's accusing Ann and refusing to deal with himself, we decided to work with them separately. Glenn needed to get through his anger to the pain and fear underneath. Only by softening could he come to understand Ann's very important reasons both for having her affair and for not telling him about it. Glenn's anger was so intense that living together became impossible; they decided to separate but continue in therapy.

Glenn explored his fears of losing her and of being inadequate, along with the humiliation of being the cuckolded husband. He also dealt with his fears of what would happen if Ann started to feel really good about herself, and the way he had withheld praise and loving words. He came to understand how, throughout their relationship, his typical pattern of getting angry and/or withdrawing into hostile silence had made Ann fearful of openly sharing her needs or her unhappiness with him. Eventually he began to soften and become ready to explore.

Meanwhile, Ann learned to respect her reasons for having an affair: her lover gave her the attentiveness and appreciation she needed. She had had the same feeling with Glenn earlier in their relationship, but it had slowly died. She also confronted her fears of being honest with Glenn and dealing with his reactions directly. She came to see that her holding back had kept the two of them from confronting the smoldering difficulties now consuming their relationship. She explored her position as a victim and her self-righteous rationalizations. As she understood her own role in the relationship better, she ceased being a victim and acknowledged that both of them had equally created their difficulties.

In opening to themselves, Ann and Glenn became more truly open to each other. Their meetings became more satisfying and more frequent as they both dropped their protections. Sex between them reached an intensity they had not experienced since first falling in love. Ann's relationship with her lover became less important as Glenn gave her more and more of what she wanted.

After six months of separation, Ann and Glenn decided to try living together again. They continued to work both in therapy and together to resolve their long-standing self-doubts. As they became more aware of their protections and the consequences, they were increasingly able to move into explorations when conflicts arose.

Over the past few years we have seen Glenn and Ann occasionally to help them when they were stuck. They have established a most unusual relationship that may be shocking to some, unbelievable to others. They have been able to share with each other their sexual thoughts, fantasies, fears, and experiences. Occasionally over the past few years, each has desired to have sex outside their relationship. A former boyfriend of Ann's stirred some unresolved memories. Glenn and she had many emotional discussions of her teen years and her early sexuality; Glenn shared many of his fears of her having sex with this man. A one-time sexual experience quickly resolved her feelings about her ex-boyfriend, but her sharing with Glenn left them feeling reassured and more in love.

Feeling very unsure of himself as he grew up, Glenn had never viewed himself as a highly sexual or "macho" man; other men seemed to have a much easier time with women than he did. He needed sex with other women to find out if he could enjoy casual, recreational sex. After a few encounters, he realized the emptiness of sex without love.

Ann's and Glenn's sexual relationship is almost always exclusive, but giving up sexual control over each other has freed them tremendously. For both, knowing they can pursue their sexual desires without retribution has greatly diminished their longing. Not fearing each other's sexual freedom has freed both of them to explore other areas of their lives. In exercising their freedom while maintaining their openness, their intimacy has grown, their sex together has become more intense, and they feel more in love. In other words, both the partners and their relationship are evolving.

Some of you may fear that giving up the traditional values of responsibility toward others will lead to social chaos with people doing what they want at others' expense. This can happen only when people are protected, thus denying their softer feelings. Personal responsibility means trying for greater harmony between our outer behavior and our inner nature — expressing the way we really feel inside, under our protections. *The goal is to become a more loving person.* As we open to our strong and gentle natures, we care very deeply and so do not need to be kept in line by guilt and fear. Only when we are protected do we cease caring about others. We always have the choice of treating others lovingly or indifferently. When we become aware of what makes us feel truly good and worthwhile, we see that behavior which takes advantage of another *never* makes us feel better about ourselves.

We often read about social responsibility as if it could be legislated or forced down the throat of the unwilling. But real responsibility cannot exist in a society until it grows and flourishes in the individual. Granted, being affected by another person and wanting to understand your own and the other's feelings takes courage. But, as Nathaniel Branden writes in *The Disowned Self:*

> I have observed with unfailing consistency that when a person learns to take responsibility for his own life, when he achieves autonomy and authentic self-esteem, when he ceases to practice self-denial and self-sacrifice, he experiences a degree of benevolence toward other human beings that was unknown to him in his alienated state.

Talking to couples has convinced us that the apparent increase in personal freedom that has led to casual and fleeting sexual experiences is in truth an abdication of personal responsibility — license, not freedom. We have seen in our practice and among our friends more and more couples who move from protected positions or from transient relationships to shared exploration, the choice of responsible actions, and the intent to know and learn. They succeed in shaping Evolving Relationships strong enough to weather the vicissitudes of real life and fulfilling enough to satisfy the most ardent nature.

·12·

The Evolving Relationship

. . . Allowing ourselves to be more loving
is a most beautiful journey.
BARRY NEIL KAUFMAN
To Love Is to Be Happy With

When each of us is willing to lower our protections, we connect with each other in that special kind of love we've called Intimate Love. Intimate Love is an adventure of shared warmth and spontaneity. Partners share playfulness, laughter, and love in large portions. We feel free to be ourselves. We are loved not for how we "should" be or what we accomplish, but for ourselves as we really are.

When people say, "I've accomplished everything I thought would bring me happiness, but something's missing," they've noted the absence of Intimate Love — the ultimate connection, the "real thing." Intimate love heightens living. Without it people feel a vague sense of emptiness. With it there is joy and satisfaction in almost everything. One's mate, children, job, the world around — all take on a new meaning. It's possible to live without this kind of love, but hardly possible to live as well.

Partners in an Evolving Relationship weave in and out of deep connection. They are not always extremely intimate, but once they have been, they are willing to work through the difficult times.

Commitment in the Evolving Relationship

The Evolving Relationship is a committed relationship, but this commitment differs from the security-oriented pledges sanctioned by custom. Most relationship models expect the kind of loving behavior that can only occur from a person who is already secure. This leads to very unrealistic expectations for a relationship. None of us can honestly guarantee we will be more loving — more accepting, more tolerant, or less judgmental — but we can commit to engaging in a process of discovering why we are not.

In the Evolving Relationship, we recognize that our fears and insecurities are what create the limits and problems in our relationship and the task of overcoming them is a major focus.

The primary commitment in the Evolving Relationship is to explore conflicts until personal learning and resolution occur. Any actions or desires are openly discussed.

Although this kind of openness may seem too frightening, it is actually the only way of achieving the security we long for in our relationships. Rather than a false security based on promises, obligation, or fear, an Evolving Relationship endures and becomes permanent from the matchless value gained from being with another person who wants to be with you, wants to understand you, and wants to facilitate your emotional growth.

Our Partner's Integral Role in an Evolving Relationship

Like any healing process, an Evolving Relationship will be at times a *therapeutic partnership*. "Therapy" comes originally from the Greek *therapon,* meaning comrades in a common struggle, and in that sense accurately describes an Evolving Relationship.

A professional therapist tries to give a client enough unconditional positive regard so the client can feel safe in exploring vulnerable areas of the psyche. A partner can also provide this kind of support and acceptance when he or she is willing to do so.

You do not need to be a trained therapist to help your partner in this way — you need only be open to learning. When you have a vested interest in changing the other while maintaining your own position, it is hard to be a "therapon." On the other hand, *when your intent is to understand rather than to change your partner,* you can really promote his or her growth, not limit it. Barriers to helping your partner in this way come more from fear than from lack of training.

Although your partner can never be responsible for your growth, engaging with him or her in a process of exploration and discovery can reach into the depths of your consciousness. Your partner can tap into your deepest fears and insecurities. When you love a person deeply, his or her approval is as crucial to your self-respect as was your parents' in childhood. Conflicts in adult relationships often call up issues and feelings from childhood; working through them as an adult with an understanding partner lets you put to rest the traumas of your childhood relationships when your dependence made you excessively vulnerable.

It seems to be part of Nature's design that you tend to choose a mate whose qualities make up for those you lack. Admittedly, this design makes life more difficult on a day-to-day basis as you come up against your partner's differences, but many rewards emerge. Your partner, that other who often represents a side of yourself that you find both attractive and threatening, can serve as a mirror in which to see more clearly the deeper parts of yourself. As you see yourself judging your partner, you can learn about your fears and self-doubts. Your differences then become catalysts for exploration and growth, rather than reasons for estrangement.

Many people welcome intellectual growth, the learning connected with work or school. Some have become fascinated with learning about themselves through discussion, therapy, self-help books. But, few people have opened to the learning about themselves that occurs through understanding how they respond to their partners in conflict. Yet the most potent force to either block or further our inward search lies in our primary relationships.

An Evolving Relationship Takes Time

Like any challenging situation, an Evolving Relationship needs time, effort, and understanding. Most of us realize that we have to work hard to master a new sport or be successful in a career; we don't, however, tackle our personal relationships with the same high energy. But the rewards of an intimate relationship can be just as good if not better than those of the most stimulating career. We are most fulfilled when we feel successful in *both* our relationships and our careers.

One of our cultural myths says that people fall in love, get married, and "live happily ever after." But as Carl Rogers points out in *Becoming Partners,* "The dream of a marriage 'made in heaven' is totally unrealistic . . . Every man-woman relationship must be worked at, built, rebuilt, and continually refreshed by mutual growth."

Our Own Evolving Relationship

Although we've been married nearly twenty years, our own Evolving Relationship really began about twelve years ago. At that point, we hit the "troubled waters" that come to every couple. The following pages describe the shift in our relationship from a situation where conflict threatened our marriage to a place where conflict became an experience from which we could learn and grow.

MARGIE:

Falling in love with Jordan was like everyone's fantasy of being in love. I felt joy and passion such as I had never known. However, the intensity began to wear off even before we married. At first, I didn't pay much attention. Instead, I got more involved in my schooling, my career, and my interests. When our children came along, I had a whole new life to adjust to.

Our marriage seemed fine. We liked each other. We sometimes fought but always managed to patch up our conflicts. Our sex life was okay. Not often passionate, but okay. What more could anyone want? But somewhere in the back of my mind I vaguely missed something. Some of my energy and aliveness was gone. In some subtle way, I was losing myself.

Then, after eight years of marriage, everything came unglued. I began doing things that threatened Jordan, especially going back to school and making new friends. We started to fight — and we fought and fought. No clear issues, I only knew he always seemed angry at me and I was angry at him for being angry at me. He seemed to think that everything I did and wanted and felt was wrong and I felt he was being too damned uptight.

JORDAN:

When I fell in love with Margie, our love stirred up things in me I never knew were there. I felt freer and freer as the lids holding down my spontaneity came off. Incredibly intense joy and sexual feelings filled me. Every day was an adventure. We shared our hopes and pains from the past and the resulting intimacy was enormously exciting.

Soon, however, the very things that attracted me to her began to threaten me. I began to feel that maybe she was too intense, too intelligent, too emotional. Would I be enough for her? Was she too free? Would she do things that might embarrass, humiliate, or lessen me in some way?

Many difficulties we met head-on and managed to work through to good feelings. But we didn't begin to touch the fears underlying our trouble — the fears that led us both to inhibit ourselves and try to control the other. As we became more protective, the special intensity in our relationship dimmed. We settled down to safe, routine, but distant ways of relating. It wasn't bad; it was better than most marriages I had seen. It wasn't what we had when we first fell in love, but I guessed maybe that happened to all long-term relationships.

I could probably have gone on like that for the rest of my life, with a "good marriage," three wonderful children, and an exciting career. Few things had ever sparked my curiosity. I wasn't interested in looking inward. I was content. Well, almost. I would have liked Margie to be sexier, but I was working on that.

Margie occasionally voiced her dissatisfaction. She wanted more. She was always taking classes and workshops, discussing her dreams, talking about her feelings, confronting problems. She even loved being in therapy since she found tackling problems and learning about herself exciting. Shaking my head in disbelief, I rated her strange behavior on a sliding scale somewhere between weird and stupid. I saw her as a malcontent troublemaker. Why couldn't she be happy? (Often, in my practice, within the first three minutes of an initial session I can spot the troublemaker. Frequently it is the woman wanting more life, deeper involvement, better communication. I know what it's like to be married to a woman like this when all you want is a little peace and quiet, some good food, some nice light conversation, and good sex.)

Each time Margie got out of line, I always managed to straighten her out, but I felt as if I were holding the line against an inevitable explosion. I was afraid of her intensity and her wanting. I was afraid of losing her if she broke out of the limits she and I had imposed.

The dam finally broke when she became unwilling to settle for what we had. Our marriage went into turmoil. Margie began to develop relationships with people who appreciated and valued her free spirit and her intensity. Although I wouldn't admit it, I was scared. My attempts to control her doubled. The more I tried, the harder she rebelled. I was trying to change her and she was fighting to stop me from trying to have control over her. Neither of us would give in so we became locked in a deadly power struggle. (I finally understood the double meaning of a stalemate.) In the middle of a terrible crisis, we battled on; as soon as one argument was patched up, another erupted. I often thought, "This is ridiculous. I can't stand these fights. I hate her. Maybe we should get a divorce. It would be much easier to start over with someone new." Years later we realized that we had been in the middle of the struggle that breaks up most marriages.

All I knew at that time was that Margie was making me very unhappy. If she would only change, everything would be all right. Meanwhile she was letting me know that I needed to get my act together. We each knew exactly what the other was doing wrong and neither understood how each of us was contributing to the trouble. (You can imagine how embarrassing this was for a couple of marriage counselors.) Our marriage, our family, our marriage counseling practice all hung in the balance. We were at a crossroads and I was scared stiff.

MARGIE:

I finally realized that I was trying to make Jordan feel wrong for trying to control me. I was trying to control him out of controlling me! Instead of trying to understand why he felt so insecure and what I was doing that was contributing to our difficulties, I just wanted him to change. One day I realized that I couldn't do a thing about what he chose to do. I could only control what I chose to do. I decided then and there that every time he got upset with me, I would try to understand why he felt that way. If he didn't want to look inward, I would simply walk away and not argue. If he wanted to understand me, I would be available for that, but I would no longer try to get him to see things my way. I saw that my anger, tears, and explanations were all ways to get Jordan to change. And none of them worked.

Those were all my awarenesses. Putting them into practice was another story. Even with all my determination, I could not put my program into action right away. First I needed to respect what I wanted for myself, believe it wasn't wrong even when Jordan made me feel wrong about it. Unable to do this for myself and with Jordan definitely not available to help me, I decided to go into therapy. I focused my therapy on my need for others' approval and my own self-doubts about being right for wanting what I wanted. After much hard work, I reached the point where I was far less vulnerable to being put down and giving myself up. I could say to myself, "I can't stop Jordan putting me down and labeling me as wrong, but I sure don't have to stand there and listen to it." I followed through with that resolve.

When I stopped pulling at Jordan to keep him from trying to control me and to force him to deal with himself, and when I was no longer available to being controlled, our fights subsided and we both softened. We discussed things instead of fighting over them, sometimes talking late into the night. We began to see how each of us had contributed to a system of relating that left us feeling unloved and insecure. We explored with each other the fears that led us to try to control each other or to give ourselves up to get each other's approval. Although we didn't know it at the time, we had begun our Evolving Relationship.

JORDAN:

Although I didn't give up easily, I finally realized that Margie needed to learn and grow and wouldn't settle for less. I knew our marriage would fail if I remained withdrawn and she kept on learning and growing. I realized there were only two possible ends to that process: the best was a widening distance between us; the worst was that she would eventually meet someone who shared her openness, and that terrified me. Neither of these outcomes was acceptable to me — Margie was too important.

When I gave up the hope of controlling her, I had only one choice left — to deal with myself and confront the reasons I was threatened by her being so open to new experiences and so free. I had to find out why new situations, knowing about myself, and deep emotional involvement were frightening.

There are easier things in life than being married to my wife. Only in the past eight or nine years have I begun to appreciate this burden as a gift. She has given me the opportunity to confront and overcome fears that had plagued me my whole life, limiting my potential, and creating a great deal of unhappiness. This continuing task has occupied much of my inward search, but as I inch along I feel better and better and we grow more deeply in love.

MARGIE:

After beginning to talk things through instead of fighting, I started to realize that Jordan's differences from me could be liberating rather than restricting. As I influenced him to be more open, he taught me a lot about myself, about how my urge to grow and learn sometimes communicated itself as criticism of him and others. Jordan helped me to confront my hardness and become a less critical person. As I softened toward Jordan, I found myself being softer and gentler with everyone. With every shared experience, our relationship has kept evolving and with every passing day I look forward eagerly to the joys ahead of us.

Today our Evolving Relationship has many more highs than lows. The years of hard work are now reaping the benefits that have come from our continuing open explorations which have helped us become less fearful and less protected. We rarely fight (our worst recent fights have been over writing this book — writing together is really hard), and our few fights are short-lived. We still have plenty of conflict, but it becomes easier and easier to go from conflict to exploration. More important, the more deeply we know ourselves, the more self-confident and secure we each have become. We feel we have significantly changed. We each feel happier and more peaceful most of the time as opposed to the insecurities and tension we had lived with for so long.

Personal Evolution: A Better Relationship with Ourselves

Personal evolution, an essential ingredient of an Evolving Relationship, requires awareness of self. *If we are not learning about ourselves, we are not evolving.* There are two basic reasons why it's important to learn about ourselves, one practical, the other philosophical. The first reason, much discussed in this book, is that almost all of the pain and misery in our lives and the difficulties we encounter in our relationships is the result of things we do when we are not open to learning.

The second reason embraces our personal spiritual philosophy. We find ideas such as *God is love . . . The kingdom of heaven lies within . . . Know thyself . . . To thine own self be true . . .* contain a universal truth: As we look inward and discover our natural selves, we become more loving human beings and therefore more one with God. Continuing explorations and deepening self-knowledge, then, give a special, compelling purpose to life — achieving harmony with our natural selves, with the God within us. The more we live with love, the more peaceful, flowing, and right we feel. When we drop our protections and connect with each other from our natural selves, we experience the spiritual dimension of Intimate Love.

Knowing our natural selves is an essential part of being able to answer our original question: "Do I have to give up me to be loved by you?" Many of us do not know "who we are" and so give ourselves up unwittingly. In other words, we may make concessions in a relationship, then feel uncomfortable but not know why.

The typical process of acculturation increasingly alienates us from our natural selves. Our natural expressions of joy, sadness, fear, and sexuality are often disapproved of. We try to become what we are "supposed" to be, hoping to be loved and not rejected. But denying our natural selves and trying to live up to an image (our protected selves) only makes us anxious and unhappy.

As we know our selves more deeply and gain a greater self-respect, we become more whole. The parts of our selves we've hidden out of fear can be integrated into our personality. Then we feel a sense of relief, no longer having to cover up and pretend. What we gave up because we needed approval can now be reclaimed as we connect deeply with our true, softer nature. We evolve from anger, defensiveness, withdrawal, and depression to joy and fun; from deadness to aliveness; from the need to protect against feared pain to the deep desire to learn about ourselves, even in the face of pain; from only needing love to being able to give it; from fear and self-doubt to a fundamental feeling of self-worth and self-trust.

The more we trust ourselves the more open we can be with others. People often hold back from being open with their partners with the implication, "I can't be open until you prove that I can trust you." By trust they mean being able to predict their partners' response, guaranteeing that their partners won't hurt them if they open up and are vulnerable. One of life's hardest realities is that this kind of guarantee is impossible. However, the more we trust that our feelings are okay, the more we are willing to be open, to risk another's free response to us and know that we can handle it.

The more we trust ourselves, the less devastated we are by disapproval. The stronger we feel inside, the less we need to protect against losing ourselves; *we can then be both strong and sensitive.* We can be intimate without needing control over others. The more we learn to trust ourselves, the less we need to take responsibility for others; when we know that we do not intend to hurt another, we can care about another's pain and help with it.

As we come to trust ourselves, we feel ourselves equal to other people. We are less prone to measure our adequacy solely by our achievements or by others' standards. We are freer to move in and out of another's world without fearing we will be carried away (lose ourselves) or get stuck in a situation we do not want to be in. We look less to others to tell us how to act and feel, for as Goethe said, "When you trust yourself, you will know how to live."

Seeking self-knowledge is a lifetime pursuit, one we can engage in as actively or as cautiously as we choose. It makes no difference where we start or how far we go. Evolving puts us on the path toward enlightenment, a goal we will probably never reach, but a place that we can be moving toward. The goal is not so much in getting there; what is important is to be on the way.

Family Evolution: Better Relationships with Our Children

The question "Do I have to give up me to be loved by you?" can be extended to any relationship. In parent-child relationships, a "Yes" answer brings on the same power struggles, rebellion, resistance, arguments, emotional distance, and feelings of being unloved that plague couples.

A "No" answer leads to an Evolving Family in which all members are helped to understand and respect each other. Conflicts are explored so that each person involved in the conflict can learn more about himself or herself.

Exploring family conflicts adds a rarely acknowledged but highly valuable reason for having children in our lives: to deepen our own self-knowledge and resulting ability to love. Understanding our reactions to our children helps us become aware of many important issues. When our child is "loud," "disrespectful," "impolite," wants to stay out late, will not do homework, or does anything that upsets us, we have an opportunity to examine our fears and the values and beliefs that have created them. When we are unwilling to see our own fears and values clearly, we react to our children in either authoritarian or permissive ways. When we do that, no one learns very much and everyone loves each other a little less.

Families can enjoy being together, even when children reach those usually difficult teen years. The rebellion typical of adolescence does not have to occur when understanding and acceptance rather than control is present. Neither is there the peace that occurs when either the child or the parent has given themselves up. There *are* conflicts, for children must test their limits and thus collide with their parents' values, but conflicts approached with an intent to learn can always be resolved in ways that do not frustrate the child's search for personal identity. Exploring areas of conflict can help a child feel respected and loved while increasing the intimacy of the family unit.

Families based on mutual respect can have a great deal of fun laughing and playing together. Mealtimes and bedtimes can be intimate, loving moments rather than tense struggles. Vacations can be exciting events that enhance family intimacy. Learning can be a satisfying, exciting, joyful process. When parents are willing to really *know* their children and learn from them, rather than try to mold and change them, child-raising becomes a joy, not a burden. It is as difficult to give up trying to control our children as it is our mates. But when we wish to understand our children and ourselves, the relationship takes on a unique and pleasing equality. Neither parent nor child has to give himself or herself up to be loved, for the needs and rights of each are respected. Each person is a part of a learning, growing, loving experience — an Evolving Relationship, family-size.

Human Evolution: A Better Social Order

The more we work with the model of the Evolving Relationship the more we can see that its application is really unlimited, and though it is not the domain of this book, we'd like to close this section with a brief comment on our vision. In nearly all relationships — teacher-student, employer-employee, nation-nation — conflict is met with a protective intent rather than with an intent to learn. In fact, all major systems — political, religious, educational, and familial — use fear and guilt to dominate, control, or teach. The resulting interactions produce rebellion, resistance, distrust. Many of the same negative symptoms that infect primary relationships permeate most other relationships as well. Learning, personal growth, mutual respect, and cooperation become thwarted.

Through the process of understanding and dissolving our protections our world can change. This process must start in each individual home, with each primary relationship. As Robert Pirsig says in *Zen and the Art of Motorcycle Maintenance:*

> I think that if we are going to reform the world, and make it a better place to live in, the way to do it is not with talk about relationships of a political nature . . . The place to

improve the world is first in one's heart and head and hands, and work outward from there.

As all of us relate to our mates in more loving ways this love will spread. We can be like pebbles hitting the surface of a lake; as we realize our essential nature and touch others with that love, they are changed. When people encounter genuine understanding, softness, and strength, they are unexpectedly touched. The experience may be fleeting, but it is profound.

Things will not change rapidly, but through our own relationships, we can take significant steps up the Evolutionary ladder. We can relate more lovingly with our mates. We can give our children a wonderful beginning. And slowly, as we express more of our true Human Nature, we can live with love and in peace.

Section Three

Exercises on the Path of Evolution

Section Three is designed to help you put the theory of exploration into practice. Although conflict is usually the catalyst that touches off exploration, you don't need to wait for a conflict to begin your own personal journey. You do need the desire to learn about yourself and the willingness, when you get stuck behind your fears and the resulting blindness, to encounter some rough times, to hang in there and, if need be, to seek help. To help you continue your explorations we have prepared a series of exercises related to the subject matter discussed in this book. These are exercises that we, as counselors, our clients, and our friends have found helpful. *Doing these exercises is the best way to integrate into your relationship what you have begun to learn.* The section is divided into two chapters: The Process — How We Explore; and The Content — What We Explore.

·13·

The Process — How We Explore

In this chapter, we focus on some basic, but critical guidelines and ideas to help manage the process of exploration. There are two fundamental exercises that will facilitate your communications: establishing a sharing-understanding format, and processing your explorations.

Sharing-Understanding

This exercise is designed to give you a basic communication technique. Partners sit facing each other. A few moments of relaxation exercises before you begin may be helpful, i.e., deep breathing, tensing and relaxing your muscles. One partner at a time will share his or her thoughts and feelings while the other carefully listens and attempts to understand. The understanding listener does not defend, answer, comfort, or interrupt, unless needing clarification.

Understanding does not necessarily mean agreement. The understanding listener will have an opportunity to share and be listened to and understood later in this same exercise. At that time, any disagreements with what his or her partner has said can be voiced.

The sharing partner pauses every few minutes and asks the understanding listener, "Do you understand what

I'm saying (or feeling)?'' The understanding listener then feeds back what he or she thinks the other is saying: "Are you saying that you feel . . . ?'' "It seems as if you're saying that you want . . . ?'' If the sharing partner feels understood, he or she continues. When the sharing partner does not feel understood, he or she says "No," and the understanding listener continues trying to understand. The sharing partner's responsibility is to clarify communication by saying the same thing with more detail, description, or feeling, or writing out his or her thoughts and sharing them with the partner. For the sharing partner, the value of this exercise is both to learn more about himself or herself and to experience feeling understood. When the sharing partner feels understood, the partners switch roles. When both partners feel understood, the exercise will have reached a satisfying conclusion.

If understanding does not occur, partners could do one of the following: wait a few days before attempting to get back into that discussion; process their communication (the following exercise); and/or explore the very good possibility that they're stuck in a power struggle (exercise on p. 279).

This exercise is not an exploration since explorations are give and take, free-wheeling discussions with *each* partner asking probing questions and attempting to understand his or her own feelings. It is, however, a good way to practice listening, can be a door-opener to explorations, and is a good technique to use when your explorations break down.

Processing

When communication breaks down during an exploration, it is usually necessary to stop talking about the issue and explore your process — *how* and *what* you are communicating to each other, i.e., the intent and resulting behavior, thoughts and feelings behind your communication.

One way to grasp the difficult idea of processing is to imagine that you and your partner have a videotape of an exploration you've just completed. During the exploration there were several shifts in intent, a lot of feelings were involved, and occassionally the interaction became heated. You and your partner are now going to watch the videotape and stop it at critical times to analyze *how* you were communicating, what kinds of *feelings* you were having at a particular moment, and what your *intent* was at different times during the interaction. You're not going to talk about the issue any longer (the *what* you were discussing), but only the *how* of your communication — the things that were happening inside each of you and between you, *the process rather than the content*. (This is sometimes referred to as metacommunication — communication about communication, rather than about issues.)

Unfortunately, since you will probably not have an instant replay available, you will have to rely on your own feelings, impressions, and observations of what is going on. Processing can occur while you're talking by changing your discussion focus from the content to the process; or immediately following an interaction as an attempt to look back and better understand where you have been together; or even days or weeks after an interaction when you feel safer and more secure. After some processing, you may find yourselves getting back into the content of the issue. Occasionally this is useful, but generally it is counterproductive.

Processing is like any other learned skill. It may feel cumbersome and difficult at times, especially initially, but the more you do it, the better you become at it.

Becoming Aware of Your Intent

Since exploration cannot occur when you are protected, staying aware of both your own and your partner's intent is a critical part of processing. Answering the following questions will help you recognize intent.

1. Do you want to learn or do you want to convince your partner or defend your position?

2. Are you afraid if you open to learning about your partner or let your partner in to knowing you that you'll end up being wrong? If so, are you willing to risk that or are you protecting against it?

In becoming aware of your intent, it is helpful to pay attention to the physical signals your body is always transmitting. You may have learned to ignore your body's communications, but emotions are always registered in the muscles. If you are unaware of the protective screen that thoughts create between body sensation and awareness, you may be living with the misconception that you feel nothing. Since learning to feel your feelings is crucial to knowing your intent, in this exercise, start by closing your eyes, turn your attention inward, and concentrate.

a. Listen to your body: start at the top of your head and go down to your toes, or vice versa. Do you feel tight anywhere? Is anything hurting? Is anything shaky? Are your hands shaking? Is your stomach in a knot or feeling queasy? Does your head hurt or feel heavy? What is the message from your gut? Is it saying, "I'm scared," "I'm nervous," "I'm hurt," "I'm excited," "I'm frustrated," "I'm peaceful," "I'm happy"? Are you open to these feelings or are you protecting against showing them?

b. Perhaps you feel a general sense of nervousness or tension. It's okay to feel tense — just pay attention to it. If you are nervous or tense, there's good reason for it. Talking with your mate about your tension may lead you to an understanding of it.

c. Recall the times you and your mate argue. What physical feelings do you have when you feel defensive? Stomach unsettled? Cringing? Muscles bunched up ready for an attack? Head pounding? Choked up? Stay with these feelings for a while before moving on to the next questions. By paying attention to these bodily sensations, you can become aware of their presence and can then explore their source.

d. What are you aware of when you are closed off and feel nothing? Many people are so used to feeling nothing they are not aware that they are depressed. Ask your mate to tell you when he or she feels shut out or disconnected from you.

To become more aware of your own hardness or openness, ask your mate to tell you when you seem closed and hard or soft and open. Once you decide to open to learning, it is much easier to put aside judgments, criticism, and blame.

Becoming Aware of Your Partner's Intent

Exploring the following questions will help you become more aware of your partner's intent.

1. Do I feel defensive or tense in reaction to my partner's tone of voice and body language, or do I feel open and curious?

2. Is my partner trying to get me to see things differently, to change my mind, to get me to feel wrong or guilty?

3. Is my partner attempting to defend his or her position?

4. Am I feeling that my partner is caring about me by wanting to understand my position and feelings?

5. Is my partner wanting to understand more about his or her own feelings and reactions?

Feedback

Since it is usually very difficult to see ourselves and our partner clearly when we're protected, we often need help. Tape recording (video or audio) your interactions can provide some useful insights into your communication process. Therapists can often provide valuable feedback to help you discover protective barriers. Michael and Paulette Liebman in their Couples' Workshop report a new potential for working with this process — couples helping each other. As people gain an understanding of intent, they can clearly see protective interactions in others even when blind to their own. By pointing out each other's protections, they are able to help each other identify problem areas.

The following example from a Couples' Workshop session was told to us by the Liebmans. Karen and Joe, whose relationship had been in turmoil for some time, had been brought to the workshop by their close friends, Robert and Mimi. In the third session the two couples were working in a group as Karen and Joe attempted to explore an issue. As usual their communication deteriorated into a blaming match, but this time Robert and Mimi were there to help Karen and Joe see how and when they were protected. As a result they dealt with their protections, dropped them, and wound up connecting with each other for the first time in months. It was a powerful moment which brought intimacy and hope. As Karen and Joe embraced, tears of joy streamed down Robert's and Mimi's faces as they felt a sense of partnership in the process that brought their friends together.

Another powerful tool is having couples switch partners for an exploration. Since it's much easier to explore with someone other than your partner, this is a way to get a deeper sense of what it's like to explore yourself and another. It will help you focus the picture of what's getting in the way of doing this with your spouse. It may also give your spouse a previously unseen picture of you.

A note of caution — danger lies in how easy it is to feel loved by someone who's interested in listening to you. Just don't kid yourself into thinking that if you were married to that person he or she would have any easier a time listening to you than your present partner.

The potential for friends helping each other learn this process is an exciting one. While we don't need others to tell us what we're doing wrong or to solve our problems, we do need help in seeing ourselves accurately. We are *all* struggling to understand relationships and to work through the difficulties of maintaining freedom and intimacy, and couples who are willing to get involved can provide valuable assistance to each other.

Processing Guide

This guide is a check list to help you know where to look when your communication has broken down. You may find it convenient to copy the guide to keep it more available. It is designed to be used over and over again. Some of the material, therefore, is repeated here from other sections for your convenience. The more you and your partner do processing together, the more natural it will become and the less you may choose to rely on this form. You will think of your own processing questions and statements which are more appropriate to your specific situation and combine them with the questions in the Processing Guide.

Whenever you become aware that your communication about some issue has begun to break down (become protective), you can shift to processing. Some good indicators that it's time to begin processing are:

- A loss of sustained eye contact.

- A breakdown of exploration.

- A change in your own or your partner's body posture from an open, accepting position to a closed, detached posture.

- A change in your internal body sensations (an increase in tension, tightness, drowsiness).

- Any time you feel stuck, defensive, scared, misunderstood, wrong, attacked, interrogated, unheard — any time you feel protected or you experience your partner as protected.

Note: We did not list silence as an indicator of a breakdown in communications because even though silence may make you feel uneasy, it is often an important part of meaningful communication. Be patient, hang in there, and learn from the silence by switching to process-ing if it becomes a problem.

Listed below are a series of questions which are designed to help you and your partner in processing your interactions. They are not in any particular sequence so select the one or ones that seem most important to deal with at the time.

There are two ways to use each question: you can ask your partner the question to find out what is going on with him or her; you can tell your own response to the question so your partner can know what is going on with you. Of course, a combination of both will probably produce the best results.

The processing questions are organized into four parts for clarity: exploring the exploration; exploring the sharing-understanding exercise; exploring your feelings; and exploring intent. As stated earlier, you can move from part to part, question to question in any order that seems appropriate to your needs at the time. When you hit upon a processing question that yields a lot of important information stay with it and continue to explore it.

Exploring the Exploration

1. How would you describe what has been happening? To me? To you? Between us? What have you experienced that has led to these thoughts?

2. At this point, what do you think is going to happen with this exploration? Why?

3. How would you summarize what you and your partner have dealt with so far?

4. How do you see yourself in this exploration? How do you see your partner in this exploration?

5. What are you doing that is interfering with the exploration? What is your partner doing that's interfering with the exploration?

Exploring the Sharing-Understanding Exercise

1. Do you feel understood, listened to, visible, to your partner? Do you feel you're being clear when you talk?

2. What happened during the exercise that caused either good or bad feelings for you? Your partner?

3. Are you really trying to listen and learn about your partner? Are you focused on understanding him or her or are you thinking/talking about your own issues?

4. What is your body posture communicating to your partner? What is your partner's posture saying to you?

5. What things was/is your partner doing non-verbally which are affecting your feelings?

Exploring Your Feelings

1. How do you feel now? How do you feel about your communication so far? How did you feel when the protective block arose, causing the present difficulty?

2. What body sensations are/were you aware of? Tense? Relaxed?

3. What do you sense your partner's feelings to be now? When the protective block occured?

4. Do you feel good about being in this interaction or would you rather stop and do something else?

5. How do you feel toward your partner now? Do you feel close or more distant than when you first began this interaction?

Exploring Intent

1. Do you want to learn or do you want either to convince your partner or defend your position?

2. Are you afraid if you open to learning about your partner or let your partner in to knowing you, that you'll end up being wrong? If so, are you willing to risk that or are you protecting against it?

3. Do you feel defensive or tense in reaction to your partner's tone of voice and body language, or do you feel open and curious?

4. Is your partner trying to get you to see things differently, to change your mind, to get you to feel wrong or guilty?

5. Is your partner attempting to defend his or her position?

6. Are you feeling that your partner is caring about you by wanting to understand your position and feelings.

7. Is your partner wanting to understand more about his or her own feelings and reactions.

Of course, the communication in processing can also break down just as the communication of an issue can. When this happens, you can begin processing the processing. If you still find yourselves stuck you need to explore the possibility that you're in a power struggle (exercise on p. 279). Anytime communication becomes too difficult and overwhelming, you may need to take a break and/or seek out a neutral third party to help you get unstuck.

·14·

The Content — What We Explore

Understanding ourselves on a deeper level will require journeys into the areas we discussed in Chapters 6 - 11. This section is designed to correlate with those chapters so you might find it helpful to reread the chapter or parts of it before or during the time you're working on an exercise. Since you can continue this journey for the rest of your life, you needn't feel pressured to rush through the exercises. Below are some general ideas for using them. By trial and error, you can discover how they can be used most effectively by your partner and you.

1. Pick one question at a time to explore. Ponder that question at various times throughout the day.

2. Set aside about twenty to thirty minutes to discuss the question with your partner. Answer questions in as much detail as possible.

3. Two useful techniques to help initiate exploration are:
1) use the Sharing-Understanding exercise; and 2) have each partner write out the answer to the same question and then trade papers and discuss what each has written. Note: Some people feel their feelings more deeply by writing them and then reading them to their partners. It's important to respect your differences and use whatever method is best for you.

4. Even if these questions lead to fights, you don't have to shy away from them. The fight can be a learning experience when

you work through it and get back into exploration. At that point, you can explore why you fought (i.e., why you both protected) by using the Processing Guide.

5. As you answer the questions, attempt to visualize your responses. Visualizing and feeling your answers on a gut level will make your experience more than just an intellectual exercise.

6. Before doing any exploration, it is helpful to relax and become aware of your body. You will get one set of answers when you engage your mind, and another set when you engage your body. This is because your feelings are in your body, not in your mind. You must be aware of your body to get a feeling response. Once you are relaxed, you can ask questions and get answers from both your mind and body. (While relaxation exercises can facilitate exploration and help you become more aware, they cannot change your intent.)

7. Relaxing will also help you become aware of the intuitive knowledge in the right side of your brain. The left side of the brain is the intellectual, rational, linear side — the part called the mind. The right side is the intuitive, creative, emotional, and spiritual aspect. It's important to engage both sides of the brain when exploring.

Exercises for Exploring Childhood

Part One

These exercises are meant to touch off memories from your childhood so that you can understand more of how your past has shaped your present. Use your answers to begin explorations with your partner to deepen your awareness. When answering these questions with your partner one of you might, at times, assume the role of an interviewer. You are not an interrogator or a disinterested collector of data, but involved, curious, and supportive. Your mission is to learn as much as you can by helping your partner recall as much as he or she can about the significant events, relationships, and feelings of his or her childhood.

1. Who in your immediate and extended family (parents, siblings, grandparents, aunts, uncles, cousins, good friends, neighbors, teachers) did you feel loved, appreciated, respected, valued you?

    a. What did they do that made you feel loved?

    b. What did they do that made you feel important?

2. Among those in your immediate and extended family whom did you dislike, fear and/or hate? How did they hurt or frighten you?

(Answer each of the following questions twice, considering your mother and father separately.)

3. What did your mother/father do that made you feel loved or unloved?

    a. Was your mother/father approving, nurturing, affectionate with you?

    b. Did your mother/father seem interested in how you felt about things?

    c. Did your mother/father stand up in support of you?

d. When you were excited about something, did your mother/father share your enthusiasm and interest or did she/he seem disinterested or indifferent?

e. Did your mother/father promise you things and not follow through?

f. Did you feel important to your mother/father or burdensome? Did you feel she/he liked having you around or that you were a nuisance?

g. Did you feel that your mother's/father's love or affection was withdrawn at some definite time, such as when a sibling was born or when you reached puberty? How did you react at the time?

h. How did your mother/father deal with your feelings:

— When you were upset or crying, did she/he try to understand your feelings or attempt to talk you out of them?

— Did she/he try to stop your pain by solving the problems, by commands, or in some other way?

— Did she/he tell you there was nothing to be upset about?

i. In what ways did your mother/father encourage or erode your trust in yourself and your judgment?

— What did your mother/father do to show respect for your wants, needs, perception, likes and dislikes?

— What did your mother/father do to try and talk you out of your feelings, deny your perceptions, belittle your likes and dislikes, your wants and desires?

j. How did your mother/father behave when you did something she/he did not like, something that was upsetting to one or both of them?

— Did she/he become cold, angry, withdrawn, indifferent?

— Was she/he interested in working out the problem with you?

k. Was your mother/father pleased with your achievements or did she/he always seem to expect more of you than you accomplished?

— In what particular areas did you receive the most disapproval and feel the most wrong and inadequate. social, intellectual, physical (looks, health, cleanliness, sex, sports), chores and responsibilities, consideration towards others?

— What were your mother's/father's attitudes toward your "shortcomings"?

4. How did your parents behave towards each other and how did this affect your feelings about yourself and your beliefs about relationships, masculinity/femininity?

   a. Were they approving, loving, happy, nurturing, affectionate with each other?

   b. Were they cold, angry, distant, indifferent with each other?

5. Was the general atmosphere around your house relaxed, tense, serious, solemn, light-hearted, boring, exciting?

6. Did you have any sense that something was being covered over or denied, such as money, sexual, emotional problems?

7. Over what issues did power struggles arise in your house? Did you fight over neatness, household chores, school work, clothes, bedtime or curfew, taking the family car, talking on the telephone, watching TV, dating, eating, drinking, drugs, music, length of hair, cleanliness?

   a. How did you resist or rebel?

   b. How do childhood power struggles affect your relationship with your mate, children, and your present relationship with your parents?

   c. Was your mother/father authoritarian or permissive?

      — Did your mother/father try to control what you wore, how much you ate, when you went to bed, when you did your homework, how you kept your room?

      — How have your parents' child-raising practices influenced your ideas about child-raising?

8. How did you react when you felt rejected, put down, humiliated, controlled?

a. Did you get angry or have a temper tantrum? Did you scream and yell?

b. Did you kick, bite, and/or destroy things?

c. Did you cry and feel sorry for yourself?

d. Were you a "good" boy or girl and give yourself up in order to go along with what others wanted from you?

e. Did you indicate you would comply and then resist (passive resistance)?

f. Did you talk about your feelings, express your pain, and explore the difficulty?

g. How are any of these behaviors a part of your adult life? Can you remember what it felt like to behave in any of those ways? Do you ever feel like that today?

9. How did your mother/father attempt to teach you responsibility?

a. Are you a responsible person today? What does that mean to you?

b. If so, how did you learn to take responsibility?

c. If not, why not?

d. How did you respond to your mother's/father's attempts to teach you responsibility?

e. Explore your beliefs about responsibility and how it should be taught to children.

10. How are you like your mother/father? How are you different from them? For example, if your parents were angry and critical, are you also that way? How do you feel about these characteristics?

11. Were you a spontaneous child, freely showing your intense enthusiasm or pain?

a. If not, why not? What were your fears of being spontaneous?

b. Recall the times you were spontaneous with joy and/or pain? What were the reactions of those around you?

12. Explore what you learned and may still believe about sex.

a. Where did you get your sex education — family, friends, school?

b. What did you learn about yourself sexually and about the opposite sex?

c. Do you think your parents were sexual with each other?

d. What were their individual attitudes regarding sex?

e. What did you learn about how sex relates to love?

f. Do you recall any sexual overtones or sexual experiences with members of your immediate family?

— If you did have sexual experiences with members of your family, were you a willing or unwilling participant?

— What effect has this had on your adult life?

13. If you had siblings, what was your relationship with each of them?

a. How has your relationship with each of your siblings affected you both positively and negatively?

b. What was your position in your family (oldest, middle, youngest) and how did this affect you?

14. If you were an only child, explore the questions that follow:

a. Were you lonely? How did you learn to protect yourself against loneliness?

b. Did you enjoy being an only child?

c. What effect do you believe being an only child has on your relationships today?

15. Did someone you loved die as you were growing up? (Parent, grandparent, sibling, aunt or uncle, very close friend.) Take plenty of time with this question.

a. Try to picture that person in your imagination. Can you feel what it was like to love that person?

b. How old were you when he or she died? Recall what it felt like to be that age and lose a loved one.

c. What were the circumstances surrounding the loss? What did you see happening around you at the time of the death? What did you hear people saying?

d. Recall how you felt. Did you cry or did you hold back expressing your pain and grief?

e. Were you able to say goodbye or was the loss sudden? If the loss was sudden, have you ever wished you could have said goodbye? Try writing or saying out loud the words you would have liked to say. Do you still miss the loved one? What is it that you miss the most?

f. Were you willing to love again after that death? Have you loved as deeply since? Could you have made an unconscious decision not to love that deeply again, or let anyone become that important to you again?

16. If possible, find out about your birth experience. What effect do you think that may have had on your life?

17. Which periods of your life — early childhood, middle childhood, early adolescence, high school — were the happiest? Unhappiest? Attempt to relive your feelings during the most intense periods.

18. How did you feel about school?

a. Were you generally accepted by teachers or did you often feel put down?

— Recall those times a teacher hurt or humiliated you. How did you feel inside and how did you react?

b. How do you think these experiences affected your feelings about yourself?

19. How did you get along with your peers?

a. Did you find it hard to make or keep friends?

b. Were you laughed at or made fun of by other children?

c. Recall those times you felt hurt, left out, or humiliated by other children. How have these experiences affected your feelings about yourself today?

Part Two

Being angry and blaming parents (or others) is just another way to protect yourself. Letting go of anger toward parents, an important step toward emotional well-being, often requires three separate processes: 1) expressing your anger; 2) understanding your parents; and 3) forgiveness. True forgiveness usually occurs through understanding. This requires seeing your parents from an adult's perspective — understanding that your parents' behavior was motivated by their fears and they were unaware of the negative effects their behavior might have on you.

Since most people can't just let go of anger, you might have to get through your anger towards your parents before you can understand them. Expressing anger directly to parents serves little positive purpose. It only hurts them and cannot change anything that has already been done. If you believe it's necessary to express your anger directly, check your intent. Are you still trying to change them? If so, you can learn some very important things about yourself. What do you hope to gain with your anger? Are you still hooked in to wanting their approval? What is your part in the resulting power struggle and what are the negative consequences of the power struggle?

Expressing anger, when your intent is to learn about yourself, need not be done directly. You can use a rolled up towel and pound a bed, chair, or floor. You can scream and pound until you are exhausted. Express what you were/are most unhappy about. Describe the most painful events you remember that illustrate your unhappiness. Getting deeply into your anger will release you from it. You will not go crazy or die, but you will function and feel better when you reach a deep release. If you feel tense, you haven't opened fully. That can feel worse than when you began. Keep pounding and yelling until you reach a deep and cleansing emotional release, until you either feel exhausted or you get to a different feeling — sadness.

Underneath your anger is a great deal of sadness, your non-blaming pain. When you get to that sadness, you have taken a big step toward ridding yourself of your protective anger. The more feelings you get out, the more profound and releasing will be your experience. It helps if your partner is present so that he or she can better understand your feelings and comfort you afterward.

If pounding and screaming your anger seems too difficult, try writing your anger in a letter. Write over a number of days, weeks, or even months, until you feel your anger is spent. Once your anger is spent and you are experiencing your sadness, you can open to learning and understanding, and finally to forgiving. This can be accomplished in a number of ways:

1. You can talk directly to your parents about their beliefs and fears as well as about their childhood and how it contributed to shaping their lives. Talking to other members of your immediate family may also help you to understand more.

2. If your parents are dead, or if they are emotionally unavailable to talk to you, then you can use the Gestalt technique of speaking to an empty chair.

> — Imagine one of your parents sitting in the chair. Tell that parent your feelings — your anger and sadness — and ask this parent any questions you have in your mind. Then take the empty chair, assuming the role of your parent, and answer the question to the best of your knowledge. Even making up the answer can be helpful. *Understanding and experiencing your parent's point of view is a critical part of this activity.*

3. If you feel silly talking out loud to an empty chair, then try pouring out all your sad feelings in a letter to your parents. Then, assuming the role of each of your parents, answer the letter.

4. Talking with an understanding partner about your feelings towards your parents can further help you release your anger and gain understanding.

Once you have reached a true understanding of why your parents behaved as they did — realizing that they did what they thought was best, did not consciously want to harm you, and were guided by their misconceptions and fears — forgiveness will follow automatically.

When we forgive our parents then we can understand how we all, in our attempts to do what we think is right, unknowingly hurt the ones we love, creating emotional distance instead of the closeness we desperately want and need. We can then forgive ourselves and others while feeling the only appropriate feeling for the messes we get ourselves in — sadness.

Exercises for Exploring Fears

Since our fears run our lives, confronting fear is the heart of the entire process. Remember the instructions that apply to all the exercises and proceed slowly. Select a question and let yourself ponder it throughout the day. Take whatever time you need to go deep inside so that you can experience the answers on a feeling level. There is little value in answering the questions superficially.

As you look over the list of fears below, write down those that apply to you. Do you fear being and/or feeling:

Afraid	Vulnerable	Incompetent	Rejected
Humiliated	Devastated	Crazy	Abandoned
Criticized	Disappointed	Successful	Lonely
Put down	Grieved	Inadequate	Dominated
Judged	Insecure	Unmasculine	Controlled
Losing face	Off balance	Unfeminine	Needy
Hurt	Violated	Unacceptable	Discounted
Weak	Out of control	Immature	Helpless
Disoriented	A failure	Neurotic	Left out
Despairing	Wrong	Foolish	Shut out

1. Take each word you wrote down one at a time and attempt to *feel* the feelings associated with that label as you explore it further:

    a. Why is it wrong or bad to be . . . (vulnerable, afraid, weak, etc.)?

    b. Where does that judgment of "wrong" come from? Recall the last time you felt judged. Now recall the time before that. And the time before that. Allow your memory to take you further and further into the past.

    c. What are your childhood memories of the label you chose to explore? What happened when you felt that way? Were you made to feel wrong? How?

2. Become more aware of what happens inside when you feel someone does not like you.

    a. Discover the place in your body — stomach, throat, chest, back, forehead — that tenses when you are disliked or disapproved of. Begin paying more attention to those feelings and realizing how they affect your life.

b. What do you feel when someone doesn't like you — scared, hurt, angry?

c. If you want everyone to like you, explore why you feel this way. Do you value yourself less if someone doesn't like you?

3. Explore in depth your fears of losing your partner.

a. Would you feel abandoned, rejected, useless? What negative things might happen to you?

b. What past experiences might have contributed to these fears?

c. What do you fear would happen to you if your partner either left you today or died?

4. Explore in depth your fears of losing yourself.

a. Under what circumstances can you imagine yourself complying with another out of fear, obligation, or guilt?

b. How do you imagine yourself behaving if someone very important to you wants something from you that you don't want to give?

c. What are you afraid will happen should you not comply with another's wishes? How did you come to fear this? Explore the reality today should the event you fear actually happen.

5. Explore in depth the following fears:

a. Fear of knowing your partner's deepest or real feelings.

b. Fear of knowing yourself, your own real fears and feelings.

c. Fear of having your partner know you.

d. Fear of intimacy.

6. Determine the places in your relationship where you feel unsure or inadequate. Complete each sentence with the word or phrase that most reflects your feelings. If you do not find the right word put in your own.

I feel unsure of myself because:

> a. I believe I am not as (intelligent) (verbal) (attractive) (interesting) (independent) (creative) (social) (open) (important) as my partner or as I should be.
>
> b. I am too . . . (old, young, sensitive, timid, etc.)
>
> c. My mate (earns more money than I do) (does not need me as much as I need him or her) (feels ashamed of me) (does not understand me).

What do you do when you feel any of the above feelings? What effect do these feelings and behavior have on your relationship?

7. This is an exercise that we call "And then what?" For each of the situations listed below, develop your own scenario of what might take place. For example, to the question, "What would happen if your partner stopped attempting to have control over you?" your immediate answer might be, "I would feel terrific, freer, more in love, sexier, more intimate." But as bad as your current situation may be and as wonderful as it seems in your fantasy, some very powerful fears are trapping you in it. To become aware of these fears continue to ask yourself, "And then what?" For example, "Feeling so free and in love would be wonderful . . . And then what? . . . Well, it might be a little scary . . . Why? . . . I might do something my partner didn't like . . . And then what?" If you have difficulty continuing the scenario, ask your partner to share any insight he or she may have into the fears you are hiding from.

What would happen if:

> a. your mate suddenly stopped trying to control you?
>
> b. you stopped trying to control your mate?
>
> c. you stopped being a victim?
>
> d. you let yourself feel freer, less inhibited; you more fully express your natural feelings — pain, joy, and sexuality?
>
> e. your partner felt freer in the same areas?
>
> f. you let yourself love your partner more deeply, and he or she became even more important to you?

g. you let yourself want what you want, feel what you feel, do what you want to do?

h. you dropped your protections and became open, soft, vulnerable to your disappointments, hurts, or anxieties?

i. you worked hard at something and failed?

j. you worked hard at something and became successful?

k. your partner worked hard at something and became successful?

l. you tried to understand your partner's feelings in a conflict?

m. you become more sexually turned on to your partner?

And then what?

When you get to the bottom of your fears and receive support and nurture from your partner, you have taken the first step toward a confrontation, not only with your fears but also with the problems they have been creating in your relationship. And then you may feel strong enough to take the next step which is testing out your fear.

Exercises for Exploring Protections

Part One

Below is a brief review of the ways we protect. Read them over and refer to them as you work through the discussion questions. When working through the questions take them slowly and carefully.

A. Compliance — giving yourself up by going along with what another wants out of fear, obligation, or guilt, hoping to avoid conflict and resulting disapproval.

B. Attempting to change and control your partner by instilling guilt and/or fear through disapproval. You may use:

> anger, irritation, annoyance
>
> threats of leaving, of violence, of suicide, of illness, of financial withdrawal, of exposure to others
>
> criticism and guilt inducing-body language — the disapproving look, raised eyebrows, "tsk, tsk," sighing, shrugging shoulders, shaking head
>
> silent treatment
>
> angry tears, "poor me" tears
>
> explanations, lectures, nagging
>
> accusations, blame
>
> sarcasm
>
> complaints, illness

C. Becoming indifferent so as not to be affected by the other person and withdrawing sexually, emotionally, and/or physically. Shutting the other person out by means of:

work	illness
TV, newspaper, books	food
drugs, alcohol	sleep
sports, hobbies	meditation

D. Resisting and rebelling by not making your own decisions

first, but waiting for your partner to decide and then resisting the decision.

Questions

1. How do you show your disapproval and attempt to change/control your partner? (Look over B above.)

2. Ask your partner to describe how he or she thinks you show your disapproval.

3. How and in what areas do you shut your partner out? (Look over C above.)

4. Ask your partner to describe how you shut him or her out.

5. How and in what areas of conflict do you resist or rebel against your partner?

6. Ask your partner how he or she thinks you resist or rebel.

7. Explore your response to being told how you protect.

   a. Did you feel wrong?

   b. Was your partner seeing you as wrong? What did he or she do that led to your feeling that way?

   c. Explore your own feelings of being wrong and/or feeling guilty.

8. Explore how you make your partner wrong for his or her protections.

   a. Do you blame your partner for blaming you, judge him or her for judging you?

   b. Do you shut your partner out when he or she criticizes or disapproves of you in any way?

   c. Do you criticize or disapprove of your partner in any way when he or she shuts you out?

9. Other than when your partner protects, explore when you make him or her feel wrong:

   a. when he or she disappoints you by not meeting your expectations?

   b. when his or her desires, beliefs, or feelings are different from yours?

     c. when he or she does something that hurts, frightens, irritates, or upsets you?

10. How and in what areas do you change yourself, give yourself up, to behave the right way?

11. Next time you feel angry or closed off, ask yourself what happened that hurt your feelings, frightened you, made you feel wrong or unimportant.

Part Two

The following questions are designed to help you explore the effects of set-ups (see page 172 for a definition of set-ups) in your life.

1. Becoming aware of how we set up others is not easy, but you can begin by paying careful attention to how others respond to you. Do others respond with warmth and openness or do you feel them shutting down slightly, pulling away, looking uncomfortable, or getting angry when you:

    a. greet them or say goodbye to them?

    b. ask them a question?

    c. compliment them?

    d. give them a gift?

Since most of us resist seeing how others respond to us, this exercise is tough. Ask your partner if he or she ever feels set up by you. Ask how he or she feels that others react to you. This can extend your awareness of the effect you have on others.

2. How do others set you up? Pay attention to how you feel when your mate or others who are important to you:

    a. ask you a question.

    b. greet you or say goodbye.

    c. praise you.

    d. give you a gift.

If the question is manipulative, if the greeting, praise or gift has an expectation attached to it, then you may feel pulled at, defensive, uncomfortable, scared, anxious or tense, shut down.

    a. By paying attention to these feelings, you can become aware that the good reason you have for feeling as you do is that you are being set up.

    b. If you feel warm and open in response to the above behaviors, then either you are not being set up, or you know that you are not available to being manipulated and therefore have no reason to pull back and protect.

Exercises for Exploring the Consequences of Protections

Part One

From the following list of negative consequences, check those that frequently occur in your relationship. Feel free to add your own:

No sex
Boring sex, no intensity
Infrequent sex
Boring routine relationship, little excitement or intensity
Feeling unloved
Feeling unloving
Lack of satisfying communication
Liking yourself better when you are not around
    your partner
Little fun with your partner
Feeling freer when your partner is not around
Feeling trapped
No discussions without arguing
One or both having an affair, or wanting to
Feeling your partner is not your friend, not on your side
Emotional distance between you
Feeling lifeless, nothing seems important or exciting
    any more
Partner lifeless, nothing seems important or exciting
    any more
Feeling resistant, rebellious, resentful a lot of the time
Partner often resistant, rebellious, resentful
Lying or not telling things to partner
Partner often lying or not telling things to you
Feeling insecure about your partner's love
Partner feeling insecure about your love
Feeling tense often
Partner often feeling tense
Often not knowing what you want or feel
Partner often not knowing what he or she wants or feels
Often feeling guilty around your partner
Partner often seeming to act out of obligation

Feeling manipulated
Often in a power struggle, each wanting only to win
Often feeling on guard around your partner
Not feeling valued for your accomplishments
Not sharing your partner's enthusiasms
Partner not sharing your enthusiasms
Frequent illness

1. Which protective circle(s) can you identify in your relationship and which one(s) predominate? (See pages 184-193 for definitions of the different protective circles.)

   a. Control-Compliance

   b. Indifference-Indifference

   c. Control-Control

   d. Control-Indifference

2. How does each of the negative consequences you checked above relate to your protective circles?

3. Write down the issues in your major conflicts and explore whether or not you are engaged in a power struggle around this issue.

4. If you find yourselves primarily in the Control-Control or Control-Indifference circles, talk over or write out a description of the resulting power struggles. What consequences are a direct result of this power struggle?

5. How does each of you feel about your protective circle, the consequences you both suffer, and your power struggles?

   a. Does one of you seem to want control more often and one of you seem more resistant than the other?

   b. Try to understand more about your part of the power struggle. (The exercise for dealing with power struggles is on page 279.)

6. Many adult relationships simulate parent-child exchanges, with one person as the controlling, judgmental parent and the other as a wrong, irresponsible, resistant, incompetent, or rebellious child. One partner may be parental in some situations and childlike in others.

a. In what circumstances do you see your partner as the child? How does this affect your feelings toward your partner? Your behavior?

b. In what areas do you see your partner as the parent? How does this affect your feelings toward your partner? Your behavior?

c. If you see yourself as sometimes in the role of the child, what are the very important reasons you have for assuming this position (fears about being controlled, more responsible, or competent)? How does your behavior affect the relationship?

d. When you sometimes act the part of the judgmental parent, can you identify the situations in which you take this position? What are the very important reasons you have for assuming this position (fears of relinquishing control)? How does this affect your relationship?

7. How do you feel when your partner protects? Jot down as many words describing your feelings as come quickly to mind (shut out, unimportant, unloved, blamed, hurt, in pain, angry).

a. Reflect on these feelings for a few moments, then share them with your partner.

b. If your partner reacts defensively, you can explore why. Have you tried to make him or her feel wrong or guilty for protecting?

Part Two

Breaking or Preventing Power Struggles

Each of us, at times, attempts to have control over others and, at other times, resists being controlled. Some of us, however, have become very controlling while others have become very resistant. This exercise is particularly important because you can work with both sides of the power struggle — controller and resistor.

To break a power struggle you must first realize you're in one. Anytime your partner or you resist each other's requests, especially when they seem reasonable on the surface, you are very likely in a power struggle. Each of you is capable of meeting the request if something isn't blocking the way. The block may be a resistance to being controlled and/or a personal fear that inhibits meeting the request. It is unlikely that a person will open to dealing with his or her personal fears until the power struggle is broken.

Breaking a power struggle requires a shift in intent from protection to wanting to learn. Learning will center around attempts to understand what you are each doing that is perpetuating the power struggle, why you and your partner are feeling and behaving as you are.

Understanding the Controlling Position

1. How do you try to get your way — do you attempt to make your partner feel guilty or afraid or do you become indifferent? How do you do that? (You can use the exercise to help you explore protections on page 272.)

2. When your partner doesn't do what you want, how do you feel? Angry, disappointed, sad, sadness tinged with anger?

3. What fears block your willingness to feel your feelings and attempt to learn more about why you feel as you do?

4. What if you stopped trying to *make* your partner meet your needs or desires? What fears would you have then?

a. Do you believe that, in general, another person will *want* to meet your needs if at all possible?

b. If not, explore why you don't have that faith. Where does your lack of faith come from?

5. If you believe that you have tried in the past to get your needs met without any manipulations, re-examine that belief with your partner. With your partner's help you can become more aware of the subtle ways you may have tried to manipulate others.

6. What are your options for taking care of yourself when your partner doesn't want to do what you want him or her to do? Are you stuck or are you free to get your needs met by others? (This is not to suggest that you should or shouldn't get your needs met by others but only to deal with whether you are willing to.) If you are not, there are certain values, beliefs, and fears that are keeping you stuck.

a. What values are getting in the way of you meeting your own needs? These are your beliefs about your role as a man/woman, husband/wife. A married woman/man should never . . .

b. What fears are getting in your way? For example: a fear that if you don't make something happen it won't happen; a fear of the problems that might be created should you get your needs met elsewhere (the fear of your own or your partner's freedom); a fear of failing should you try to get your own needs met?

7. What happens when you are successful at getting your partner to give in?

a. Other than the elation over winning (or the relief from not losing), become more aware of what's missing that keeps you from feeling completely satisfied?

b. Do you lose respect for your partner?

c. Does your partner seem to keep score and attempt to get even in some way?

d. What might your partner be withholding from you that's related to his or her giving in? Sex? Emotional involvement? Time spent with you? Money?

8. Why are you unwilling to understand your partner's feelings and behavior?

Understanding the Resistant Position

This is the most difficult position to work with because when we resist we see ourselves as merely reacting to another. We thus give up all personal power and become helpless victims. We must strongly desire to be personally responsible to look at our resistance.

1. Why do you resist and what happens as a result of your resistance?

2. Why don't you tell your partner when you are resisting and initiate an exploration to understand more about why he or she is needing to be in control?

3. Why are you closed off to the things your partner is interested in? While it's true that not everything will be interesting to you, you can learn a great deal by considering this question.

   a. Even if you're not interested yourself, why aren't you interested in what your partner is thinking, feeling, and doing?

   b. Do you put down what he or she is interested in? If so, why?

   c. When did you learn to respond this way?

   d. What purpose is this response serving in your life today?

   e. What are the negative consequences of this response in your life today? What happens to your partner when you respond this way? What happens between you? What limitations does this response create for you?

   f. Aside from your struggle not to be controlled, what are your fears of doing what your partner wants you to do?

     — Being inadequate? Concern over what others might think?

     — Jumping into something new, making a mistake?

     — Furthering your partner's involvement and/or freedom?

The patterns of controller-resistor are deeply ingrained and your responses will probably never go away *completely*. However, through awareness and exploration, your need to be in control and to resist will slowly lessen, thus greatly alleviating the negative consequences of your power struggles.

Exercises for Exploring Values, Beliefs, and Expectations

Part One

Below is a list of issues. Write down those issues that create conflict in your relationship:

Time — how it is spent
Outside relationships — non-sexual
Outside relationships — sexual
Sex within the relationship
Affection
The past
Communication
Child-rearing — differences in philosophy, responsibilities
Dress, cleanliness, grooming, weight
Money
Housekeeping — neatness, meals and food, chores
Promptness — always being late or compulsively punctual
Behavior at social functions or around other people
Vacations — how and where they are spent
Work — attitudes toward
Roles — male/female, husband/wife
Interest and enthusiasm
Use of stimulants such as alcohol and drugs
Health
Hobbies
Gift-giving
Holidays and special events — if and how
        they are celebrated
Religion
Politics
Ways of being

1. After taking the time to relax and become aware of your body and feelings, take each of the problem areas and discuss them with your partner, or write down for yourself exactly how you expect, or want, your partner to feel and/or behave.
2. How do your partner's values, beliefs, and expectations differ from yours?

3. Why are these values, beliefs, and expectations important to you?

4. Explore the source of your own and your partner's values, beliefs, and expectations.

    a. What major values and beliefs do you share with your parents?

    b. What major values and beliefs are opposite from those of your parents?

    c. Are your professed values consistent with the true values of your inner self?

5. What purpose does it serve you to continue to hold the values and beliefs that are causing you and/or your partner difficulties? What negative things do you fear happening if you do not believe or behave according to these values?

6. Do you believe that your values apply only to you or do you believe that others should feel the same way you do?

    a. If so, why?

    b. What negative things do you fear happening if your mate does not believe or behave as you do?

    c. Why do you believe that what you fear will happen will actually occur?

    d. Are you willing to test out whether your fear will come true? If not, why not?

7. Taking each of the problem areas, discuss what could make you feel loved and why, and what makes you feel unloved and why.

Part Two

Below is a list of common expectations. Write down those that apply to you and add any of your own that we have not included.

"If you really loved me, you would . . . ":

include me in everything.
give me what I want.
know what I want without my having to ask for it.
do what I say.
want the same things I want.
be on time.
remember my birthday and/or our anniversary.
help around the house.
have the house neat by the time I come home.
be sexually attracted to me most of the time.
help support the family financially.
want to listen to my feelings.
want to spend more time with me, less time working.
want to spend more time with me and less time
    with the kids.
make more money.
spend less money.
buy gifts for me that I really like.
be interested in the things that interest me.
never do anything that hurts or threatens me.

1. If you are meeting each other's expectations, are you giving yourself up out of guilt, fear, or obligation, or are you doing it out of genuine caring? If you are giving yourself up, you can explore your fears of conflict and the negative consequences for you, your partner and your relationship.

2. When your expectations are not met you can explore your recurring conflicts.

   a. Why are these expectations important to you?

   b. Why might they not be important to your partner?

3. Explore what may be getting in the way of the two of you not meeting each other's expectations.

    a. Explore the times when you do not both consider the same things important and your unwillingness to explore with each other to find a satisfying resolution.

    b. Explore the times when you are each rebelling against the other's control.

You will find many more of your expectations being met out of genuine caring when you can reach resolutions to your conflicts and reduce your power struggles.

Part Three

On a sheet of paper write down the words and phrases from List #1 (below) that describe you and on another sheet the words and phrases that describe your partner. On a third sheet, from List #2 (below) write down the phrases your partner says to you or you think he or she thinks about you and on another sheet write down the phrases you think or say to your partner. Put a check by those areas on your list that you see as problems for yourself and/or for your relationship.

There are no right or wrong answers. Answers describe in general your own and your partner's behavior. Use the lists freely and loosely; they are only examples to touch off your own thoughts. Where there is more than one phrase, chose the one that most applies. Add your own words as you go or at the end. Change sentences as you wish adding qualifying words like "sometimes" or "usually" where they fit. If you wish, go through quickly and just mark those words that leap out at you.

After your lists are completed, you can use the discussion questions which follow List #2 to further your exploration.

List #1 — Ways of Being

Spontaneous — deals well with the unexpected, quick
Scheduled — planned, systematic, methodical, decisive
Lively — intense, fun-loving
Calm — moderate
Acts like a kid — silly, conspicuous, makes a fool of self
Uptight — rarely lets go, rarely has fun, rarely is silly
Enthusiastic — jumps into things, goes to extremes
Reserved — lacks enthusiasm
Rebellious — individualistic
Conforms — acts in accepted ways, conventional
Talks about feelings — easy to get to know
Reserved — hard to get to know, keeps feelings to self
Has in-depth relationships with others

Has superficial relationships with others
Imaginative — creative
Realistic
Impractical
Practical — uses common sense, reasonable, rational
Changing — experimental, trying new ideas
Permanent — stays with the known, stable,
    feet on ground
Drifts from thing to thing
Stays in a rut
Emotionally up and down — very reactive
Emotionally even — non-reactive
Socially detached — bored and/or anxious
    at social gatherings
Sociable — at ease socially
Feeling person
Thinking person
Deals with ideas
Needs to experience things in order to believe in them
Deals in theory
Sentimental
Trusting of feelings
Logical — needs facts
Emotionally very sensitive
Emotionally insensitive — sarcastic, critical
Namby-pamby — butters people up
Takes responsibility for self
Puts responsibility on others — blames others
Judges new ideas to be right or wrong
Open to new ideas — inquiring and curious about
    new ideas
Inflexible — locked in, opinionated, perfect, correct
Open-minded — hangs loose, casual, flexible
Finishes whatever is started
Easy-going
Anxious — worries about the future
Relaxed — in the moment
Leader — wants things own way
Leader — open to new directions and ideas
Follower — difficulty making decisions
Interested primarily in success — achievement

Interested in having fun
Interested in emotional satisfaction
Undertakes too much
Holds self back
Can never be wrong — argumentative
Lets others win too easily — good girl/nice guy
Reliable
Unreliable
Organized
Disorganized
Judgmental of self
Judgmental of others
Selfish and self-centered
Self-sacrificing — a martyr

List #2 — *Judgments About Ways of Being*

You talk too much.
You talk too loud.
You are too quiet and reserved; you never talk to me.
You are too outrageous, out of bounds, impulsive.
You are too controlled, systematic, predictable.
You always make a fool of yourself.
You are so conventional.
You act like a kid, silly.
You are so uptight, you never let go.
You like everyone, no discrimination, namby-pamby.
You are too critical, always blaming others for everything.
You always drift from one thing to another.
You are always in a rut.
You have no common sense.
You are too practical.
You always want things your way.
You never make decisions.
You live too much in the moment.
You are always worrying about the future.
You are too reactive.
You are always so even.
You are too sensitive.
You are too insensitive.
You are too much of a perfectionist, so inflexible.
You are so disorganized.

All you think about is accomplishing things.
All you think about is having fun.
You can never be wrong, always have to win.
You are too wishy-washy, always letting people
    run over you.
You are always biting off more than you can chew.
You never really get into anything; you are so lazy.
You are so opinionated.
You never have anything to say about anything.
You are always interrupting; you never listen.
You embarrass me in front of others.
You expect me to read your mind.
You never appreciate me.
You are self-centered and selfish; you care only
    about you.

Discussion Questions

1. Take any word or phrase from List #1 and discuss why it is a problem.

2. From List #2, discuss those ways of being that your partner does not like about you. Since the very important reasons you have for being as you are come from your values, beliefs, and fears, that's what you can discuss.

   a. What are the values and beliefs that lie underneath your behavior? (Example: *Behavior* — you are methodical, decisive, careful. *Value* — it is better to think before you act.) Where did you get these values?

   b. What are the fears that lie underneath your behavior? (Example — If you act impulsively, you might make a mistake and people may think less of you.)

3. Discuss those ways of being you do not like about your partner:

   a. What negative consequences occur or do you fear will occur from your partner being this way?

   b. Why are you afraid of those consequences?

Part Four

Sexual Behavior and Attitude Inventory

Because the many values, beliefs, and expectations surrounding sex create so many conflicts, we have developed this inventory. It consists of many statements that can focus your thoughts, feelings, beliefs and wants. But, since there are no right or wrong statements, when conflicts arise you may need to gain additional information to continue your explorations. If so, you can consult some of the many excellent books on sexuality. We particularly like *Male Sexuality* by Bernie Zilbergeld, and *For Yourself* by Lonnie Barbach.

For each of the statements in the inventory choose the word, or phrase, (or insert your own) that makes it correct for you and write down the statement. We suggest that you plan on doing only one section at a time. After completing a section, circle the one or two statements that are most important to you. Think or write about what's important to you in this issue: What's upsetting to you? What fears, values, beliefs, and expectations are being tapped into? What does this issue say about you? What's your history with this issue?

Set aside an appropriate time to explore, and one partner begin by reading his or her statement. The Sharing-Understanding format can be used to begin your discussion and exploration could continue for days. Alternately choose the statement to be explored. There's enough material in these statements for years of exploration, so be patient with yourself and your partner. The greatest benefits will be reaped with a willingness to take risks, be vulnerable, and work through any conflicts that occur.

Section 1 — Emotional Involvement

1. How I am feeling emotionally about myself has (great) (minimal) (no) effect on our sex.

2. Emotional involvement with my partner before we make love is (very) (minimally) (not) important.

3. Talking about our feelings before making love is (important) (unimportant) (helps me to feel sexual) (bores me).

4. Doing something fun or interesting together before making love (helps me to feel sexual) (is unimportant).

5. Saying "I love you" with genuine feeling is (uncomfortable) (comfortable).

6. Having my partner say to me "I love you" with genuine feeling is (uncomfortable) (comfortable).

7. Loving looks and smiles between us while we are making love are (important) (unimportant) (enjoyable) (unenjoyable) (uncomfortable).

8. Expressing our feelings about each other while we are making love is (important) (unimportant) (enjoyable) (unenjoyable) (easy) (difficult).

9. Sharing what we like and dislike sexually is (important) (unimportant) (difficult).

10. Talking about sex is (important) (unimportant) (enjoyable) (difficult).

Section 2 — Initiating Sex

1. Initiating sex is (difficult) (easy).

2. I would like my partner to initiate sex (more often) (less often).

3. When my partner initiates sex it (arouses me) (creates problems for me).

4. When my partner initiates sex and I do not feel like it, saying "No" (does) (does not) create problems for me.

5. When my partner is sexually aroused I should (feel like making love) (make love whether I feel like it or not) (do what I feel like doing).

6. When I am sexually aroused my partner should (feel like making love) (make love whether he or she feels like it or not) (do what he or she feels like doing).

7. I think sex should be (spontaneous) (planned).

Section 3 — *Affection: Sexual and Non-Sexual*

1. Receiving affection is (important) (unimportant) (pleasurable) (difficult).

2. Giving affection is (important) (unimportant) (pleasurable) (difficult).

3. If I am not affectionate, it is because (there is always an expectation that it will lead to sex) (I am afraid of being rejected) (it is not adult) (I am often angry at my partner).

4. Should I become aroused while we are being affectionate (I want to make love) (I can sometimes enjoy being aroused without feeling the need to make love).

5. Affection is important to me (throughout the day) (only when we are going to make love).

6. Having my partner caress my body, other than breasts and genitals, is (unimportant) (important) (pleasurable) (uncomfortable).

7. Caressing my partner's body, other than breasts and genitals, is (unimportant) (important) (pleasurable) (uncomfortable).

8. Having my partner caress my genitals is (unimportant) (important) (pleasurable) (uncomfortable).

9. Caressing my partner's genitals is (unimportant) (important) (pleasurable) (uncomfortable).

10. Having my breasts caressed orally and manually is (unimportant) (important) (pleasurable) (uncomfortable).

11. Caressing and kissing my partner's breasts is (unimportant) (important) (pleasurable) (uncomfortable).

12. Some of the difficulties I encounter when caressing my partner's body are (I don't get much pleasure) (my partner does not respond) (I get embarrassed) (I find it hard to give in that way) (I feel bored).

13. Some of the difficulties I encounter when my partner caresses my body are (I find it hard to receive pleasure) (I don't get much pleasure) (my partner does not seem to like it) (I get embarrassed) (I feel obligated, bored, pained, uncomfortable).

Section 4 — *Body*

1. Having my partner admire my body, other than my breasts and genitals, is (important) (unimportant) (pleasurable) (uncomfortable).

2. Admiring my partner's body, other than breasts and genitals, is (important) (unimportant) (pleasurable) (uncomfortable).

3. Having my partner admire my genitals is (important) (unimportant) (pleasurable) (uncomfortable).

4. Seeing my partner's genitals is (important) (unimportant) (pleasurable) (uncomfortable).

5. (Women only) Having my partner admire my breasts is (important) (unimportant) (pleasurable) (uncomfortable).

6. (Men only) Seeing my partner's breasts is (important) (unimportant) (pleasurable) (uncomfortable).

7. Some of the difficulties I have admiring my partner's body are I (do not like the way parts of his or her body look) (am embarrassed) (think he or she is uncomfortable) (feel it is wrong).

8. Some of the difficulties I encounter when my partner is admiring my body are I (feel embarrassed) (feel it is wrong) (am worried that if I respond he or she may want to have sex).

9. I believe (your/my) breasts are (too large) (unappealing) (okay) (beautiful) (too small) (poorly shaped) (perfect).

10. I believe (your/my) penis is (too large) (too small) (perfect) (okay) (unappealing) (beautiful).

11. I believe (your/my) vagina is (too large) (too small) (too tight) (unappealing) (beautiful) (perfect).

12. I do not like the hair on your (face) (arms) (chest) (legs) (underarms) (pubic area) (nipples).

13. I like the hair on your (face) (arms) (chest) (legs) (underarms) (pubic area) (nipples).

14. I do not like the hair on my (face) (arms) (chest) (legs) (underarms) (pubic area) (nipples).

15. I do not like the (shape) (firmness) (weight) (color) (distribution) (texture) of parts of your body.

16. I like the (shape) (firmness) (weight) (color) (distribution) (texture) of parts of your body.

17. I do not like the (shape) (firmness) (weight) (color) (distribution) (texture) of parts of my body.

18. I like the (shape) (firmness) (weight) (color) (distribution) (texture) of parts of my body.

Section 5 — *Environment*

1. I like to make love (with some light) (in the dark).

2. Making love in different places and environments is (difficult) (easy) (exciting) (unimportant) (important).

3. Making love at certain times of the day — morning, midday, evening — is (difficult) (easy).

4. I do not like it when my partner comes to bed (not ready to make love) (unclean) (breath smelling) (looking unattractive).

Section 6 — *Nudity*

1. I believe being nude in front of other people is (wrong) (okay).

2. I believe being nude around our children is (wrong) (okay) (important).

3. Sleeping nude is (important) (unimportant) (enjoyable) (unenjoyable).

4. For my partner to sleep nude is (important) (unimportant) (enjoyable) (unenjoyable).

Section 7 — *Children*

1. When we are making love and the children are awake, it is (impossible) (uncomfortable) (okay).

2. It is (important) (unimportant) (uncomfortable) for me that our children know we make love.

3. The way we handle birth control is (acceptable) (unacceptable) (inhibits me) (worries me).

Section 8 — *Masturbation*

1. I believe masturbation is (wrong) (normal).

2. I masturbate (often) (occasionally) (never).

3. If my partner masturbates it would (bother me) (be okay) (arouse me).

4. Masturbating in front of my partner is something I (like) (would like) (would not like).

5. My partner masturbating in front of me (is) (is not) (would be) (would not be) enjoyable.

6. Masturbating as a part of love-making would (bother me) (be okay) (excite me).

7. My partner masturbating as a part of love-making would (bother me) (be okay) (excite me).

8. Masturbating with a vibrator is (wrong) (okay) (exciting) (repulsive).

Section 9 — Fantasy

1. I believe having sexual fantasies is (wrong) (okay) (enjoyable) (unenjoyable).

2. Sharing my sexual fantasies with my partner is (unacceptable) (okay) (pleasurable) (difficult).

3. Having my partner share his or her sexual fantasies with me is (unacceptable) (okay) (pleasurable).

4. In my partner's sexual fantasies (anything would be okay) (some things are not okay).

5. In my sexual fantasies (anything would be okay) (some things are not okay).

6. While we are making love I (never) (sometimes) (often) fantasize.

7. For me to have a fantasy while making love is (wrong) (okay) (exciting) (never happens).

8. For my partner to have a fantasy while we are making love would be (wrong) (okay).

9. Sharing our sexual fantasies during love-making would be (wrong) (okay) (a turn on) (difficult).

Section 10 — Oral Sex

1. Having my partner stimulate my genitals orally is (unimportant) (important) (pleasurable) (uncomfortable).

2. Stimulating my partner's genitals orally is (unimportant) (important) (pleasurable) (uncomfortable).

3. Some of the difficulties I encounter when my partner is having oral sex with me are that I feel (it is wrong) (my partner

does not like it) (obligated) (little or no pleasure) (separated and alone) (irritation) (pain) (embarrassed) (bored).

4. Some of the difficulties I encounter when I am having oral sex with my partner are (sight) (taste) (smell) (size) (semen) (pubic hair) (texture) (feeling that my partner does not like it) (no response from my partner) (I do not get much pleasure) (I feel it is wrong) (I feel inadequate).

Section 11 — Orgasm

1. When we make love I have an orgasm (each time) (often) (sometimes) (never).

2. When we make love my partner has an orgasm (each time) (often) (sometimes) (never).

3. I should have an orgasm (each time) (often) (sometimes).

4. My partner should have an orgasm (each time) (often) (sometimes).

5. Occasionally not having an orgasm during love-making would be (okay) (not okay).

6. Simultaneous orgasm is (important) (not important).

7. Orgasm for a woman should be through (intercourse) (clitoral stimulation) (any means).

8. A woman should have (many) (a few) (one) orgasm(s).

9. Orgasm for my partner occurs too (quickly) (slowly).

10. My orgasm occurs too (quickly) (slowly).

11. My orgasm (is) (is not) a problem for me.

12. When my partner has an orgasm I (always) (sometimes) (never) know it.

13. I would like to (know more about) (not know more about) my own and my partner's orgasm.

Section 12 — Erection

(For men only)

1. Having an erection is (difficult) (easy) (worries me).

2. Maintaining my erection is (difficult) (easy) (worries me).

3. Should I lose my erection during love-making, I (never) (rarely) (sometimes) (almost always) (always) get it back.

4. Should I not be able to get an erection (there is something wrong with me) (I am not wanting to get an erection) (I feel guilty).

5. Some of the reasons I may not want to get an erection are: I am (worried) (angry) (hurt) (not wanting to make love).

6. Should I have difficulty with my sexuality my partner is (usually understanding) (usually not understanding) (neither of the above but I fear that she will not be understanding).

(For women only)

7. When my partner has difficulty with his erection I usually (feel responsible) (get angry at him) (pretend nothing is wrong) (feel hurt) (want to understand what he is feeling) (ask him what he is feeling) (feel warm) (feel cold).

8. A man's erection is something I (do not) (would like to) understand more about.

Section 13 — Intercourse

1. The length of time we have intercourse is too (short) (long).

2. The rhythm of our intercourse is too (fast) (slow) (uneven) (okay).

3. Once we begin to have intercourse we (continue to move until orgasm) (can stop moving and enjoy other pleasures while coitus is maintained) (can stop having intercourse, enjoy other pleasures, then return to intercourse) (can express our feelings freely).

4. Intercourse for me is usually (fun) (serious) (romantic) (tender) (passionate) (loving) (vigorous) (expressive) (pleasurable) (unpleasurable) (a separate feeling) (a together feeling) (creative) (routine) (experimental) (restrictive and tense).

5. Intercourse for my partner seems to be (fun) (serious) (passionate) (a duty) (expressive) (non-expressive) (pleasurable) (unpleasurable) (restrictive and tense).

6. During intercourse I am usually into (my own feelings) (my partner's feelings) (flow back and forth between my partner's and my own feelings).

7. During intercourse my partner is usually into (my feelings) (his or her own feelings) (able to flow back and forth between my feelings and his or her feelings).

8. The position(s) that we use during intercourse are (varied) (comfortable) (confining) (pleasurable).

Section 14 — Feelings About Sex in General

1. The frequency of our sexual encounters is (okay) (not okay) with me.

2. Having sex is (relatively unimportant) (very important) to me.

3. I wish my partner was interested in having sex (more) (less) often.

4. I like my partner to be sexually (aggressive) (passive).

5. I like to (be serious) (have fun and be serious at times) while making love.

6. Good sex is mainly a matter of (technique) (our emotional involvement) (other factors).

7. I feel our sex is (routine) (creative) (passionate) (satisfying).

8. For me, sexuality is connected with feeling in love (always) (sometimes) (never).

9. I usually feel (bored) (intense) (unimportant) (special) (unloved) (loved) (inhibited) (flowing) (relaxed) (tense) during our love making.

10. I feel my partner is usually (bored) (intense) (inhibited) (flowing) (relaxed) (tense) during our love-making.

11. I often want sex in order to (be close and involved with my partner) (release my anxiety) (prove my adequacy and lovability) (feel intimate without having to expose my softer and more vulnerable feelings) (prove that my partner loves me).

Section 15 — Sexual Power Struggles

1. I (often) (sometimes) feel like having sex and my partner does not.

2. I take it personally when my partner rejects me sexually and I become (withdrawn) (angry) (tense) (annoyed) (hurt).

3. I feel (anxious) (scared) (unloved) (angry) (tense) (withdrawn) when I want to make love and I am worried that my partner does not.

4. I believe my partner should (always) (sometimes) (never) attempt to make love with me when I want to, even if he or she is not feeling turned on.

5. I generally feel (resistant) (turned-off) (annoyed) (imposed upon) (tired) (tense) when my partner wants sex.

6. I (often) (sometimes) (never) think about having sex with my partner when we are apart, but then feel turned-off when we are together.

7. When I feel my partner is hovering over me wanting to have sex, I feel (tense) (anxious) (turned-off) (scared) (angry) (rebellious) (resistant).

8. When I am not feeling sexual and I refuse my partner, I want him or her to (let me know it is okay) (cuddle me and be warm) (stay open and want to know why I said "No").

Section 16 — Relationships with Other People

1. Platonic intimate relationships with other people are (important) (not important) to me.

2. My partner having platonic intimate relationships with other people is (acceptable) (not acceptable) to me.

3. I would seek outside platonic relationships for (intellectual stimulation) (emotional intensity) (fun) (common interests) (acceptance).

4. A restriction for me not to have sex with anyone else is (okay) (not okay).

5. It is okay for me to have sex with others if I am (discreet) (open) about it.

6. It is okay for my partner to have sex with others if he or she is (discreet) (open) about it.

7. If I found out my partner was having sex with someone else, I would feel (afraid of others' finding out) (afraid of losing the relationship) (devastated) (humiliated) (scared) (inadequate) (sick) (disgusted) (deceived) (untrusting) (unloved) (our sex is not very special) (turned on) (freer).

8. If I were to have sex with someone else, I would feel (it is wrong) (afraid that my partner would find out) (scared) (disgusted) (okay) (more turned on to my spouse) (freer).

9. The reasons I might have sex with someone else are because I want more (sex) (affection) (affirmation) (variety) (love) (intensity) (fun).

Exercises for Exploring Personal Responsibility

Part One

Since the entire issue of personal responsibility is central to one's evolution and yet difficult to confront, it might be helpful to take each part of the following questions separately, spend some time writing about it, and then share your insights with your partner.

1. Explore the areas in which you believe you are a victim of your partner's behavior. In what situations or areas do you:

    a. think or feel you would not withdraw were your partner not trying to control you?

    b. think or feel you would not try to control your partner if he or she did not always shut you out?

    c. think or feel you are helpless to do anything about your unhappiness?

    d. think that if only your partner would change, everything would be fine?

    e. believe your partner is more responsible for the difficulties between you than you are? Or that you are just reacting to your partner?

    f. believe your partner generally starts the problems by trying to control you or shut you out and that your partner is more to blame than you are?

2. Make a list of all the things you do and the ways you spend your time that lead to good feelings about yourself, and of those that lead to bad feelings and unhappiness. Explore these lists with your partner.

    a. Explore the purpose of continuing to behave in ways that make you feel bad about yourself.

    b. Discuss what you could do to help you to feel better about yourself. Explore the good reasons you have for not doing these things.

3. Explore your feelings of responsibility towards others and others' responsibility towards you.

a. When you unintentionally hurt another's feelings or do something for yourself that puts another in pain, do you feel wrong? Guilty? If so, why?

b. What happens when your partner does something for himself or herself that hurts or threatens you?

Do you believe your partner is wrong?

Do you feel like a victim?

Do you have any desire to understand the good reasons for your partner's feelings and behavior?

Do you have any desire to explore why you are hurt or threatened by your partner's feelings and behavior?

4. What fears do you have of recognizing each other's freedom?

a. Do you fear if your partner were free from fear, obligation, and guilt that he or she would not care about you?

Would leave you?

Would never spend time with you?

Would never want to make love?

Would have affairs?

b. If you were free of fear, obligation, and guilt, how do you imagine yourself acting or being?

Part Two

Below is a list of statements we believe to be true. You will find yourself in agreement with some and disagreeing with others. Your partner and you may disagree with each other and you will even find controversy among qualified experts. The value of this exercise will be in learning more about why you believe as you do and how your belief shapes your life. Explore each statement fully, preferably with your partner. Be sure to give yourselves plenty of time to understand each statement. Going through them quickly will bring little benefit. Discuss exactly what each statement means to you and why you believe as you do. What events led you to your conclusions? Are you willing to hear opposing points of view? If not, why not? Trace the effects that believing or disbelieving each statement has on your life. To further your own thinking, are you willing to seek out through reading, attending classes, etc., both other points of view as well as supporting points of view? If not, why not?

1. When protecting ourselves is our number one priority, caring for another becomes secondary. Our behavior, even when it hurts another, is primarily *for ourselves* rather than *against another*. Likewise, when our partner is protective, his or her behavior is primarily for himself or herself and not against us.

2. We are all judgmental and all judgments are a result of fears.

3. There is nothing wrong with being judgmental. We can become aware of the reasons we are judgmental and of the consequences of being judgmental.

4. We are all very sensitive people and feel bad when we are not affirmed by those most important to us.

5. Our mate's approval is very important to us and therefore he or she has a great deal of power over us and vice versa.

6. There are always very important and appropriate reasons for our own and others' behavior. Therefore, our feelings and

behaviors, other than those that intentionally harm others, are neither right nor wrong.

7. Almost all of our behavior comes from our hopes and fears — the hope that things will change, and our desire to protect ourselves from the things we fear.

8. Our unwillingness to experience pain blocks our awareness.

9. Since there are no guarantees in life, promises and contracts are meaningless.

10. We can only have control over another as long as he or she is willing to be under our control; therefore, we must face one of life's most frightening realities — we are powerless to control others. We only have control over ourselves.

11. When we have sincerely attempted to explore why another is angry, and he or she has shut us out or not met our requests, or refuses to explore with us, we are helpless to change the other's intent.

12. Our attempts to get another to do what we want carries with it many negative consequences.

13. Much of our behavior with another person is manipulative.

14. When we expect safety before we are willing to let go and be vulnerable, we are holding the other person responsible for what we do.

15. Blaming another person for putting us in pain denies us the opportunity to learn more about ourselves.

16. Our individual nature is determined before birth and then is influenced and shaped by our life's experiences. This does not, however, prevent us from making significant changes in our personalities.

17. The essence of a human being is good. Negative behavior is learned and comes from the protective, defensive, insecure, part of ourselves.

18. Our natural feelings are non-blaming pain, frustration and rage, joy, sensuality, and sexuality. Being angry at another person is learned.

19. Real strength lies in the willingness to express our natural feelings and deal with any negative consequences that occur.

20. Many factors, other than psychological, contribute to our moods and resulting emotional difficulties. Therefore, we must

also give our attention to what we put into our bodies and our level of physical activity.

21. To feel at peace and self-satisfied we must find fulfillment in two areas: 1) a productive pursuit that challenges our intelligence and creativity; and 2) a relationship in which we are both giving and receiving love. One without the other will leave us feeling like something is missing.

22. Although we all bring a history of difficulties into a relationship, what goes on in the relationship either helps to alleviate or to perpetuate these difficulties. Therefore, we need to look both to our past and our present to understand any particular difficulty.

23. Relationship difficulties are equally created.

24. We are not responsible for how another person feels or behaves in reaction to something we have said or done. We can, however, care for the difficulties that person may be having without feeling responsible.

25. Feeling bad about something we've done that has upset another and feeling guilty or wrong for having done it are two separate things. It is possible to feel bad without feeling guilty.

26. Guilt feelings mean we believe we have done something wrong. When we feel guilty we are not respecting that we have very important reasons for our behavior.

27. We are essentially free to make our own choices within the limits of the law, our physical structure, and our awareness of other possibilities. No one is to blame for how we respond; therefore, we are fully responsible for our choices and for the consequences of those choices.

About the Authors

Drs. Jordan and Margaret Paul hold doctoral degrees in psychology and are licensed marriage, family, and child counselors. Married to each other for twenty-two years, they are the parents of three active teenage children. Their unique ideas are the basis for Intention Training seminars and workshops taught throughout the United States and Canada. Authors of two best-selling books, *Do I Have to Give Up Me to Be Loved by You?* and *Free to Love*, the Pauls were awarded the California Association of Marriage and Family Therapists Educational Foundation's 1986 Clark Vincent Award for outstanding literary or research contributions to the profession.

The down-to-earth, entertaining, humorous, and very personal presentation of Jordan and Margaret Paul has made them popular radio and television talk show guests on national shows such as Merv Griffin, Hour Magazine, and Sally Jesse Raphael as well as guest hosts for Dr. Toni Grant and Susan Forward.

In addition, the Pauls teach professional training workshops throughout the United States. Organizations sponsoring Intention Training workshops for professionals include: Southern Regional Institute of The National Association of Social Workers; The Mountain Area Health Education Center in North Carolina; and The Spokane Community Mental Health Center.

If you would like to:
- receive more information about Intention Training and the dates of future workshops;
- arrange for the Pauls to speak to a group in your area;

- help bring an Intention Training Workshop to your area;
- have the Pauls answer your relationship questions—

    Call or write:

    Intention Training Institute
    2531 Sawtelle Blvd., Suite 42
    Los Angeles, CA 90064
    (213) 390-5993

Index

312

For price and order information, or a free catalog,
please call our Telephone Representatives.

HAZELDEN EDUCATIONAL MATERIALS

1-800-328-9000 (Toll-Free, U.S., Canada & the Virgin Islands)
1-612-257-4010 (Outside the U.S. & Canada)
1-612-257-1331 FAX

**Pleasant Valley Road • P.O. Box 176
Center City, MN 55012-0176**